"Insightful . . . invest the time to read this book."
—*USA Today*

"A fascinating study . . . a two-fisted tale about real men running a real organization—straight into the ground."
—*Chicago Tribune*

"A lively, colorful account . . . Stevens is a skilled writer and reporter."
—*Kirkus Reviews*

"Shocking!"
—*The San Francisco Chronicle*

(Please turn the page for more extraordinary acclaim.)

DISCARD

MARK STEVENS is the author of such business books as *The Accounting Wars, Land Rush, The Insiders,* and the bestseller *The Big Eight.* His syndicated financial column runs in over 100 newspapers and magazines, and he is a contributing editor to *Sylvia Porter's Personal Finance* and *Dun and Bradstreet Reports.* He lives in Chappaqua, New York.

"A SUPERIOR ACCOUNT, RICH IN ANECDOTE AND PERSONALITY DEVELOPMENT."

—*Business Week*

"STEVENS HAS DUG DEEPLY INTO THE HUMAN SIDE OF THE DISASTERS THAT RESULTED IN THE DEMISE OF THE ONE-TIME GIANT BROKERAGE FIRM."

—*Copley News Service*

SUDDEN DEATH

THE RISE AND FALL OF E.F. HUTTON

Mark Stevens

A PLUME BOOK

PLUME
Published by the Penguin Group
Penguin Books USA Inc., 375 Hudson Street,
New York, New York 10014, U.S.A.
Penguin Books Ltd, 27 Wrights Lane,
London W8 5TZ, England
Penguin Books Australia Ltd, Ringwood,
Victoria, Australia
Penguin Books Canada Ltd, 2801 John Street,
Markham, Ontario, Canada L3R 1B4
Penguin Books (N.Z.) Ltd, 182-190 Wairau Road,
Auckland 10, New Zealand

Penguin Books Ltd, Registered Offices:
Harmondsworth, Middlesex, England

Sudden Death previously appeared in an NAL Books edition.

First Plume Printing, May, 1990
10 9 8 7 6 5 4 3 2 1

Copyright © 1989 by Mark Stevens
All rights reserved. For information address Penguin Books USA Inc.
Published simultaneously in Canada by Penguin Books Canada Limited.

 REGISTERED TRADEMARK—MARCA REGISTRADA

Library of Congress Cataloging-in-Publication Data

Stevens, Mark, 1947–
  Sudden death : the rise and fall of E.F. Hutton/Mark Stevens.
    p. cm.
  ISBN 0-453-00673-6
  1. E.F. Hutton & Company. 2. Stockbrokers—United States.
3. Securities—United States. I. Title.
HG4928.5.S74   1989
364.1'63—dc20   89-9454
0-452-26438-3 (pbk.)   CIP

PRINTED IN THE UNITED STATES OF AMERICA
Set in Times Roman
Original hardcover designed by Sherry Brown

BOOKS ARE AVAILABLE AT QUANTITY DISCOUNTS WHEN USED TO PROMOTE PRODUCTS OR
SERVICES. FOR INFORMATION PLEASE WRITE TO PREMIUM MARKETING DIVISION, PENGUIN
BOOKS USA INC., 375 HUDSON STREET, NEW YORK, NEW YORK 10014.

DEDICATION

To H.B. and J.B.

Research by:

Carol Bloom Stevens

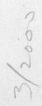

SUDDEN DEATH

Chapter 1

Robert Fomon couldn't believe his ears.

Seated in his baronial offices high atop the pink marble and granite monument he'd built as a symbol of his personal power, he was a prince in his court. A handsome man whose battle-weary face made him look slightly older than his sixty-two years, he was resplendent as usual in a chalk-stripe suit, a pale blue shirt trimmed with a white collar, and black shoes that shined more brightly than a hand-waxed Rolls Royce. A passionate Anglophile, he'd come to see himself as an extension of British royalty: Sir Robert Fomon, Duke of New York.

After running the venerable brokerage firm of E.F. Hutton for seventeen years, guiding it in his imperious way from a modest wire house into a Wall Street giant, he had just been fired by the board of directors, banned from the company he'd come to think of as his own.

Just three years before, Fomon had sat at the pinnacle of the Wall Street hierarchy and the Manhattan/Southampton social scene so closely aligned with it. As the absolute monarch of E.F. Hutton—the firm made famous by the advertising slogan "When E.F. Hutton talks, people listen" —Robert Fomon was rich, powerful, prominent, as much at home on the society pages as on the cover of *Fortune*. He was the kind of corporate Renaissance man America

1

worships. But now, after years of drinking, philandering, cronyism, management neglect, and most recently jealous infighting with his hand-picked successor, Fomon was being kicked out. Major league baseball commissioner and Hutton director Peter Ueberroth summed up the board's feelings.

"Look, Bob, this feuding simply has to stop. The board just can't tolerate it any longer. We've tried everything. Nothing's worked."

As point man for the lily-livered board of directors, Ueberroth took on most of the tough jobs, in this case leveling the coup de grace to the man who'd built the modern Hutton.

"Bob, we have to demand that you give up your office in this building."

Fomon sat motionless, numbed by Ueberroth's message. Only the capillaries around his eyes, twitching like netted butterflies, gave any sign of the emotions raging inside.

"Don't get me wrong, Bob, we're not going to leave you out in the cold. You'll have to give up your office here, but the board's agreed that you can arrange for space anywhere else in the city and the company will pay—"

Fomon raised his hand in the air. Hobbled by the strains of age and of a crippled leg, he paced the room.

"Anywhere else in the city? What the hell are you talking about? Don't you understand that there is nowhere else? I built this building. I built this company. What are you saying?"

Ueberroth didn't have to answer. Fomon knew exactly what he was saying: his reign at the top of E.F. Hutton had come to an end. The last vestige of his power was being stripped away. Even as the board acted to remove him from the premises, Fomon was a deposed chairman, his fall caused not only by his failure as a chief executive, but as a human being.

For nearly two decades Fomon had run Hutton like an

eccentric dictator whose actions shocked even his closest aides.

"The power went to Bob's head," says former Hutton vice president and head of the syndication department, Humbert Powell. "I mean, the guy started thinking he could do anything, no matter how bizarre.

"Let me give you a case in point. At one time I got him to take up bird hunting in Nebraska. The next year, when the hunting season began, he brought his rifle into the office and called me in to help get it in shape. Well, I thought that was a strange request during business hours, but he was the boss, so I did as he asked. I went to his office, set the gun up, made sure it was in good working order, and handed it back.

" 'Here, Bob,' I said. 'You're all set.'

" 'Will it work?' he asked.

" 'Of course it will,' I told him.

" 'How do you know, Hum?'

" 'Trust me, Bob.'

" 'I don't want to trust you, Hum. I have to be sure.'

"With that, the maniac takes a goddamn shell out of his pocket, loads the shotgun, and heads for the window.

" 'Bob, what in Christ's name are you doing?'

" 'I'm going to test fire it.'

"He's going to test fire it! Believe it or not, the lunatic is going to fire a rifle into Battery Park. That's crazy enough under ordinary circumstances, but doubly, triply crazy at that moment because the pope is scheduled to speak there the next day. Hell, the park is crawling with secret service agents and cops and FBI men and SWAT teams, and there's the chief executive of E.F. Hutton getting ready to point a rifle out the window!

" 'Bo-o-ob-b-b, you can't do that,' I screamed, rushing over to slam the window on him.

" 'Just watch me,' he says as he marches headlong toward the window.

"Well, I wasn't about to do that. So I wrestled the gun from him and removed the shells myself. But let me tell you, if I hadn't stopped him, he would have blasted that rifle right into the park. That there were police and secret service all over the place—none of that bothered Bob Fomon. As the chief executive of E.F. Hutton, he thought he was above it all."

Crushing as it was to hear the board's final eviction notice, it could hardly have come as a total surprise.

"For months Bob had been behaving badly, like a child who wasn't getting his way," recalls a former board member. "He'd seen his power slipping away, but he refused to let it slip gracefully. He was annoying and obnoxious and unwilling to heed the board's warnings that he had to move into the background. He had to know that we were reaching our breaking point (some of his friends on the board told him this in confidence) and that if he didn't alter his behavior, his days at Hutton were numbered."

Adds a former Hutton senior vice president active in lining up limited partnership investments: "Bob came to me shaken, angry, frightened that there might be a move afoot to kick him out of the company. He said, 'Let them try it, I'm not moving.' But I said, 'Bob, you can't do that. When someone wants you out of their house, it's undignified to stay. It's beneath you, Bob. You'll have to go.'"

Although Fomon had had years of greatness when he presided over Hutton's emergence from a small quasi-partnership to a major player in the securities business, its assets growing under his stewardship from $260 million to $23 billion, in the mid-1980s he'd become a bumbling Nero, fiddling while Hutton burned. Only six months before, in November 1986, Fomon had relinquished the title of chief executive officer, reluctantly passing the baton to Hutton's president Robert R. Rittereiser.

The move had come after an emotional board meeting in

which the directors had wrestled with an offer by Wall Street competitor Shearson/Lehman Brothers to buy Hutton for $50 a share. With the discussions having collapsed over the board's demand for $55, a demand Shearson's chief executive Peter Cohen would reject, Ueberroth took the floor. His mission, spelled out beforehand in secret backroom meetings, promised to be a watershed for the firm. Aware of what was coming, the members of the weak, indecisive board fell silent.

While some sympathized with Fomon, they knew something drastic had to be done. Hutton was a public company being torn apart by two men who had come to view it as a fulcrum for their personal goals and ambitions.

The problem dated back to June 1985, when Rittereiser—a highly touted star in the Wall Street management galaxy—had left the executive vice-presidency of brokerage giant Merrill Lynch to become Hutton's president and soon after its chief operating officer. With Hutton's once pristine image tarnished by a front-page check-kiting scandal—culminating in a guilty plea to two thousand counts of fraud and conspiracy—the call had gone out for a clean-as-a-whistle executive to restore confidence in the firm's good name. Rittereiser's all-American good looks and unblemished record made him a natural for the job.

From the start, he found himself sandbagged by the man he reported to. Unwilling to share control with anyone, least of all an outsider trying to encroach on his personal domain, Fomon countermanded Rittereiser's orders, belittled him publicly and privately, and encouraged subordinates to detour the president's office and report directly to him.

"When I would go to see Rittereiser, to enlist his help in structuring a deal, Fomon would call me on the phone and bitch about it," says Andre Backar, a former star in the Hutton pantheon who orchestrated big ticket real estate transactions. "He'd say, 'Why are you helping that guy? I thought you were my friend. If you need something, come to me.' "

Finding himself president in name only, Rittereiser began to lobby the board for the position he had sought to achieve at Merrill, Lynch: to be elected chief executive officer. Fearing a brawl with Fomon, he pleaded and cajoled behind the scenes, buttonholing the directors, reminding them one by one of his mandate to turn around a troubled firm and of their fiduciary responsibility to clear the way for him to do so. The message was clear: for the savior to perform his miracles, he would have to be installed as CEO.

"You had all the players in a Greek tragedy," says Paul Bagley, a veteran of Hutton's corporate finance department, widely considered one of the brightest minds in the firm. "A blind and arrogant monarch, namely Bob Fomon, proclaiming his rule over the kingdom. A supposedly loyal aide in the character of Bob Rittereiser, plotting to overthrow him. And a counsel of elders, call them the board of directors, proving themselves incapable of mediating between the warring factions.

"The feud began, Rittereiser will tell you, when Fomon refused to give his second-in-command operating authority, sabotaging whatever decisions he made. And while the charges may be valid, Rittereiser has to share the blame. As a seasoned corporate executive—as a man who rose to the number three spot at Merrill Lynch and who knew where the power lies in a major securities firm—he should have known that parachuting into Hutton without being named CEO was tantamount to committing corporate suicide.

"Fomon's personality was no secret. Everyone on the Street knew that he was as close to an absolute dictator as you can get in a major public corporation. Walking into that environment with little or no power base of his own was a terrible blunder. Fomon may have intimated that he'd step down shortly after Rittereiser came on board, but he had no intention of doing so.

"Rittereiser should have read the writing on the wall. He should have known that Fomon would try to destroy anyone with the audacity to succeed him. Guys like Fomon don't give up without a fight. That's the first lesson of corporate politics."

By the time Rittereiser learned the lesson, he was an angry and frustrated man, the butt of jokes in his adopted company. Unable to gain control of the eighty-two-year-old brokerage firm he was supposed to be running, he used the Shearson proposal to press his case with the board. Following a divisive board meeting, where Fomon and Rittereiser clashed openly over the Shearson bid, the directors were prepared to act. It was then that Ueberroth ordered Fomon to speak with Rittereiser and to settle the leadership issue.

With that, Ueberroth set the wheels in motion for a changing of the guard.

"It's time that the two of you sort it out," he said. "We can't allow things to go on this way."

To Fomon, the message was as clear as a shot to the solar plexus. He would have to step down as CEO, allowing the subordinate he'd come to detest to succeed him. The thought left him sick. In the "battle of the Bob's," Rittereiser had won.

Or had he? Though Fomon had clearly lost the battle, he hadn't yet ceded the war. But that was a secret he kept to himself.

At a breakfast meeting held at the Westbury Hotel, Fomon played the dutiful employee for the first time in his tenure as chief executive (he was, he claims, simply heeding the board's directives). His tone was calm, complacent, subdued—enough to frighten Rittereiser that this was a trap in the making. The idea of Bob Fomon simply abdicating the throne was hard to accept. Something had to be up his sleeve.

The warring executives had never trusted each other. From the day they'd met, both men had manipulated each other in a high-stakes game of corporate chess.

Rittereiser took a humble, selfless approach.

"I don't think he'd been with Hutton for more than an hour when he comes up with this bullshit story that title and salary and perks and office size and all the other trappings of executive life don't mean shit to him," Fomon recalls, the smoke from a chain-lit Marlboro streaming out of his nostrils. "Then he comes on with his pathetic melodrama that pictures him as the poor New York kid up from the gutters who played ball with the black boys and who grew up rough and tough and streetwise. God, you could take out a violin.

"Then to cap it all off, he disclaims the need for any personal gain and says, 'Bob, I only want to work with you. To help you make this a better company. That's all I ask.' "

If that was true, the man had undergone a dramatic transformation. Throughout his career at Merrill Lynch, Rittereiser had been protective of his executive turf. When Merrill's chairman William Schreyer took a two-month leave of absence for bypass surgery in 1984, he left a six-member caretaker committee, Rittereiser included, to manage the company's affairs. Although his role was more of a back-office lieutenant than a commander-in-chief, Rittereiser began to picture himself as Schreyer's heir apparent. In a top-secret meeting with Fomon in mid-1984, when the two men first discussed the Hutton presidency, Rittereiser cited his stint at the helm as evidence that he could run a major brokerage firm.

While Rittereiser painted a self-portrait he knew would appeal to a beleaguered monarch ("I only want to help you, Bob"), Fomon was hardly more candid about his intentions. Though he promised that Rittereiser would be more than a figurehead—that he would have wide latitude in managing Hutton's day-to-day affairs—his intentions were to sabotage the new president, proving to the board, and to the world, that the incumbent alone was capable of running the firm he'd come to think of as E.F. Fomon & Co.

In short, what was meant to be a balanced team, the seasoned chief executive and the rising management whiz, turned into a bitter rivalry leading, just hours after the board demanded a showdown, to a breakfast table at the Westbury.

Fomon recalls the meeting: "So you want to be CEO," Fomon said, barging into the issue in the same headstrong way he'd always run the company.

Taken aback by Fomon's offensive, Rittereiser fiddled with his coffee cup. Could the prize he'd coveted since rising to the inner circle at Merrill finally be within his reach? Could Fomon be trusted?

"Do you want my job now?" Fomon pressed, forcing Rittereiser to reveal his ambitions. "Do you want to be CEO?"

Rittereiser squirmed in his seat. A product of the Merrill Lynch bureaucracy, he was used to wielding his power behind the protective cover of a corporate memo. Open warfare, Hutton style, left him feeling weak and vulnerable. Nonetheless, he summoned his courage.

"Yes," he told Fomon. "I want to be CEO."

Hearing the impact of his words said aloud and fearing the confrontation they might provoke, the CEO-to-be promptly sugar-coated his response.

"If I'm going to have a fair chance to run this company, Bob, I have to be chief executive. But that doesn't mean I want to force you out. You'll work beside me as chairman. As the firm's elder statesman, its leader emeritus. You are E.F. Hutton, Bob. No one can ever take that from you."

Convinced that there would still be a place for him in his castle—that he might still run it, title or not—Fomon agreed to abdicate. With the board finally closing in, he had little choice.

At ten that morning, Bob Fomon stood before the board of directors and nominated Robert Rittereiser to succeed him. He would be Hutton's newest chief executive.

And he would be Hutton's last.

Chapter 2

"I'm J. Paul Getty and E.F. Hutton is my broker."

The saga of E.F. Hutton & Co. traces back to the Horatio Alger tale of its founder, Edward Francis Hutton. The son of a Cincinnati farmer who migrated to New York, young Edward was raised in Manhattan and educated in the city's public school system. It was in P.S. 6 that he befriended an older classmate, Bernard Baruch, who would become an early influence on his thinking and a lifelong friend.

Drawn to finance the way his ancestors had been drawn to the rich Midwestern soil, Hutton gravitated to Wall Street, landing at age seventeen a five-dollar-per-week job in the mailroom of a prosperous mortgage company. Displaying a brash irreverence that would remain his hallmark throughout his career, E.F. took leave on an unauthorized vacation, only to find on his return that he'd been fired from his ground-floor position.

Undaunted, young Edward, who impressed prospective employers with his unique mixture of all-American enthusiasm and urban savvy, landed his next job as a check writer for the Manhattan Trust Company. The lowly position proved to be a turning point in Hutton's fledgling career. When the firm's president, John Waterbury, criticized Hutton for his sloppy penmanship, suggesting that the young clerk attend night school to improve his handwriting, Hutton resigned in a huff. Determined to move out of the Dickensian back offices of the city's financial institutions and into a position of power, he enrolled in Packer's Business College, taking management courses and spending evenings poring over books on economics and finance.

Imbued with the spirit of a dynamic young country first feeling its oats as an industrial power, Hutton was convinced that a young man with drive and ambition would find himself inexorably hooked to the engines of capitalism, achieving great personal wealth as the nation itself prospered. Indentifying the brokerage business as an especially promising opportunity, Hutton made his first bold move, purchasing—along with his friend Arthur Harris—a membership on the Consolidated Stock Exchange. Thus was born the firm of Harris, Hutton & Company.

A strikingly handsome bachelor-about-town whose chiseled face and trim physique turned women's heads, Hutton charmed his way into New York's social scene, where his name became a permanent fixture on the Who's Who of Manhattan party lists. It was in this upper strata that he met and fell in love with Blanche Horton, a stunning debutante whose father, H.L. Horton, was one of the leading members of the New York Stock Exchange. After a brief and passionate courtship, Hutton approached H.L. for his daughter's hand, only to be dismissed as an unworthy suitor. The reason? Hutton's membership on the Consolidated Stock Exchange, which was viewed by Big Board members as a street bazaar for third-rate brokers and investors, would be an embarrassment to the Horton family. Putting romance before business, Hutton promptly dismantled his partnership, sold his interest in the Consolidated Exchange, and proceeded in June 1902 to marry the woman he loved.

It was an impulsive move, but one that would have a

beneficial impact on Hutton's career. While honeymooning with his bride on the West Coast, Hutton was struck by the dearth of quality brokerage services in San Francisco and Los Angeles. Minus a direct link between Wall Street and the West, investors had to wait for stock prices to make their way through a patchwork of telegraph feeds that started in New York and made local stops across the heartland. As a result, California traders were operating on stale information, hours behind their peers (and sometimes investment competitors) in New York.

Sensing a classic void in the marketplace, Hutton decided to establish a New York Stock Exchange firm capable of serving investors on both coasts. Returning to New York late that summer, the budding brokerage tycoon accepted a partnership with W.E. Hutton & Co., a sleepy, Cincinnati-based bond house owned by his cousin. His goal: to convince the partners to take his vision from drawing board to marketplace, launching a bicoastal trading operation. But his words fell on deaf ears. More comfortable with bonds than equities and fearing the risk of expansion into virgin territory, the ranking powers turned thumbs down to the new partner's plan, prompting Ed Hutton to pursue his dream elsewhere.

Turning to his friend George Ellis, Jr., the son of a prominent banker and bond trader, Hutton suggested that they form a company, buy a membership on the New York Stock Exchange, and promptly expand to the West Coast. When Ellis agreed, Hutton rounded up a small group of partners willing to finance the new venture. A born salesman blessed with infectious optimism, Hutton enlisted a cast of powerful allies, including Uncle William D. Hutton, who offered to contribute his Big Board seat for a stake in the firm, and Edward's older brother, Franklyn L. Hutton, then married to the daughter of F.W. Woolworth.

Though all agreed to join E.F.'s fledgling operation,

George and Franklyn needed time to tie up their personal affairs. Unwilling to wait, Ed Hutton proceeded without them, forming E.F. Hutton & Co. as a two-man partnership (Edward Francis Hutton and William D. Hutton) christened on October 12, 1903. When Ellis and brother Franklyn joined the firm six months later, offices were taken at 33 New Street at the corner of Exchange Place, just one block from the New York Stock Exchange. The date was April Fool's Day 1904.

"Success was almost instantaneous," states Donald Phillips, a long-time Hutton employee and the firm's unofficial biographer. "E.F. and Franklyn scoured the city for new accounts, W.D. Hutton busily engaged in executing the firm's orders on the Exchange, and Ellis maintained his contact with banks and institutions and oversaw the operations phase of the business."

Though the founders' personal talents contributed mightily to the firm's explosive start, another major factor came into play. An enlightened employer clearly ahead of his time, Ed Hutton's philosophy was: "Secure the best available talent, pay them generously, and, most important, make them a part of, not apart from, the family." The sense of belonging proved critical to the Hutton culture, evoking extraordinary employee loyalty and thereby giving the firm a decided advantage over its competitors.

By the time the thriving little firm that bore his name approached its first anniversary, Ed Hutton had begun to shift his attention from the local scene to the vision of a national firm based on a technological bridge linking the east and west coasts.

At this juncture only one firm, Chicago's Logan & Bryan, offered direct quotes from Wall Street to Los Angeles or San Francisco. But the service left much to be desired.

As Don Phillips notes, Logan & Bryan was essentially a commodity house that gave preference to commodity quotations and news at the expense of stock quotations, which were supplied over the wire at infrequent intervals and then only on a few of the most actively traded and prominent securities. Local West Coast firms who were not "cut in" on Logan & Bryan's wire had to depend on Western Union's CND Service, which was an hourly service on a predetermined list of New York Stock Exchange and Curb Exchange securities, with a periodic transmission of commodity quotes.

The setup was hardly ideal. Orders entered from San Francisco or Los Angeles frequently required an hour or more for the round trip and in active markets it was not surprising for an execution to be affected several points above or below the quotation available at the time the order was entered.

According to Phillips, "Logan & Bryan's service was substantially better than CND but because of the number of 'drops' on the wire—the firm maintained its own offices in Des Moines, Kansas City, Omaha, Denver, Salt Lake City, Los Angeles, and San Francisco—as well as correspondent drops at smaller cities across the country, there was always a 'fight' by the telegraphers to seize the circuit to clear the traffic of their own offices with consequent delay to other business. It was this situation that E.F. was determined to correct."

His master plan called for stringing a private telegraph wire linking Hutton's New York and San Francisco offices, giving the firm a monopoly on timely transcontinental stock quotes. With this bold stroke E.F. Hutton & Co. would leapfrog its brokerage competitors by assuring customers of a decided advantage in securities trades. Because time was always critical to investors, E.F. saw his private wire as the better mousetrap that would bring the investment community banging on Hutton's door.

But there were obstacles to overcome. When E.F.

pitched his plan to Western Union president Newcomb Carleton, the skeptical executive threw two barriers in his path. Based on the telegraph equipment already in place, a private wire could extend only as far west as Salt Lake City. What's more, even if the hookup could be extended to San Francisco, an expansion Carleton was not about to suggest, the cost of maintaining the wire would be prohibitive.

But Hutton was determined to proceed. According to Phillips, E.F. asked, "How much would it take to string additional telegraph wire from Salt Lake to San Francisco?"

"One hundred thousand dollars," Carleton bellowed.

"If I pay half the cost, or fifty thousand dollars, whichever is the lesser, do I get my wire?" Hutton asked. "I'll worry about generating enough business to pay the rental after I have it."

Stunned by E.F.'s gutsy response, Carleton asked for twenty-four hours to consider the offer. When Hutton returned to the Western Union offices the following day, he had the news he'd been hoping for.

"Young man," Carleton said, "I am impressed by your enthusiasm and confidence, and although I have misgivings as to your judgment, if you are willing to make such a commitment, my associates and I are prepared to accept your proposal. Work will start immediately."

Thus was born Western Union Lease #1 for the first private transcontinental telegraph wire.

It would prove, as had the New York operation before it, an instant success. When E.F. Hutton & Co. launched its San Francisco office on the corner of Bush and Montgomery Streets in December 1904, it boasted the startling ability to execute customer orders in minutes, as opposed to an hour or more for established brokers. Quickly some of the biggest players in San Francisco were in the Hutton camp. The roster of wealthy and socially connected clients included the Fairs, Crockers, Fleischhakers, Stanfords, and Haywords. In just two months of operations the office moved into the black, generating substantial profits and giving birth to Hutton's image as the brokers of choice to the carriage trade. Quickly the reputation fed on itself, creating in privileged circles a Hutton mystique.

Stories of Hutton's brokerage magic abounded. Don Phillips tells of a time when legendary New York stock speculator "Bet a Million" Gates was visiting San Francisco on a business trip. He gave Hutton's office manager Richard Mulcahy an order to buy a big block of stock.

"I'll stop by in an hour or so to see how you made out," Gates said.

Mulcahy could hardly contain himself. "If you'll wait a *couple of minutes*, Mr. Gates, I'll have the report of your purchase."

"What?" Gates blustered. "I'll bet you a thousand dollars you can't get me a report in fifteen minutes, let alone two or three."

"Mr. Gates, I cannot accept your wager, but I'll make you a proposition. If I'm able to confirm your purchase in three minutes, will you give a portion of your business to my firm when you return to New York?"

"Done," Gates replied.

As Mulcahy predicted, the order was confirmed within the allotted time and Gates, who kept his end of the bargain, remained a lifelong Hutton client.

During this startup period, E.F. Hutton & Co. was blessed by the brilliant stewardship of its first great management team: Edward Francis Hutton and George Ellis. Not for another seventy years would a management duo rival their skills and success in building the firm. Polar opposites, E.F. and Ellis complemented each other, creating a management unit that was far superior to the sum of its parts. Whereas Hutton was impulsive, unorthodox, and flamboyant, Ellis was methodical, cautious, and reserved. Whereas E.F. was driven by an aggressive approach to the marketplace and by an overriding faith in his ability to generate commissions no matter where the firm opened offices, Ellis played the devil's advocate, tempering E.F.'s ambitions by demanding that growth and expansion be commensurate with business conditions. While Hutton was always prepared to take a risk, Ellis demanded that the firm base its bets on more than a hunch.

Although the conservative Ellis carried great weight in the firm, the man whose name was on the letterhead, and whose personality was the driving force behind the business, could not be contained. Where there was opportunity, Hutton would seize it. His unflagging optimism, combined with an unrelenting commitment to growth, led to a network of retail brokerage offices that would become the envy of Wall Street. By 1909 the Hutton marketing map boasted branches in Los Angeles (run by Mulcahy's son-in-law, Robert Burns), San Francisco, New York's Woolworth Building, and, in what would become a Hutton tradition, the Plaza Hotel.

"In those days, when affluent travelers wanted to make investments, communicating with their hometown account executives was difficult," says Bob Bacon, a veteran of fifty-four years in the brokerage business. "So they needed local brokers to execute their trades while they were on the road. By opening offices in some of the finest hotels, we hoped to get their accounts.

"It was a modest investment that paid off handsomely. The hotel branches, which were little more than a salesman and a telegrapher, brought in substantial business and further positioned us as the premier brokers. Anyone could wait for their clients to come to them, but we went to our clients. The world saw that distinction and rewarded us for it."

*   *   *

As E.F. Hutton & Co. sailed through the second decade of the twentieth century, the founder took great satisfaction in watching his firm expand and prosper. It was a rewarding payoff for his entrepreneurial gamble.

But then tragedy struck. In 1919 Hutton's fourteen-year-old son, Harcourt, a bright and effervescent boy who had inherited his father's good looks and exuberance for life, died when he was thrown from a horse. For E.F., who'd dreamed of creating a Hutton dynasty, the death left a void he tried the rest of his life to fill.

"Father always wanted to turn me into the son he'd lost," recalls actress Dina Merrill, Hutton's daughter from a subsequent marriage. "First he tried to make me a hunter, taking me with him into the duck blinds in South Carolina. But I hated that. The thought of killing those lovely creatures left me . . . well I just couldn't bear the thought. Next he tried deer hunting, but that didn't work out, either. I'd say, 'Oh, Daddy, look at the lovely deer . . .' and the deer would run away.

"I remember one time he bought me a pony from a circus that was passing through town. He thought it would be a good idea if I learned how to ride. But the pony turned out to be a trick horse. When I cried, 'It runs away with me—it does whatever it wants,' Daddy looked at me as if I were dreaming it up. 'That's because you don't know how to ride,' he answered. 'I'll show you what to do.'

"Did he ever. He gets on the horse and it runs away with him.

"That was it. We got rid of the pony."

Soon after Harcourt's tragic death, the first Mrs. Hutton (the former Blanche Horton) died as well, leaving her husband, now forty-five, a widower. An incurable romantic happiest when in the company of women, Hutton tried vainly to drown his loneliness in work. But making money, which he did with ease, was never enough. In 1922 he married again, this time to Marjorie Post Close, the daughter of Charles W. Post, founder of the Postum Cereal Company. The marriage, pairing a glamorous woman with a rich and glamorous captain of Wall Street, seemed made in heaven.

But it didn't work out that way. Mrs. Hutton, a stiff, dour patrician always mindful of her station, could never accept her husband's flamboyant personality and distaste for social convention.

"Daddy lived in the South quite a bit and always wore pastel suits, white jackets, and pink pants, while everyone else was still wearing classic navy," Dina recalls. "Mother thought that was crude. She also loathed the way Daddy used to unbutton his jacket cuffs and roll them up. His T-shirts also drove her mad. He had these big white T-shirts that he loved to wear around the house. The only problem was, people were more proper in those days. Mother for one. She absolutely deplored the T-shirts. She said they smelled."

Although Edward and Marjorie were less the perfect couple than the newspapers pegged them to be, the marriage proved to be a turning point in the history of E.F. Hutton & Company. A strong-willed woman, Marjorie convinced her husband to leave the firm he'd launched and assume the chairmanship of Postum Cereal, her family's business. Sensing the opportunity to turn the prosperous health food company into a corporate giant, Hutton accepted the challenge, hoping to build the second great business of his life.* In 1923 he stepped down from the senior management of E.F. Hutton & Co., accepting the designation as a special partner.

It was the end of an era.

"When Edward Francis Hutton relinquished active con-

---

*He would ultimately transform Postum into the General Foods Corp.

trol over the firm he'd founded, he left behind a small partnership more prominent in California than in New York," says Bob Bacon. "In those days you could shout the name of E.F. Hutton on Wall Street and people would hardly know who you were talking about. But in San Francisco or Los Angeles, people thought E.F. Hutton *was* the Stock Exchange."

Hutton's stature three thousand miles from Wall Street traced back to its origins as the first brokerage house hooked by Western Union wire to the Big Board in New York. "Investors used to congregate in our San Francisco office," Bacon recalls. "It was a bustling place filled with the sounds of Morse code clicking over the wire and of men calling out prices across the trading room. The way the system worked, a telegrapher in New York would tap out the latest stock quotes, sending the prices along a transcontinental line that ended in the Hutton office. As the dots and dashes came in from Wall Street, they would reverberate loud enough—thanks to a tin cigar box placed over the wire—for a team of six men called 'markers' to hear the code and to chalk the numbers on a huge blackboard, then the largest of its kind in the world.

"You could always feel a buzz in the room. For investors, Hutton was the place to be."

Throughout the 1920s the Hutton company had prospered, buoyed by a stock market that took off like a shot and continued to skyrocket throughout the decade. With stocks reaching new highs on a daily basis, the nation succumbed to speculative fever, gobbling up securities as if they were one-way tickets to the American dream. Brokerage firms fueled this frenzy, opening offices and promoting investments on the heady assumption that the roaring bull market would never end. Caught up in the euphoria, they expanded at a dizzying pace.

As Don Phillips recalls, during this period of intense,

worldwide speculation, stock exchange firms enjoyed undreamed-of prosperity and branch offices were opened by the hundreds, new firms were formed by the score (often by men who had no previous experience other than their own personal speculative successes), and the slogan "A chicken in every pot and two cars in every garage" became the catch-phrase of the nation. People in humble walks of life became wealthy as the result of following "tips" on the market, and every manicurist, bootblack, barber, and cab driver considered himself a market expert.

But the bubble was about to burst. On Black Friday, October 29, 1929, the market nosedived, wreaking havoc on the New York Stock Exchange and on a nation of investors that had come to worship at its altar. By mid-1930 the price of an NYSE membership, up to $625,000 before the crash, sold for $17,000. During this financial crisis fortunes were wiped out, banks went belly-up, and broker-age firms, which only months before were riding the crest of confidence, were forced to liquidate.

Incredibly, E.F. Hutton came through the debacle virtu-ally unscathed. The firm's ability to weather the storm is testimony to co-founder George Ellis's prudent manage-ment style. A conservative businessman who kept his wits about him despite the reckless abandon of his competitors, he behaved like a savvy investor, recognizing that when the little guy is on a buying spree, the smart money sits on the sidelines. During this decade of pell-mell growth in the brokerage industry, Ellis kept Hutton in check, holding the firm's expansion to seasonal offices along the gold coast vacation circuit from Palm Beach (where Hutton had five offices) to Miami and across the continent to California's Del Monte Hotel. The only year-round offices launched during the period were limited to small satellites of the Los Angeles and San Francisco outposts.

Credit this prudent policy to insight and perception.

Whereas his Wall Street peers saw the market's giddy boom as reason to cut ribbons in dozens of new markets, Ellis, always cognizant of the market's cycles, saw the wild speculation as a red flag. As Don Phillips notes, in the midst of the euphoria, he told his executives: "This is not the time to spend money on expansion. Everyone has money today; the time to expand is when no one has money."*

Equally important, Ellis demanded that Hutton respond to the market fever of the late 1920s by tightening its margin requirements and denying all credit for the most speculative trades. Though clients were free to gamble, Ellis had no intention of sharing the risk. Naturally, this tight-vested policy proved unpopular with investors, prompting many to take their business elsewhere. But from Ellis's standpoint, this was more of a blessing than a curse. Yes, the firm would lose commissions, but should the market collapse, as he feared it would, Hutton's exposure on high-margin accounts would be minimal.

He turned out to be a seer. When the market went to hell in a hand basket, prompting investors to bail out of windows and brokerage firms to dissolve overnight, Hutton lost less than $50,000 on unsecured accounts. It had survived the first stock market crash with hardly a tremor.

In the 1930s a new generation of Hutton men began to wield power in the firm. Prominent among them were the Crary brothers, Allan and Gordon, who would contribute enormously to the Hutton wealth and mystique and who would become leaders of the increasingly powerful West Coast faction.

Old hands at the brokerage business, the brothers had cut their teeth in their father's commission house, Crary & Sons, going from there to a stint with E.A. Pierce & Co.,

---

*This contrarian approach, pursued by Bob Fomon forty years later, would account for Hutton's greatest growth.

a leading securities firm of the day. By the time they joined the Hutton partnership on April 1, 1928, the Crarys were able to bring a substantial clientele into the firm's Los Angeles office. None of them was more important than the oil tycoon who would become the richest man in the world: J. Paul Getty.

During their prep school years at the Harvard Military Academy in Los Angeles the Crarys had befriended Getty, then a bright entrepreneur operating in the shadow of his oilman father, George F. Getty. The relationship, which continued as the Crarys went on to attend Stanford and Getty pursued his business interests, bore fruit when George Getty died, leaving J. Paul as the trustee of his estate. Using his position as a major shareholder in the Pacific Western Oil Co., the junior Getty launched a bold campaign to create a giant oil business that would ultimately dwarf his father's holdings.

Fortunately for the Crarys, the campaign was built around a stock market strategy executed by E.F. Hutton.

Don Phillips notes that in the depression period of the early 1930s, with California crude oil selling for less than twenty-five cents a barrel and oil security prices depressed to levels where market quotations were frequently lower than the new quick cash per share in companies' treasuries, Mr. Getty aggressively purchased through E.F. Hutton & Co. in Los Angeles shares in companies he had chosen as most suited to his ultimate purpose, particularly Tidewater Associated Oil Co.

By mid-1934 Mr. Getty's position with the Los Angeles office had reached such proportions that Gordon and Allan Crary felt they could continue buying for Mr. Getty only with the specific authorization of the New York senior members, and accordingly suggested that Mr. Getty come to New York and lay before Mr. Ellis, Mr. Adams, and Mr. Cutten (Hutton's ranking partners) his financial position and his plans for future market activity.

Mr. Getty set forth in the minutest detail his financial position and the step-by-step program he had evolved to secure control of the companies he sought. In view of the enormous sums of money involved, there was lengthy discussion among the New York partners.

When the firm's leaders emerged from their private meetings, Mr. Getty was told that E.F. Hutton & Co. was prepared to "play the string out to the very end."

Brokerage commissions generated by the Getty account helped to keep Hutton afloat during the deeply depressed securities markets of the 1930s. But it did more than that. From the beginning, the Getty/Hutton relationship added immeasurably to the firm's evolving image as the brokers to the rich and famous. Over the years the Getty connection acted like a magnet, drawing well-heeled clients into the Hutton fold and polishing the firm's mystique as the brokers of choice.

It was an image Hutton courted. Whereas the firm's competitors began to look beyond the individual investor, allocating ever greater resources to investment banking divisions that financed corporate clients, Hutton stuck to the knitting, expanding its network of retail offices, adding to its mix of financial products, weaving its way into the fabric of affluent America. To playboys and dowagers, to Main Street merchants and to captains of industry, the Hutton broker was as indispensable as a friendly banker and a savvy CPA. As clients saw it, he would add to their wealth. "If they can do it for Getty," the thought went, "they can do it for me."

For decades Hutton would cash in on the Getty magic again and again. After a series of setbacks soiled the firm's image in later years, Bob Fomon had the brainstorm of asking J. Paul—then living in virtual seclusion on his Sutton Place estate in England—to appear in a television commercial for Hutton. With this in mind, Gordon Crary, Jr., the second-generation Crary to run the Los Angeles office, was dispatched to see the eccentric billionaire. Posing the question to Getty, wondering anxiously if he would take the request as an honor or an insult, Crary felt the weight of the world leave his shoulders when the firm's most valued client agreed to go before the cameras, stating in his own inimitable manner:

"I'm J. Paul Getty and E.F. Hutton is my broker."

Chapter 3

"In the early sixties, a group of guys who'd joined Hutton about the same time and who'd become close friends, would go out on the town almost every night. We weren't married, we didn't have kids, and the only thing on our minds were partying and meeting women. If we needed any lessons, Bob Fomon was a capable instructor."
— *a former Hutton vice-president*

Bob Fomon never expected to run anything. He certainly wasn't groomed for it.

Born in Chicago in 1925, the third and youngest son of Samuel and Isabel Fomon, Robert was only four when his mother died, leaving a cold, disinterested father in charge of the household. Having known that her husband was not cut out to be a single parent, Isabel had arranged during her long bout with cancer for her sister Marie Sherman to take custody of the boys, raising them in her hometown of Appleton, Wisconsin.

And so the Fomon boys were shipped off to Appleton shortly after the funeral, moving from bustling Chicago to rural Wisconsin. To Frank Capra's America. To a place Bob Fomon would come to hate.

It wasn't just the small-town trappings, the church suppers, and the Saturday night bingo games that he detested, but also the pious lifestyle Aunt Marie tried to create for her adopted sons. A devout Catholic, she was

27

determined to make religion the central force in their
lives, dispatching them to parochial school and shepherding
them to mass seven days a week. While young Robert
played the role of the good choirboy, accepting Marie's
religious regimen as the price of pleasing the sole parental
figure in his life, it was only a matter of time before he
rebelled.

From Robert's earliest recollection, his father was a
remote figure. A physician who made his living teaching
review courses to medical students, his life took a dramatic turn when an interest in plastic surgery (then a
fledgling science in the United States) led him to Europe to
apprentice under the great masters in Austria and Germany. Returning to the States, he published extensively
on surgical techniques and emerged as the leading practi-
tioner of his time. His book *Surgery of Injury and Plastic
Repairs* became the definitive work in the field.

Over the years his sons were out of sight but not
completely out of mind. He continued to support them,
sending Marie monthly checks for their care, but he offered little in the way of parental warmth. When he showed
up in Appleton, he played the role of guiding patriarch,
summoning his offspring before him, plotting out the course
of their lives as if he'd earned the right to do so. For young
Robert the visits were torturous, creating a deep-seated
resentment against authority.

"I never liked my father," he says, musing. "And I
never saw why I should lead my life according to the plan
he'd set for me."

By the time Robert was dispatched to the Campion
Jesuit School for Boys in Prairie du Chien, Wisconsin, a
rebellious streak was starting to peek through the clean-
cut Midwestern demeanor. Far from the pious-minded
cleric his aunt had set out to raise, he emerged as a
campus cutup who thumbed his nose at anything smacking
of authority. Rules, to this free spirit, were meant to be

broken and he did so with impunity. By his junior year the list of Fomon infractions had made him a legend among his peers.

Though they were innocent pranks, rites of passage for a fatherless young man living away from home, this was a religious school. The secret trips off campus, the waterbag bombardments from the dormitory roof, the repeated violations of curfew—all were too much for the Jesuits to accept, innocent or not. Rules had to be followed. An example had to be set. Robert Fomon, Campion's public enemy number one, would have to go.

"They reached the breaking point and booted me out," Fomon recalls, thoughts of his youthful bravado bringing a mischievous glint to his eye. "Being a godly woman, my aunt saw my dismissal as a sin, a disgrace, a cause for great shame. But I didn't share any of that. To me, getting kicked out of that place was a badge of honor."

Returning to Appleton to complete his studies at the public high school, Fomon found himself without a shred of ambition or a clue as to what he wanted to do with his life. All the standard options—law, medicine, business, accounting —left him cold. With little drive or direction, he was Appleton's unanimous choice as "least likely to succeed."

That distinction was hardly lost on Dr. Samuel Fomon, who promptly traveled to Appleton to rekindle an old and by now ridiculous notion: Robert would become a priest.

"My father's thinking had nothing to do with religion," Fomon says. "To him it was a business decision. He saw the church as a quasi-corporation. Get the right management training and you rise to the top. Because I didn't look like the kind of candidate any sane-minded corporation would accept, he saw the church as a court of last resort.

"So he put an offer on the table. If I agreed to pursue the priesthood, he would pull strings on his end, doing whatever it would take to get me into the American College in Rome. It was like he was preparing me for some kind of executive post. With a little luck and a little work, I'd become a cardinal. He had it all figured out.

"But, hell, that wasn't my idea of the priesthood. The way I'd always heard it, you were supposed to have a calling for that. You know, someone whispering in your ear about God and heaven and earth. A mystical experience. That hadn't happened to me—and I had good reason to doubt that it ever would.

"So I canned the priesthood idea. Anything, I told my father, anything but the priesthood. I can't be a man of the cloth."

It was then that Dr. Fomon, who may have anticipated his wayward son's rejection all along, presented plan number two:

"You'll be a lawyer."

The menace of Appleton High had about as much interest in practicing law as in leading high mass, but the idea was infinitely more palatable than pledging himself to a life of celibacy.

Beginning his undergraduate studies at the University of Southern California—chosen because it was worlds away from small-town Appleton—Fomon majored in English literature, switched to archeology and anthropology, and then flip-flopped back again to English lit before graduating with mediocre grades in June 1946.

Remaining in school more for the shelter it provided than the academic challenge, Fomon, still unfocused and immature, enrolled in law school, joining a group of young Turks eager to call themselves attorneys. Bob was never one of them.

"He figured out pretty quickly that law wasn't for him," recalls one of Fomon's close friends during his first and only year at USC Law. "In every law school class you get a good chunk of the student body that's there because they can't figure out what else to do. Bob fitted that mold.

"It was funny. He'd contribute in class, but not on legal

matters. That never interested him. Instead he served as
our translator. Having written a thesis on the obscure
Scottish poet William Dunbar, he was good at deciphering
the old English verbiage used in case law. That kind of
work he loved. But the law itself made his eyes glaze
over."

Now twenty-three and a law school dropout (he quit
before the first year was up), Fomon remained on the USC
campus, teaching English classes and seeking refuge in the
archeology and anthropology courses that captured his
fancy and fed his fascination with the glorious civilizations
of the past. But it was also at this time that he developed
another fascination, one that would shape his personality,
playing a key role years later in his management style, in
his success as a brokerage executive, and in his ultimate
undoing as the chief executive of E.F. Hutton & Co. It
was his blind, arrogant obsession with the rich, powerful,
and socially connected men and women who ran Los Angeles, hosted the great lawn parties and the debutante balls,
and whose regal faces were permanent fixtures on the
society pages.

"Unlike many of his peers who came to the USC campus
with a suitcase full of clothes, a few books, and little else,
Bob Fomon came with social connections," his former
college friend recalls. "His father—then an eminent name in
the medical profession—had paved the way for Bob's arrival, making introductions with the crème de la crème of
Los Angeles families. At the time I first met Bob, he was
living with Dr. George Davidson, minister of the most
prominent Episcopal church in L.A. Bob's father had set
this up, and it opened the doors to an even wider range of
social connections."

These connections Fomon cultivated with great zest.
Like the archetypical country boy who arrives wide-eyed
in the big city and is swept away by its size, splendor, and
elegance, the college man from Appleton recognized im-

mediately that he was in his true element. Dining in the fashionable homes of his college friends, invited to their golf clubs for weekend formals, he was hypnotized by the red brick driveways lined with glistening Mercedes; the mansion walls covered with Picassos, Klees, and Matisses; the black-tie parties that ran until dawn. This glimpse of a charmed and privileged lifestyle captivated Fomon like nothing before.

It wasn't just the money. Equally important were the trappings that came with it. Style, taste, breeding, elegance: this was the world he yearned to inhabit. These were the people he wanted to befriend. He would join the American aristocracy in the only way that was open to an outsider with middle-class credentials: by gaining wealth and power of his own. It would become a lifelong obsession.

"When I went out to dinner with my friends, they would pick up the tab," Fomon recalls. "When we went to a party, it was at their homes, not mine. And when we went for a drive, it was in their Packards and Cadillacs. I didn't even have a car.

"At first, I didn't care whose money it was. Why should I? We were young and free and having a ball. Who paid for what seemed immaterial. If I couldn't afford the good life, I was happy that someone else could and that they were taking me along for the ride.

"But that changed. One day something just clicked inside of me. I didn't want to remain the group pauper. I didn't want to keep taking, taking, like some kind of charity case. I wanted equal status with the people I called my friends. It was time to get rich myself."

This was more than a healthy ambition. Soon Bob Fomon would become the worst kind of snob, a middle-class social climber determined not only to rise from his roots, but to turn his back on them. By wiping the slate clean, by pretending that he was to the manner born, he hoped to join the social elite he'd come to lionize. But first he would have to "get rich," and like E.F. Hutton a half century before him, Fomon saw the brokerage business as the shortest route to personal wealth.

Determined to land an entry-level job with a prominent securities firm, he made the rounds at the leading Wall Street houses, starting with Dean Witter and working his way to the E.F. Hutton building on South Spring Street in the heart of L.A.'s financial district. After setting up an interview with a senior Hutton partner, Fomon returned on the scheduled date, only to find that his contact had passed away in the interim. But what seemed at first like a bad omen turned out well enough when another partner agreed to interview the young applicant and hired him on the spot. Five days later Robert Fomon began his career at E.F. Hutton & Co.

He went to work for an intimate partnership split between the New York headquarters at 61 Broadway and two highly profitable brokerage offices in San Francisco and Los Angeles. Though it had been in business for more than fifty years, Hutton was still a modest enterprise. The entire L.A. staff worked on a single floor, knew each other by name, and felt (as Ed Hutton had hoped they would) like family.

Entering "the family" rather inauspiciously, Fomon began his career as a back-office functionary called "a computer." In those days, tradition required that young brokers earn their stripes in the trenches, learning the nitty-gritty of the securities business before they were allowed within ten feet of a customer. In this baptism by fire the impatient social climber from Appleton, Wisconsin, found himself toiling away in a dimly lit room, recording buy/sell figures on thousands of stock trades. The work was grueling and tedious. Making life even more intolerable, a bank of pointy-nosed clerks assigned to supervise the young "computers" delighted in finding errors in their worksheets and ordering them to recalculate columns of figures from scratch.

Miserable in his role as a back-office grunt, Fomon learned that brokers-to-be could move through the mire of the training program by reminding superiors that "I was hired to be a broker not a clerk." After taking his message up and down the management line, Fomon's persistence paid off. At the end of his third month as a "computer," he was moved up a notch to the "interest desk." Another numbers-crunching outpost, this job called for figuring the current balance on customer accounts. Here too the work was excruciating. If the account balance changed twenty times a day, reflecting a corresponding number of trades, the grunt on the interest desk had to revise the figures accordingly. Without adding machines or calculators, it was sheer drudgery.

After three months on the interest desk, Fomon (who feared being left behind in this corporate Siberia) reminded his superiors again: "I was hired to be a broker, not a clerk." Again his determination paid off, leading finally to his appointment as a Hutton stockbroker.

The odds were against his success. Everything Bob Fomon had pursued until now had ended in failure. His religious education had led not to Rome, but to a scandalous dismissal from a Jesuit school. At Appleton High he had departed without a diploma. Enrolled in USC, he had proved to be an academic dilettante. At law school he had been out the revolving door before the professors learned his name.

So his arrival to the brokerage ranks was hardly a momentous occasion. Trumpets didn't sound. Seasoned brokers didn't hide their Rolodexes. Hutton executives hardly noticed the new recruit—and saw no reason to.

But history would not repeat itself. With his initiation as a broker, Robert Fomon's life would take a dramatic turn, lifting him to the pinnacle of American business.

Bob Fomon succeeded as a broker from his first day on

the job. His mission, to persuade wealthy investors to buy and sell securities through E.F. Hutton & Co., was tailor-made for a young man with a network of contacts in Los Angeles society and a penchant for hobnobbing with the affluent. That stock brokerage was still a gentlemanly calling fit hand in glove with the image he was determined to project to the world.

"Brokerage was a civilized business," recalls Charles (Bud) Crary, who joined Hutton in June 1947 at the behest of his father Allan Crary, then co-managing partner of the Los Angeles office. "We were salesmen, but there were limits on how we sold. Cold-calling clients? Never. Sure, that's standard procedure today, but we thought it unprofessional. Hell, to our way of thinking, calling someone out of the blue was an insult.

"Instead we went to see people, to deal with them face-to-face. We'd get their names through personal contacts and through lists of prospects the firm secured. Hutton was big on country club memberships. The office manager would get lists of members' names, and we'd knock on their doors at home or call on them at work.

"And we'd be creative. In a popular strategy of the time, brokers would go to the most prominent office buildings, jot down the names on the directories, and then call on the executives floor by floor. If someone refused to see you, that's all they had to say. We never pushed. We'd get in to see our fair share without that kind of hard sell. The Hutton name opened doors."

But even this kind of "meet 'em and greet 'em" soft sell was too much the Willy Loman school of sales for budding elitist Bob Fomon. Never much of a door knocker, he preferred to develop clients through his circle of friends and associates.

"I met Bob soon after I graduated from Harvard Business School," says former Hutton vice-president Al Scheid, who joined the Los Angeles office in 1959. "They'd hired me right out of school because in those days, it was L.A. chic to have a Harvard MBA on board.

"I could see from the outset that Bob was a star in the office. In a socially conscious culture—and God, that described the Los Angeles office to a *T*—Bob was among the more socially connected guys. He knew the right people. You'd hear him on the phone talking to Getty Oil and the presidents of the big banks and insurance companies. He won their trust and confidence, and they ran a hell of a lot of business through him."

At the time, Hutton's L.A. office was as much a nonstop Hollywood party as a brokerage business. Partner-in-charge Murray Ward had joined Hutton after a brilliant naval career, having served as a senior intelligence officer on Admiral Halsey's staff. A handsome, dashing man with a patrician bearing, he fit the elegant mode of Hutton leaders that had begun with Ed Hutton and would continue over the years. All of the firm's presidents appeared to be born to the role of brokerage barons.

"Murray was a very sophisticated gentleman," Scheid says. "The kind of guy who, no matter what he had on, looked like he was wearing a tuxedo. That was perfect because Hutton was the glamour firm in L.A. Movie stars would drop in during the day to talk about their portfolios and then show up at Hutton parties later that night. Jane Mansfield stands out in my mind. She was around so often you'd have thought she worked for us.

"Hutton was a fun place to be. To succeed in the firm then, you had to work hard and play even harder."

No one did that better than Bob Fomon. But it was here that the darker side of the man, a grown-up version of the high school prankster, began to reveal itself.

"To Fomon, nothing was off-limits," recalls a close friend. "If he felt like getting so drunk that he couldn't stand up, that's exactly what he'd do. On many nights he'd drink till two, collapse wherever he was standing, and then make his way back to the office the next morning, only to start the whole process over the next night."

Says another Fomon friend from the wild and woolly sixties: "Bob was always up to tricks. I remember a time he was having an affair with a married woman, and he asked me to be his beard. We'd go to parties together, only to separate once we walked through the door. My job was to talk to his lover's husband, diverting the guy's attention while Bob slipped off with his wife. A half hour later I'd get a girl, and we'd all go off and fuck somewhere in our cars.

"Bob was a rascal, but women loved it. Seeing him in action, I'd always think of the line 'and with the girls be handy.' One of the women he was screwing said to me, 'He's the kind of guy you love to be with, but not to marry.' "

Perhaps they saw the darker side. If they did, they had one up on Murray Ward. The man who'd distinguished himself as a wartime intelligence officer didn't see, or didn't care to see, that the live wire in his office was an overgrown kid who refused to see the connection between his actions and the effect they had on others.

"Murray adored Bob Fomon," recalls Scheid. "Bob was driven. All he ever talked about was making money and Murray liked that kind of raw ambition.

"But there was another factor. Bob was a superb manipulator. He could bend the organization to his will. In his own subtle way he was a superb politician. I used to tell him, 'We're both tools. I'm a wedge. I go straight through things, rather than over or around them. When I'm asked a question, I tell the truth. But you're a different kind of tool, Bob. You're a consummate politician. You can wind your way through the organization. You can make it work for you.' "

And he did.

Successful as he was as a stockbroker, Fomon found

himself drawn to the deal-making side of the securities business, to investment banking, where securities firms financed corporations, selling their stocks and bonds through syndicates of brokers. This was more than a career decision. It was also the social jockeying of a young snob who had come to view brokers as common laborers. Cogs in the wheel of finance, they were far below the station he had in mind for himself. He yearned for the white-shoe prestige of corporate finance, where the elite Wall Street firms—the Goldman Sachs, the Salomon Brothers, and the Morgan Stanleys—made their money. In what would prove to be an Achilles' heel for a man who would run a major securities firm, Fomon developed an early disdain for brokerage. He wanted out.

And he got his wish. In January 1960, Murray Ward plucked his fair-haired boy from the brokerage ranks, appointing him assistant to the firm's West Coast syndication manager.

At this stage in his career Fomon revealed a split personality that would be his trademark over the years. On one hand, he could charm the pants off the most sophisticated clients, turning them into loyal and lucrative accounts. On the other hand, he cringed in the company of common folk, a mark of contempt for everyone beneath his chosen caste.

"Put Bob in a room with ordinary people—you know, regular working stiffs, and he was like a fish out of water—awkward, groping, so uncomfortable he'd sweat through his suit," says a one-time Los Angeles-based broker. "I remember a time Bob and I attended a birthday party for one of the secretaries in the office. There were all of these clerks and receptionists wearing cheap suits and guzzling beer out of the bottle. Well, I don't know how or why Bob wound up there, but it was clear from the start that he'd made an awful mistake. I mean, you're not talking shy, you're talking closet-case shy. As soon as Fomon sees what's going on in that room, he starts mumbling something about 'bowling parties.' He wants to back out but I won't let him. Because I block the way, he tries to make the best of it, but it's a disaster. The guy sits in a corner, nursing a drink, talking to no one.

"But inject the same Bob Fomon into a ta-ta cocktail party with the art auction crowd and he'd be suave, charming, debonair."

Over the years, those who viewed Bob Fomon as an introvert failed to understand the man. What was mistaken for shyness was actually arrogance. Arrogance based on a conviction that he was superior to those middle-class mortals who had ordinary jobs and ordinary cars. By distancing himself from these reminders of his own pedestrian background, Fomon hoped to escape his past and establish himself as a born aristocrat. In every way he yearned to be the equal of the society folk he'd come to idolize.

It was a lifelong pursuit that would make him an imposter in both worlds.

Chapter 4

"Keith Wellin fit the Hutton mold to a T. He had a wealthy family, a glamorous wife, and an impressive brokerage clientele. The problem is, he wasn't very adept at running the firm. All the standard traits of Hutton management were no longer enough. The business got too complicated for the salesmen."

—Al Scheid

From the beginning, E.F. Hutton & Co. had drawn its strength from the branch office system and it remained a management priority over the years. While other Wall Street firms carved out powerful roles in corporate finance, Hutton built a savvy retail sales force that could move stocks and bonds to an affluent clientele that was the envy of the brokerage business. In time the firm became the darling of the big portfolio crowd that ran the corporations, hosted the charity balls, and wintered in Palm Beach, Palm Springs, and Zermatt. The average customer was hardly a millionaire, but he aspired to be one, and Hutton's association with the Gettys of the world made being a Hutton customer a status symbol. Capitalizing on this image, and on the proven ability to market securities products, Hutton management kept christening new brokerage offices (mostly through the acquisition of existing brokers), seizing every opportunity to tighten its grip on affluent investors.

Although the pins on the Hutton marketing map were concentrated on the West Coast, where the firm's prosperous retail system stretched from San Francisco to El Paso, senior management was based in New York. A patrician lot, the men who led the firm rose to power through the ranks, parlaying a skill for brokering into a managing partnership.

It worked that way for Ruloff E. Cutten, the man at the top when Bob Fomon joined the firm. A native San Franciscan, Cutten had traveled a serendipitous career path that took him from the front stage of the American theater, to the floor of the New York Stock Exchange, to the royal suite at E.F. Hutton & Company.

Starting out as a budding thespian, Cutten landed roles in theater companies across the country. From all indications, he'd found his life's work. But a detour through the U.S. Navy (he enlisted at the outbreak of World War I) changed that. Dispatched to the Great Lakes Naval Station, Cutten called on a distant relative, Arthur W. Cutten, a renowned commodities trader who operated out of Chicago. Taking to each other immediately, the two men were inseparable whenever young Rulie's naval duties allowed him free time.

Impressed by the elder Cutten and fascinated by his work in the financial markets, Rulie abandoned his acting career at the end of the war for a starting position in the brokerage business. Sponsored by his mentor, he won a job with Clement Curtis & Co., a Chicago-based commission house that processed its trades through E.F. Hutton in New York. After completing an intensive training program in the arcane and often mysterious world of commodities trading, Cutten borrowed money from A.W., bought a membership on the Chicago Board of Trade, and began to operate as a floor broker specializing in the grain pits. Blessed with a quick mind and the kind of sixth sense for timing buys and sells that separates top traders from the pack, Cutten earned wide recognition as a sharp operator.

With the stock markets starting to heat up in the early 1920s, Cutten decided to become a player in securities as well. Buying a membership on the Chicago Stock Exchange, he split his time between the Exchange and the Board of Trade, pulling off a financial juggling act that would swamp all but the most accomplished traders.

Don Phillips recalls that as A.W. expanded his activities in securities, Ruloff was called upon to execute orders of greater and greater magnitude, and it was not long before his services as a broker were being sought by many large traders, not only in the Midwest, but in New York as well. He was entrusted with the responsibility for "making the market" on the Chicago Stock Exchange in such prominent issues as Union Carbide, Montgomery Ward, Armour, and the Insull group.

Because many of his orders were placed through E.F. Hutton & Co. (which for years had maintained A.W.'s Big Board accounts), Cutten was well-known by the firm's New York partners, who asked him to join them as a peer. Accepting the offer to move up to Wall Street, Cutten transported his trading skills to the epicenter of brokerage, the floor of the New York Stock Exchange, where he carried on the tradition that had made Hutton famous: executing substantial trades for rich and prominent clients.

With his success in consummating large sales and purchases on clients' behalf, and with his loyal following among high-rolling investors (both corporate and personal), Cutten emerged as a powerful force in the firm. And so when George Ellis relinquished the management reins in 1939, Cutten succeeded him as Hutton's senior partner.

Convinced that Hutton was overly dependent on retail sales, Cutten developed a smorgasbord of investment banking services, beefing up the firm's capabilities in international arbitrage, securities underwriting, corporate and municipal bonds, mergers and acquisitions. Though Hutton would remain primarily a wire house, it developed limited capabilities in this wider range of markets.

Cutten respected the importance of the retail business, both as a money machine and as a source of the Hutton mystique, but he believed that the future of the securities business belonged to those firms that through diversification could serve the full sweep of corporate and individual clients.

It was a visionary outlook his successors failed to share. While they paid lip service to investment banking and corporate finance, their hearts were on the retail side. Selling stocks and bonds was the business they knew best and the one they remained loyal to.

Another luminary in the Hutton pantheon, Sylvan C. Coleman, took control of the firm in 1961. True to the Hutton's leadership tradition, Coleman was regal and debonair, a Wall Street baron with Hollywood looks. As a graduate of Harvard Business School, he was the first of the Hutton's managing partners to be trained for the role.

Starting out as a securities analyst, Coleman compiled an impressive track record for selecting growth stocks. Convinced that informed investors were successful investors, he persuaded management to create a full-scale research department, one of the first of its kind on Wall Street, staffing it with a corps of Ivy League grads from Wharton, Harvard, and Dartmouth's Amos Tuck School of Business.

After service as a naval officer in World War II (he was assigned to the Department of the Navy in Washington, D.C.), Coleman returned to Hutton as a highly placed partner, assisting Ruloff Cutten as he ventured into the complex areas of corporate underwriting, mutual funds, arbitrage, and private placements.

Unlike Cutten before him, who had been viewed as the heir apparent years before he became senior partner, Coleman had to battle his way to the top, fighting off another top contender, Ted Weichert. But once in control, he was a tough taskmaster whose sharp tongue and testy impatience created a climate of fear on executive row.

"Coleman was intimidating," recalls former regional vice-president and Hutton board member Michael Judd. "When he wasn't pleased, he'd express himself in no uncertain terms. People were scared of him—and no wonder. He chewed their asses off with great regularity."

Adds Clarence Catallo, former head of the Great Lakes region: "When I joined the firm in 1965, all new brokers were sent to New York to be trained. The classroom sessions they put you through were demanding, but the real torture test came on graduation day, when you'd have the honor of meeting Sylvan Coleman. On this momentous occasion all of the trainees would be marched into the boardroom and seated around a big table with Mr. Coleman at the center. Addressing us one by one, he'd ask a series of brain-teasing questions about the stock market, the economy, and our role as brokers. I always thought he did it more to scare us and to test our mettle under fire than to see what we really knew."

A towering personality, Coleman was the kind of leader subordinates worked overtime to please. Sometimes their efforts backfired. When they did, the patrician in Coleman would come to the fore.

"I recall a time when a contemporary of Bob Fomon's had performed an assignment quite well, and as a reward was invited to spend the weekend at Coleman's Connecticut estate," recalls a former Hutton lawyer. "Wanting desperately to make a good impression, the guy decided to buy a box of chocolates for Mrs. Coleman.

"Well, he drives out to the country, only to have the car break down on him twenty miles from the Coleman residence. Being that it's a blistering summer day, his biggest concern is that the chocolates will melt before he gets them to Coleman's wife. But he's in a jam. His car is out of commission, he's out in the sticks, there are no cabs to be found. So when someone offers him a ride in a pickup truck, he accepts.

"A half hour later he pulls up in Coleman's long driveway, propped on the back of the truck, the box of chocolates beside him. Looking up at the house, he notices from the corner of his eyes that Coleman is looking out the window, observing his grand arrival. Naturally, he's mortified, but over the course of the weekend Coleman never said a word about it. It was as if nothing unusual had happened.

"A dignified gentleman just didn't recognize that sort of thing. And in a social setting Sylvan Coleman was a gentleman's gentleman. That was the kind of man you had to be to run Hutton. It was the firm's tradition."

But there was a secret lurking in Coleman's past, one that violated the most deeply ingrained Hutton tradition: no Jew would ever run the firm.

"Only a few people knew that Coleman's real name was Sylvester Cohen," says Hutton's former chief financial officer Tom Lynch. "I discovered it when filing with the Securities and Exchange Commission. Years later, when I was attending a social function, a woman who knew Sylvan from his college days and had learned that he was running Hutton, asked me, 'How's Sylvie Cohen doing?' "

"When Sylvan started in this business, a young man had to choose between the WASP firms and the Jewish firms," says Hutton's former general counsel Tom Rae. "Because Sylvan wanted to work for Hutton, he changed his name to fit the firm. From that day on he lived the life of an Episcopal, marrying an Episcopal woman and ultimately arranging for his burial in an Episcopal service. But that didn't change the fact that he was a Jew. Few people in or outside of Hutton knew it, but he was."

"Sylvan used to try to camouflage his Jewishness by singling out other guys in the firm and claiming that they were Jews," Lynch recalls. "I remember the time he took

me aside, saying, 'Did you know that George Ball's a Jew?
You may not think so, but it's true. His wife Molly's a Jew
and so is he.' When I told him he was wrong, he wouldn't
hear of it. By casting the spotlight on others, he hoped to
keep it off of himself.''

Coleman's announcement that he would retire from Hutton
in September 1970 came at a turning point for the firm and
the securities industry. An explosive rise in equities trading had created an avalanche of paperwork and a back-
office logjam that the brokerage houses, first experimenting
with computers, were struggling to control. At the same
time, the mix of financial services required to compete for
corporate and industrial clients was growing complex and
demanding. In this environment a new breed of professional manager was needed in the chairman's office. Although Ed Hutton and Rulie Cutten and Sylvan Coleman,
men who ran the firm as if it were a family business, were
ideal when Hutton was an intimate partnership, the times
were changing.

"When I joined the firm in 1954, the entire New York
operations were on two floors of 61 Broadway," says
former broker and board member Bill Clayton. "It was a
compact, intimate place where everyone knew everyone
else. To find out what was going on in the firm, all you had
to do was walk down the hall."

In this familial environment the senior partners served
more as role models than as full-time leaders. Still acting
as brokers themselves, the head men—up to and including
Sylvan Coleman—retained their own clientele, buying and
selling stocks for the accounts they had built up over the
years. Formal managing, what there was of it, had to be
sandwiched between telephone calls.

"Dealing with Coleman was exasperating," recalls Al
Scheid. "Because he remained an active producer throughout his presidency, he was too busy talking and selling and

writing tickets to manage. His clients always came first. Guys in the firm who wanted to see the senior partner had to wait in line outside his office."

This kind of part-time management could suffice when Hutton was a "compact, intimate place," but the sixties put an end to that. Suddenly Wall Street was forced to change from a clique of wood-paneled clubs run by grand old men to hard-nosed businesses run by professional managers who knew their way around computers, strategic plans, mergers and acquisitions, financial forecasting, and budgeting. To succeed in the new era, Hutton would have to break with its tradition.

But a major hurdle stood in the way. In 1966 Hutton's partners had chosen another of the living portraits in oil, Chicago broker Keith Wellin, to serve as president and heir apparent to chairman Coleman. A native of Grand Rapids, Michigan, Wellin had started out as a salesman in the firm's Chicago office in 1951, moving up the retail ladder to Chicago regional vice-presidency in 1963 and then to the presidency. But to many, he had a fatal flaw. Like his mentors before him, Wellin was considered too absorbed with his personal trading to serve as a hands-on manager.

With the market in the doldrums and with the firm appearing to drift, a growing chorus began chanting for Wellin's hide. The loudest voices came from a powerful new force in the Hutton hierarchy: the bright young men who had joined the firm in the 1950s and '60s and were lobbying for more sophisticated management. This quality they found lacking in Keith Wellin.

"Wellin was a good-time Charlie," Scheid says. "On a personal level, you had to like him. He was charming, gracious, a real gentleman. The kind of guy who knew the right people, who wore the right suits.

"While that made for a successful broker, it didn't matter a whit in the management department. It's the classic case of turning a top salesman into a top executive. You lose a good salesman and you get a lousy manager in return.

"Keith's problem was that he was a consensus-style politician in a job that demanded a decisive leader. He couldn't move quickly or make the big decisions.

"One day when I was dining with him at 21, I mentioned that some of our competitors were making extensive use of computers, doing neat things like figuring their trading margins right on the computers. When I suggested that Hutton should start computerizing, he sniffed and said, 'Maybe someday. After we retire.'

"That's when I knew he was in trouble. The guys who'd entered the firm with me weren't going to put up with that. We were pushing for more aggressive and enlightened leadership, and we had no intention of stopping until we got it. Our attitude was: 'Youth has to be served.' Wellin wasn't the answer."

The growing sentiment against Keith Wellin was building along geographic as well as generational lines. Ever since Edward Hutton had christened the San Francisco office, the firm had been split between mostly autonomous factions on the east and west coasts. The king was enthroned in New York, but his rule over the provinces was tempered by the power of regional vice-presidents, mostly the high lord of Los Angeles, whose office had become the command post of Hutton West.

Through the years both sides eyed each other suspiciously. Distrust, resentment, and lingering jealousies lay just beneath the surface. In part it was a classic clash between East and West, with the Californians—who viewed themselves as the real brokers and money-makers—convinced that they were under the thumb of the ivory-tower elitists engaged in arcane market strategies that brought little to the firm.

This regional resentment took on crisis proportions as

the Wellin presidency, considered a product of the eastern establishment, faced a bear market that took its toll on brokerage businesses in the late 1960s, ending a euphoric period of rising stock prices that had continued unabated since the 1950s.

"Overexpansion and other excesses of the sixties—such as the hedge fund and performance fads, the new issue craze, the collapse of Penn Central and other high-touted speculations—resulted in near disaster," recalls Hutton's former senior vice-president and resident aristocrat Henry Mortimer, who would come to serve as one of Bob Fomon's social gurus. "When the storm broke in late 1968, the industry found itself overextended and undercapitalized. The back offices of many brokerage houses and banks became incapable of processing the volume of business, adding further confusion to the picture.

"The stock market, which touched 1,000 for the first time in February 1966, failed in its second attempt to scale the magic numbers and it fell by 36 percent between December 1968 and May 1970. By then the situation had reached near panic proportions. It was destined to get worse."

"I remember taking my brokerage training in New York in the summer of 1969," says Richard Bragh, who went on to become a branch manager in San Jose. "We were brought into the infamous last session with chairman Sylvan Coleman expecting to hear that we were embarking on careers of extraordinary promise. Our classroom teachers had led us to believe that the market was in one of its routine dips and would turn up quickly. But Coleman, never a man to mince words, hit us with the hard truth.

" 'If you think this is bad, you ain't seen nothing yet,' he said. 'You might as well face it, you're in for very bad times.'

"On that alarming note, the guy next to me said, 'Shit, I hope he's wrong.' But he wasn't. The market kept sliding."

It was just the scenario the Californians feared. At a time when Hutton needed strong leadership at the top, they wanted one of their own to fill the bill. In this troubled environment, Keith Wellin wasn't perceived as the kind of man who could step in and take control."

"The guy wanted to handle his own customers," says a former vice-president and board member. "I remember one time George Ball* wrote a speech for Wellin to give to a group of our Texas brokers. You know, a pep talk from the boss.

"As Wellin's talking, he gets the pages mixed up. He's going from page four to seven and from seven to five and so on. It's all coming out like gibberish, but does that stop him? No! He just jumps from one page to the next even though what he's saying makes no sense. All he wants to do is to get the speech over with, get on the plane, and go home."

Although Wellin's popularity in the firm was falling along with the Dow Jones averages, he hardly noticed. "Wellin never saw the opposition gathering forces against him," Scheid says. "Until that point the man had led such a charmed life that he never thought anything could rain on his parade."

But the end was near. As the schism widened, growing more virulent with the passing months, it became obvious that Wellin would have to go.

Four years after assuming Hutton's presidency, Wellin would be banished from the post, the victim of a bicoastal battle that would pit the firm's most powerful offices, and its most prominent personalities, against each other.

When the dust cleared, Robert Fomon would rise like a phoenix, taking control of E.F. Hutton & Co. It would be the beginning of the firm's most spectacular growth. And it would be the beginning of the end.

---

*Then a Hutton sales manager, he would go on to become president of the firm.

Chapter 5

"It was like King Solomon and the women who claimed the same baby. In this case it was two men, John Shad and Keith Wellin, claiming the same firm. Al Jack would be the great mediator."

—Norman Epstein

The East vs. West schism that had lain beneath the surface for years grew more apparent when the Wellin regime launched a burst of retail expansion. Inspired by senior vice-president Arthur Goldberg, a brilliant marketing tactician who favored aggressive expansion of the brokerage network, the Wellin/Goldberg team began christening new Hutton offices at a breakneck pace.

"Branches were opening at such a furious pace that we ran short of managers to run them," recalls Humbert Powell. "I had had my broker's license for about a year when George Ball says, 'You've got to go into branch management.'

"Well, that was easy for him to say, but as a broker I'd always been taught that the first thing you do is build your book (a roster of brokerage clients), because you can always take your book wherever you go—and you can live by it.

"So I said, 'George, I haven't built my book yet.' But he wouldn't hear of it. There were too many jobs to fill.

" 'Just get out in the field,' he said. 'And shut up.' "

Hutton's "California mafia" had always cheered for bold expansion of the retail network, but in this case the pins on the map were dotting the East Coast rather than the West. This, they feared, would further dilute their power base, making them even more subservient to the men at 61 Broadway. And the specter of one man in particular, Arthur Goldberg, gaining power over them was anathema.

"When I trained in New York, Arthur Goldberg was the role model for all the young brokers," says Clarence Catallo. "When you looked out on the floor, he was fielding dozens of calls, writing tickets, barking out orders. The man was a freight train—and that scared the hell out of the guys out West. They knew he had grand ambitions for Hutton and that if anyone could accomplish them, it was Arthur."

But Goldberg's ambition wasn't the only thing that frightened the Hutton establishment. A darker issue lurked within this lily-white, all-male bastion of WASP supremacy, poisoning the culture and erecting invisible roadblocks against Wellin's rise to chief executive. In an ugly smear campaign launched by the California camp, supported by well-placed sympathizers in Texas, Florida, and New York, rumors spread throughout the firm that Wellin's election would bring about a first for the blue-blooded brokerage of E.F. Hutton: a practicing Jew in the presidency.

"The fear was that Arthur would ride into office on Keith's coattails," Norm Epstein recalls. "The scenario had Wellin assuming the chairmanship and then appointing Goldberg, who was widely regarded as his brain trust, to the presidency. In effect, an observing Jew would be chief operating officer. That prospect sent a chill through a lot of people."

Throughout the firm's history an unwritten rule had barred Jews from holding down the top spot. Sylvan Coleman had evaded the rule by camouflaging his Jewish identity under a false name and a membership in the Episcopal Church, but Goldberg was the real megillah.

"There was a streak of anti-Semitism there that you had to be blind to miss," says Goldberg, now a partner with the brokerage firm Neuberger & Berman. "Even though I stated repeatedly that I didn't want to be president, that I'd reject the job if it were offered to me, the rumors persisted and the opposition remained firm. They didn't want me to get within striking distance of the office."

Internal prejudice wasn't all of it. There were clients to consider, too. The second- and third-generation Hutton investors, who passed along their accounts like family heirlooms and whose image of the archetypical Hutton man was gleaned from the patrician portraits of Edward Francis Hutton, George Ellis, and Ruloff Cutten, were not prepared for a Goldberg staring down from the wood-paneled walls. With that one change the Hutton mystique, as fragile as it was effective, would be in jeopardy. It was a risk that the anti-Semites and the hard-nosed pragmatists alike refused to take. They would block Wellin's path to the top.

At this critical juncture a group of dissidents determined to block Wellin from office began to promote the candidacy of the man widely acknowledged as the brightest mind in Hutton: John Sigsbee Rees Shad.

As head of the firm's investment banking arm, Shad was a natural choice to run the firm. Creative, analytical, and authoritative, the forty-six-year-old graduate of the University of Southern California, Harvard Business School, and the New York University School of Law, had emerged as one of the most prominent and respected men on Wall Street. An astute market analyst and investor, he'd made millions for himself and for Hutton.

Shad's financial wizardry was apparent early in his career. Graduating from Harvard in 1949, he took a job as a securities analyst with the market-advisory service Value

Line, where he recommended investments in an obscure outfit called Associated Transport. With the company unable to meet its preferred dividends, the stock was selling for $2.50. But Shad, whose analytical abilities X-rayed through the company's surface problems to find hidden strength, borrowed $5,000 and bought 2,000 shares of Associated's shares. Six months later, with the stock at $9, Shad sold out, pocketing more than $13,000 in profits. It was a fit beginning for a man who liked to say he would spend "the first third of my life learning, the second third earning, and the third part serving."

Joining Hutton in 1963 as vice-president in charge of corporate finance, Shad brought new luster to an investment banking department that had been virtually dormant before his arrival. "John had plotted out a brilliant strategy that was paying big dividends for the firm," says Paul Bagley, who as a 26-year-old graduate of Harvard Business School went to work for Shad in 1968. "Rather than competing with the premier investment banks for the Fortune 100 clients everyone on Wall Street was gunning for, Shad set his sights on small-growth companies the others were ignoring. By financing these fledgling companies in their formative years—taking them through initial public offerings, arranging private placements, and doing whatever he had to to secure early-stage capital—Shad gained management's loyalty, holding onto his clients as they emerged over the years from modest enterprises into major companies.

"John's success stories included such companies as the home-building firm of Kaufman & Broad, Browning Ferris Industries, and Continental Telephone. At Continental, for example, he was intimately involved from the beginning, providing the company with periodic infusions of equity capital as well as financing its acquisitions. Over the years Continental became a major client of the firm. That was the essence of John's strategy: sink your teeth into a client and hold on forever.

"And it worked. Under Shad's leadership Hutton was a consistent winner in the investment banking sweepstakes."

Shad's genius was in filling a void in the marketplace. With the elite firms dismissing small companies as crumbs on the table of corporate finance, Shad found little competition in his search for growth clients.

Besides creating a profit center of his own, Shad's strategy fit hand in glove with Hutton's overall strength: the retail distribution of investment products. In pitching the firm's capabilities to prospective clients, Shad could point to Hutton's high-powered brokerage force, proving that the firm was in a unique position to sell the shares of stock he brought to market. Once the client went public, Hutton's investment bankers could turn the stock over to the brokers, feeding their voracious appetites for investment products. It was a true strategic fit.

Bagley continues: "Instead of saying, 'Let's become big in investment banking,' a hollow cliché that sounds good but fails to provide a means for achieving that end, Shad said, 'Let's capitalize on our strong retail network, using it to leverage our banking activities.' It may seem simple now, but the best ideas always look that way from hindsight."

As a man who moved in Wall Street's highest circles, Shad appeared to be the kind of presidential timber who could lead Hutton through the 1970s. With the brokerage business in a rough-and-tumble period, and with the firm evolving from clubby partnerships to modern corporations, a man of Shad's stature seemed tailor-made for the role. As one of the few Hutton executives with ties to the power brokers on both coasts, he was in a unique position to challenge Wellin.

With this in mind, Shad assembled a team of supporters—

led by his second-in-command, Fred Josephs*—to secretly tour the firm's offices in the winter of 1969, lobbying for support. In a ploy designed to ice the election before the annual meeting scheduled for February 1970, the Shad forces cooked up the idea of passing out "irrevocable" proxies naming their man as chief executive. In this way a vote for Shad would be iron-clad. Once a Hutton executive signed a Shad proxy, that vote was in the bank. Theoretically, their minds could not be changed.

With Shad's supporters on the march, Wellin marshaled his own hit squad, dispatching campaign teams to the same offices the Shad forces had already "sewn up."

At this point Hutton was an armed camp, pitting East against West, retail against banking, the encumbent against the challenger. Quickly the battle turned personal, with each side spreading rumors—"Shad's an opportunist: if he loses, he'll join Merrill Lynch"—and innuendos—"A vote for Wellin is a vote for Goldberg."

In the end the mudslinging backfired. By dividing the firm, both sides canceled each other out, creating a vacuum that another force, a self-professed "darkest of dark horses," would come to fill.

"While making my way through the Hutton offices on Keith's behalf, it hit me that Wellin and Shad had effectively nullified each other," recalls Norm Epstein, whose eleventh-hour campaign swing took him to Boston, Detroit, Tucson, Los Angeles, and San Francisco. "At each stop my message was the same. I told the guys that the Shad proxies were not irrevocable, and no matter what anyone had or hadn't signed, they should give Wellin a chance to present his side.

"But it was no use. With the firm split down the middle, it was apparent that neither candidate could be elected on his own."

*He is now chief executive of Drexel Burnham Lambert.

Enter Hutton's reigning patriarch, Los Angeles regional vice-president Alec Jack. A diminutive Scotsman, he had joined Hutton in 1929 and risen through the ranks.

"Al Jack was the definition of honesty," says an old Hutton hand now retired. "Let me give you an example. We once had a big producer in the L.A. office. The guy sat right in front of the room, puffed on a big stogie and represented all the top investors. He had this one customer who loved to short stocks and had an uncanny ability to buy in just as the shares were about to decline.

"Well, one time when the client was on a business trip abroad, a stock in his portfolio started to show some strength after falling nearly 15 points. Thinking the stock had bottomed out, the broker tried to contact the customer, seeking his permission to sell the shares. But he couldn't track the guy down. He called Zurich, he called Rome, he called Paris. After a half dozen tries, all without luck, he decided to sell the stock without the client's okay.

"Bad move. After a brief uptick the stock continued its slide, dropping eight more points by the day the investor returned to the U.S. and strolled into our office expecting to collect a $60,000 profit. That's when the account executive broke the bad news that he had sold the stock before the final plunge.

" 'But I didn't authorize you to do that,' the investor screamed.

" 'I was only anticipating your move—trying to protect your interests.'

" 'I don't need anyone to protect my interests. I've managed to do a pretty good job of that myself. I'd been following the stock. If I'd wanted it sold, I would have called you. You should have known that.'

"When the issue went to Al Jack, he paid the investor his full $60,000 that day. And then he turned around and fired the broker, the biggest producer in the office.

" 'We can't run this business the way you did,' Al said. 'We work for the customer, and that's something we can never forget.' "

Everyone's first choice to succeed Sylvan Coleman, Jack, sixty-three years old at the time, had removed himself from the running, insisting that Hutton deserved a younger man at the helm.

Still, he reserved the right to be kingmaker.

"By the time my campaign trip took me to the last stop in Los Angeles, it was clear that Al Jack held the election in his hands," Epstein says. "If he supported Shad, Shad would be CEO. If he backed Wellin, Wellin would be.

"But at this point I wasn't about to electioneer for anyone. The firm was being torn apart by opposing forces. We needed a stabilizing force, and only Al Jack could provide that. Whatever power I had as head of operations, I was delegating to him. I told him, 'Al, I lay my imaginary sword at your feet.' Without saying exactly what he would do, he promised to come to New York to help settle the matter."

With the election only days away, Shad, who counted the California contingent in his camp, believed he had the election won. But whether he had the votes or not, a growing concern about his management abilities began to spread through the firm. While no one doubted that Shad was a superb banker, they feared that he was more of an individualist than a team player. Absorbed in his work, committed to his own buying and selling and deal-making, he had neither the time nor the inclination to step away from his personal pursuits to lead the firm.

In addition, as successful and as respected as he was as an investment banker, Shad was still a source of considerable amusement in the executive ranks. "Shad had things percolating because he was a bright, innovative guy who had made a name for Hutton with emerging companies," says a former vice president in the investment banking department. "But as brilliant as he was, he could be equally comical. You have to picture the guy. He's kind of ugly, and he wears these terrible suits that always seem two sizes too big.

"As you can imagine, Shad wasn't much of a salesman. Not the kind of guy who could go out and do deals one on one. No, he was best barricaded in his office with his ears plugged into two phones. Still, every once in a while he'd go out on the road and try to make a pitch for new business.

"One time he accompanied me on a sales call to some Kansas utilities. At the first few stops Shad stays in the background, listening to me go through my spiel about Hutton's great strengths, its hundreds of offices and thousands of salesmen. Well, when we get back in the plane after one of these dog-and-pony shows, Shad says to me, 'Hey, that was great stuff about the Hutton offices and account executives and the like. Tell it to me again.' Christ, here was one of the most senior guys in the firm, and it was like he'd never heard any of this stuff before.

"To appease him I recited the whole speech chapter and verse and goddamn if he doesn't start writing it all down on the inside of matchbook covers. He fills one matchbook and goes onto another and another and another. Seemed strange, but with John you never knew what to expect.

"The next day, just as we're about to go into a meeting, Shad says, 'That was a good pitch you gave yesterday. Let me try it.' And lo and behold, he goes before this group of utility executives, pulls a crumpled bunch of matchbooks out of his pocket, and starts reading from them. 'Hutton has 103 offices . . .'" He puts that matchbook down and reads another: 'Hutton has 1,500 salesmen . . .' Believe it or not, that's the way he gives his speech.

"Needless to say, everyone in the meeting is stunned.

Everyone except Shad. He thinks he'd done a brilliant job."

But Shad wasn't paid for his speaking style. A legendary workaholic, he virtually lived in his Hutton office and expected others to follow the same "learn, earn, serve" regimen that guided him.

"Many times I would come to see him at 8 A.M. only to find that he had been at work all night," recalls Paul Bagley. "Others who got holed up at the office now and then on emergency projects said they'd find Shad there, too, wandering around at three or four o'clock in the morning. The man had an unlimited capacity for work.

"The problem was that he expected others to be equally driven. Were they less so, he had little use for them. He'd rant and rave and tell them to shape up.

"Some managers use diplomacy, but Shad used fear and intimidation. When subordinates presented ideas that he rejected for one reason or another, he'd tear into them in front of others, dissecting their arguments, humiliating them. Tact? The man never heard of the word.

"He was also inaccessible. You've heard of the open-door policy, where the boss keeps his door ajar so subordinates can wander in at will. Well, John's style was just the opposite. Sequestered in his office, wired into the telephones, he was harder to see than the pope.

"You can't run a firm that way. Maybe people started to recognize that. Maybe he'd made too many enemies to be elected president."

When the showdown came at the annual meeting on February 11, neither Wellin nor Shad could muster the votes to take office. The next day Al Jack arrived in New York. He came with a public mission—and with a secret plan.

"The action took place on the forty-second floor of our offices at One Chase Manhattan Plaza," Epstein recalls.

"At first Jack tried to forge a compromise. To keep tempers from flaring, he cordoned off the standing armies on separate parts of the floor. On one side there was Keith Wellin and his entourage, including Arthur Goldberg, chief financial officer Tom Lynch, George Ball, and myself. On the other side, there was Shad and his loyalists, including Midwest regional manager John Latshaw, Fred Josephs, and equity trading chief Jimmy Gahan. In the middle sat Al Jack, a symbolic buffer between the enemy camps.

"Jack's strategy was to bring together people from the opposing sides, shuttling guys around, hoping to forge a meeting of the minds. Some of the odd couples included John Shad and myself, John Shad and Arthur Goldberg, Jimmy Gahan and Wellin, and Fred Josephs and Wellin. It was a game of musical chairs that went on for hours.

"But in the end, it proved futile. Everyone who came into the room supporting a candidate left the room supporting the same candidate. We were at a tense and bitter impasse that only Al Jack could break. He could do it by giving in and accepting the presidency, or by choosing a candidate of his own. With Jack's support, that man would be Hutton's next CEO."

The stage was set. Three days after arriving in New York, the kingmaker was ready to name his king. But few expected what they were about to hear. In a move that startled the firm, Al Jack nominated Robert M. Fomon to head E.F. Hutton.

That day a showdown took place in Coleman's office. With Shad, Wellin, and Fomon in attendance, Jack asked Hutton's directors, all of whom had been informed of his choice, to name their candidate for president.

Fomon remembers it well. "It was so tense you could almost see sparks fly. One by one the directors said they wanted me. Shad looked ghostly. Trying to avert the inevitable, he launched into an impassioned plea for the job. He argued his case in front of everybody, saying that he had the skills, the experience, the stature to head the firm. Then he turned to me and asked, 'Who do you think should be president?'

"I hated being put on the spot, but I wasn't about to give Shad my support. 'Everyone in the room has just said that I should be president, John. Do you want me to tell them they're all wrong? That you should be?'

"For the first time in his life John Shad had nothing to say."

Shad's silence said it all. The contest was over.

Chapter 6

"When I heard some guy named Bob Fomon had emerged victorious from the Wellin/Shad imbroglio, my first response was 'Who the hell is Bob Fomon?' "

—*Clarence Catallo*

In the deal hammered out by Al Jack and approved by the stockholders, Bob Fomon was elected president and CEO, Keith Wellin was exiled to the vice chairmanship, and Jack, bowing to those who feared Fomon was inexperienced, agreed to take the title of chairman when Sylvan Coleman retired on September 1, 1970. Shad, his ego severely bruised, was named chairman of the executive committee, a face-saving gesture that added little to his power, and Arthur Goldberg, who had lost his mentor in Wellin, was fired.

On the surface it appeared that Jack had structured a brilliant compromise, ending the power struggle, retaining widely respected John Shad, neutralizing Keith Wellin, and bringing in new blood to head the firm. But what appeared as compromise was really the clever maneuver of a skilled politician.

From the moment the two front runners had begun creating a poisoned environment in which neither man could win, Jack had planned to install Bob Fomon as chief executive. The trip to New York, the shuttle diplomacy at

One Chase Plaza, the search for common ground—all were part of a carefully calculated plan to give Fomon the appearance of a consensus candidate. Even the early support for John Shad was little more than a ruse designed to deflect support from Wellin.

"Shad was betrayed—no doubt about it," says a former Hutton participant in the election. "The West Coast boys used him as a foil. Holding out his candidacy as an alternative to Wellin, they convinced the shareholders to abandon the incumbent, putting their votes in limbo. That done, they turned on Shad as if they had never offered him support.

"By the time John figured out what had gone on behind the scenes, he was staggered. I remember it well. It was right before the annual meeting. Thinking he had the California contingent in his hip pocket, Shad called Bob Fomon. 'Bob, we've won,' he said. 'Deliver the proxies to me because we've gained enough votes to beat the Wellin faction.' "

" 'What proxies, John?' Fomon asked, breaking an icy silence. 'What are you talking about?' At that moment John knew he'd been had.

"The truth is the West Coast mafia intended to abandon Shad all along. Because he'd never served as a broker, and because he'd never bothered to court the brokerage ranks, his candidacy was seen as investment banking's plot to dominate the retail side. To the California camp, most of whom started out as brokers and still viewed Hutton as a wire house, this was unacceptable. No way they'd let an 'outsider' run the firm."

Still, even if Shad had been born a broker, if he'd never heard of investment banking and had never set foot in New York, another factor, an invisible one, would have sabotaged his run for the presidency. That was the special relationship between kingmaker Al Jack and his fair-haired boy Bob Fomon.

"Bob and Al had more than a business relationship—it was a father/son thing," recalls Tom Rea.

Al Jack was a devoted family man who had one thing missing in his life: the son he never had. Bob Fomon, on the other hand, was a rising young executive who had one thing missing in his life: the father's love he never had. So when the two met—Fomon as a young broker in the Los Angeles office, Jack as manager of the investment department—they were drawn together, finding that they filled each other's needs.

It was a strange alliance, uniting two men with radically different lifestyles. A straight-laced conservative who'd launched his career as a marker on the old Hutton blackboard and worked his way to the top, Jack lived the moral life. Foul language, crude jokes, drunkenness, cavorting with women—all were verboten in his presence.

And all were part of the ritual of his young protegé. Divorced from his first wife, Marilyn Quinton, Fomon had become a legend on the L.A. social scene, carousing, partying, womanizing.

Why then did Jack take the young bachelor under his wing? In spite of his own high principles, he was charmed by Fomon's rakish, devil-may-care bravado. If this was the son he never had, he enjoyed watching him feel his oats. And he liked playing the role of the paternal disciplinarian.

"Jack was the only man Bob Fomon ever listened to," Rae says. "When Jack said, 'Do this,' Bob did it. When Jack said, 'Don't do that,' Bob obeyed. He'd never cross Al Jack. Never."

"Whenever Jack went to New York to visit with Bob, they'd have dinner at Christ Cella restaurant," recalls Andrew Backar. "Just the two of them, always at the same table. The way Fomon sat by Jack's side, it was like he was his little boy. If you came in when they were there, they'd ask you to join them for a drink, but you could tell they preferred to be alone. They meant the world to each other."

Bob Fomon came into office on a tide of doubt and skepticism. As an investment banker in a retail firm, as a secondary player still in the shadow of his mentors, Murray Ward and Al Jack, he was hardly known outside of the executive offices in New York and Los Angeles.

To the brokers in the field, Fomon was an unknown quantity. Mention of his name drew blank stares.

And no one was in any rush to study up on him. Almost all of them were certain he would self-destruct in six months.

There was good reason for selling Fomon short. In his nineteen years with Hutton, he'd failed to emerge as a major talent. Under his leadership West Coast corporate finance had remained a sleepy outpost of the firm. His only apparent skill, the ability to manipulate his senior partners, hardly prepared him for running a sixty-five-year-old brokerage house.

"You have to realize that Bob's election was an incredible event," says Phil Thomas, a former Hutton executive who worked for Fomon in Los Angeles and New York. "One day he was a wide-eyed California kid barely known outside of Los Angeles and then, like that, he finds himself in New York running the company. Before Bob or anyone else knew what hit them, he was the boss."

The boss of a troubled business. Still a relatively small firm with slightly more than 1,200 brokers and stockholders' equity of less than $26 million, Hutton was being battered by the slumping stock market that had dropped precipitously from its euphoric high in 1968. With investors sitting on the sidelines licking their wounds, brokers up and down the Street were plagued by the dual demons of shrinking commissions and whopping losses in house trading accounts. In this bleak environment dozens of firms were struggling to survive; some went belly-up, others were forced to merge.

"Red ink has flowed freely within the securities fraternity since the end of 1968," Hutton vice-president Henry Mortimer noted in the mid-1970s. "One need only look at the dramatic decline in the number of firms to appreciate the extent of the clean-out. There were approximately 570 NYSE member firms dealing with the public in 1969. There are now only 371. The epidemic struck in waves, the first sparked by a 350 point drop in the Dow (from 891 to 630) between December 1968 and May 1970. This followed chronicled excesses and back-office problems of the late 1960s."

In this gloom-and-doom atmosphere, Bob Fomon took his place as Hutton's chief executive.

To the true believers in the Hutton culture, those dyed-in-the-wool optimists who saw salesmanship as the perennial solution to Wall Street's woes, installing a man who'd turned his back on brokerage was a prescription for disaster.

"A lot of guys thought our only salvation was in finding an Arthur Goldberg without a yarmulke," says a former Hutton regional manager. "Someone who could get down into the pits with the brokers, who could provide them with products and promotions they needed to lure investors back into the fold.

"Of one thing they were sure: Bob Fomon wasn't the man. The way they saw it, the only thing he brought to the job was Al Jack's blessings."

But they were wrong. The new president brought a critical quality to the firm, one that would prove invaluable at this critical juncture in its history: the man could make a decision.

"From his earliest days with the firm, Fomon never shied away from putting himself on the line," recalls an associate from the L.A. days. "Both Al Jack and Murray Ward knew that if a decision had to be made quickly and decisively, with no second-guessing and no looking back, Bob was the man they could count on. In California they called him 'I'll do it, Fomon.'

"That's what people liked about Bob. He was always a gunslinger."

The rakish charm that had endeared Bob Fomon to Al Jack worked its magic once he was in office, this time with the headquarters staff, who found the new chief executive a fresh and exciting force. His was a natural leadership ability, not the blood and guts of a George Patton but more of a Pied Piper who enticed others to follow his lead.

"All Bob had to do was ask, and his agenda for the day became your agenda for the day," says Norm Epstein, who after backing Keith Wellin's losing cause found himself attracted to the man who'd defeated him. "I remember a time Bob was flying to Chicago to address a securities group. Because there were last-minute details to iron out, he asked me to accompany him on the ride to the airport. So we jumped into a limousine and drove to LaGuardia, working through a laundry list of issues along the way. By the time we got to the American Airlines terminal, there were still a few loose ends to tie up, so Bob waved me inside, the idea being that we'd finish up at the gate. But when they started the boarding call a half hour later, we still weren't done.

"That's when Bob grabs my arms and says, 'Come on, Norm, get on the plane with me. I still need you.'

"Did the fact that I had long-standing dinner plans stop me? No. Did the fact that my wife would blow up at me for ruining her night stop me? No. Because Bob Fomon asked, I flew with him to O'Hare, helped him nail down all the issues, stepped off the plane in Chicago, and took the next flight back to New York.

"In those days there was something about Bob that drew you to him. You wanted to be close to him."

*   *   *

Like other ordinary Joe's who rise to the occasion in war, politics, and business, Bob Fomon was a leader waiting to lead. As Hutton's new president, he transformed the firm that Ellis, Cutten, and Coleman had safeguarded over the years as a quasi-men's club into a Wall Street giant. He did it the old-fashioned way: with balls and moxie and flair and instinct. And with a sixth sense for motivating people and for making money.

Fomon was not versed in the textbook principles of corporate management, but at this point in its history, Hutton needed more of a business builder than a business manager. In a character trait that surfaced only after he took command at Hutton, Fomon proved to be a classic entrepreneur. A swaggering, egocentric visionary, he saw an opportunity for his company and he had the brains and the backbone to cash in on it.

Fomon's trump card was his can-do attitude. Like Ed Hutton, who told Western Union president Newcomb Carleton to string the wire "and I'll worry about generating enough business to pay for the rental," Fomon refused to let anything obstruct him. If there were legal, financial, or administrative details obstructing his path, he would blow them away, letting others fret about the repercussions.

"Fomon wasn't just good in the beginning," says Norm Epstein, "he was spectacular. His trademark was an ability to zero in on a problem and then go out and solve it post haste. I'd seen other CEOs in action, and none of them used power like Fomon. They'd hem and haw, they'd consult advisers, and in the end they'd still wind up hedging their bets. But not Bob Fomon. He made a decision and acted on it."

Fomon's decisiveness was apparent from his first days as president. It was then that Keith Wellin, who had lost the battle to run Hutton, decided to retain the big corner office traditionally reserved for Hutton's CEO.

"Bob was miserable about this and he made his displeasure known to Sylvan Coleman," recalls Phil Thomas. "Sylvan's advice? Do something about it, and do it quickly. There was a message written between the lines. As long as Keith had that office, power would flow from it. Bob had to make a symbolic move, demonstrating clearly and forcefully that he was now in charge.

"It was a delicate thing, telling a vice chairman to give up his office. But Bob just went in and laid down the law. He made it clear that a new man had taken over the executive reins."

As soon as he had taken his seat in the CEO's office, Fomon faced an immediate crisis. "We were skating on thin ice," recalls Tom Lynch, who as Hutton's chief financial officer worked closely with Fomon from the start. "Heavy losses in the bear market had battered our capital position, dropping it to a perilous low. Warning signs were flashing all over the place. If the trend continued, we'd fall below the New York Stock Exchange minimum requirements. That would be disastrous. It would mean we could be banned from hiring new account executives, or opening new offices or if capital really deteriorated, we could be closed down."

Fomon immediately moved to halt the slide in Hutton's capital base by dealing first with an internal threat. As concern grew over the stock market, and over Hutton's ability to weather the economic doldrums, the firm's major stockholders were on the verge of cashing in their stocks, thus exacerbating the capital crisis.

"Bob's first job was to block a rush for the exits, and he found a way to do it," Lynch recalls. "An obscure clause buried in the corporate bylaws permitted us to freeze capital withdrawals when the loss of funds threatened the firm. Bob took advantage of this, using his power to stop the outflow of capital. Needless to say, the shareholders protested—some even sued to get their money—but Bob held tough. It's good he did: if all the money that wanted to get out, got out, Hutton would have gone under."

With the internal threat neutralized, Fomon turned his attention outside of the firm, seeking funds to build Hutton's long-term capital base. Soon after taking office, he was out in the hustings, beating the bushes for money.

"Bob knew the senior officers at First Interstate Bank in Los Angeles, so we flew out to see them regarding an infusion of subordinated debt," recalls Tom Lynch. "Given the state of the securities markets, it wasn't the best time to be seeking investments, but Bob was superb. He reminded the bankers that Hutton had a long history of success and he assured them that we were going to be around for the long haul. Yes, our profits were weak at the time, he admitted, but he convinced them that he would change that, and so they came up with the money.

"Then Fomon made a similar pitch to the Royal Bank of Canada, promising that Hutton would come out of the current Wall Street slump stronger than ever. When he completed his presentation, we landed a $7.5 million subordinated loan."

No sooner had Fomon returned from Toronto than he took a call from regional vice-president John Latshaw, who was onto another source of capital. Word had it that a wealthy angel in St. Louis was interested in investing in Hutton.

"One of our brokers in St. Louis, a John Woods, was the son of a wealthy family, the heirs to the Ralston Purina fortune," Fomon recalls. "It seemed that Woods's mother wanted to buy a stake in Hutton and so I flew out to see her.

"She was a charming lady who'd always been impressed with the Hutton name and who was eager to invest in the firm. Because this would be the first time someone other than a partner would be allowed to put capital in Hutton, I heard voices of objection all over the place. But I ignored them. This wasn't the time for tradition or protocol. We needed money and Mrs. Woods had it. So I made a deal, giving her warrants in exchange for about one million dollars in capital."

Securing a mix of private and bank capital, Bob Fomon faced down the first crisis of his young presidency with the aplomb of an experienced hand. Looking down the barrel of a financial disaster, he simply went about his business, never doubting his ability to raise millions of dollars, and in the process prevented Hutton from falling below the Big Board's capital requirements. His confidence was contagious. Lenders and investors, traditionally a conservative and skeptical lot, were willing to buck the trend of a bear market, risking their capital in a shaky firm and a beleaguered industry. Bob Fomon's E.F. Hutton, they believed, was an investment that would pay off.

Chapter 7

"Even if you saw George Ball once in a blue moon, you felt close to him. The way he would pick your face out of a crowd, the way he would compliment you on a minor achievement you never even thought he knew about, that kind of caring and attention radiated great warmth. George was your boss, but you felt he was more than that. You felt he was your friend."

—a former Hutton West Coast branch manager

Bob Fomon assumed the Hutton presidency with little interest or experience in the retail side of the business and with the perfect opportunity to downgrade its importance. As an investment banker with the dream of making Hutton a power in corporate finance, he could hit his brokerage colleagues when their stock was down, transforming the firm from a latter-day wire house into the kind of white-shoe merchant bank that had always captured his fancy. The stage was set.

"Understand, Bob comes to power with the stock market in dismal shape," recalls Norm Epstein. "The chorus on the Street is chanting, 'Retail is dead. Retail is dead.' The consensus among the Merrill Lynches and Paine Webbers and Kidder Peabodys is that they are going to reduce retail, where the red ink is flowing, in favor of expanding the institutional side of the business. Instead of catering to individual investors, they're going to focus on the big traders—the banks and insurance companies. That's where Wall Street sees its future.

"But not Bob Fomon."

An astute contrarian, Fomon recognized, as had Hutton's co-founder George Ellis before him, that "the time to expand is when no one has money." With competitors paralyzed by fear, he believed he could seize the initiative, filling the vacuum in the brokerage marketplace. Yes, the Dow was at the bottom of the curve, taking profits and investor confidence along with it, but Fomon had seen enough market cycles to know that what goes down comes roaring back up again.

At this stage of his career Bob Fomon showed all the signs of a brilliant CEO. Creative, entrepreneurial, and independent-minded, he was able to see beyond the crisis of the moment, recognizing that the market's plight was really an opportunity in disguise. Like a savvy investor who buys into weakness and sells into strength, Bob Fomon would make his move. All he had to do was wait for a sure thing. It would come soon enough. When it did, he alone would have the vision to see it and the guts to make it work.

But first he would make a critical move, hiring a number two man to ride herd over the retail system. Having served as a broker himself, Fomon knew from experience that the men in the field needed more than a chief executive. They needed a cheerleader, a mother confessor, a rah-rah, slap 'em on the back, kind of guy. Shoehorned into claustrophobic cubicles, their ears soldered to telephone receivers, these Bible salesmen of the brokerage business spend their days in a pressure cooker world peddling the American dream to a constantly changing Rolodex of clients. Taken individually, they are disposable gremlins, bit players in the financial system. But as a unified force, they serve as the main turbine of the brokerage firms: their energy and ambition keep the stocks and bonds and puts and calls moving from buyers to sellers and generate billions of dollars in commissions.

As much as Bob Fomon relished the prospect of building Hutton into a brokerage giant, he had no intention of cheerleading the account executives, of soothing their delicate egos, or of rousing them to battle. That wasn't Bob Fomon. He was smart enough to know it and shrewd enough to hire an alter ego to play the role for him. His choice for a second-in-command would prove to be his finest decision as Hutton's CEO.

Tapping into the headquarters scuttlebutt, Fomon heard talk of a bright young meteorite streaking through the management ranks. An unlikely candidate for prominence in Hutton's galaxy of patrician executives, the up-and-comer, George L. Ball, looked more like an oddball out of the Sunday comics than an emerging Wall Street wunderkind. Painfully thin, with a freckled face and a Pinocchio nose, he looked too young to live on his own, much less to run Hutton's New York office, the job he was holding down when Fomon took over the firm.

But there was more to George Ball than first met the eye.

"Soon after I was hired by Hutton in the summer of 1969, the powers-that-be sent me to New York to attend a brokers' training class," says Rich Braugh. "While at headquarters, my group got word that this hot-shot sales manager would be addressing us, giving winning tips on making it in the real world. Because we'd heard he was a fireball, we couldn't wait to meet him and have some of his success rub off on us. So you can imagine how we felt when we walked into the classroom to find this fourteen-year-old kid standing there rattling around in his father's suit. What's going on here? we thought.

"As we found out soon enough, what was going on was that the 'fourteen-year-old kid' was really thirty-year-old George Ball. Just as we were wondering how this runt could control a training class, much less a sales district,

some snot-nosed rich kid who'd gone into brokering for a
hobby decided to crucify the pile of bones at the head of
the class. So he puts on a sideshow from the back of the
room, letting loose with loud wise-cracks every time Ball
tries to make a point.

"Well, this guy gets five minutes into his act, certain
he's going to rout the wimp instructor from the room when
Ball turns on him like a Doberman pinscher. The next
thing you know, the guy's out in the hall, his butt kicked
swiftly out of the class. No warnings, no second chances,
no nothing.

"When I look back on it now, I think George welcomed
the confrontation. It was his way of saying, 'I may look
like a kid, but I'm someone to reckon with.' And that he
was. You learned from day one that you didn't step on
George Ball."

In a prominent firm blessed with a rich lode of bright
young men, George Ball was the brightest of them all.

"The first time I met George I was a cocky, thirty-year-
old branch manager," says Clarence Catallo. "Having come
so far so fast, I had a bit of a swollen head.

"Well, that lasted until I attended a regional sales meeting, where I got my first peek at George Ball. I'd never
met him before, but judging by the other regional VPs, I
figured he was a member of the old boy's club. Gray-
haired, late fifties, a little thick around the middle.

"So imagine my shock when Ball is introduced and up
to the podium bounds this cherubic-faced stick figure who
looks like he's pushing fifteen and is already rungs above
me on the management ladder. He took the wind right out
of my sails.

"At first I wondered how this skinny kid could have
risen so far so fast. Did he know someone in the firm? But
as I sat there watching George regale the audience with a
masterful blend of jokes and anecdotes and inspirational
messages, the answer was perfectly clear. He had this
charisma, this extra dimension drew people to him."

Ball had first come to Hutton as a quote clerk during the summer of his freshman year at Brown University. The job was lined up by a family friend who served as a floor broker for the securities firm of Edwards & Hanley. After graduating from Brown with a degree in economics and serving a stint in the Navy (where he rose to the rank of lieutenant j.g.), the budding Wall Streeter returned to Hutton, launching his career in earnest as a broker at 61 Broadway.

Though Ball performed well, he was a cut below the salesmen-of-the-year types who walked away with the brass plaques and free junkets to Barbados. But he displayed a rare and precious commodity in the brokerage ranks: he was a natural manager who could lead and motivate others.

Impressed by this ambitious, talented Ivy Leaguer, Arthur Goldberg anointed him as his protegé and powered Ball through the Hutton hierarchy. He had found, he believed, the future of the firm. When Ball was in only his fourth year of his career, serving as a branch manager of the Madison Avenue office, Goldberg told his wife, "Someday George is going to be president of E.F. Hutton."

In a break that would give him firm-wide recognition, Ball was dispatched to Hutton's Beaumont, Texas, office, the scene of a local scandal in which a broker and a margin clerk had siphoned off millions of dollars from customer accounts.

"It was an ugly incident," recalls a former Hutton executive. "The money they'd embezzled had been the life savings of retired schoolteachers and ministers of the church. It was hard-earned money, working-class money, stolen in a town where things like that didn't happen. People had trusted Hutton and Hutton had double-crossed them. By the time Ball arrived, the firm's name was mud there.

"Which is exactly why headquarters sent him there. Because he looked like an eighteen-year-old choirboy, the people of Beaumont could trust him on sight. One look at him and they knew he wasn't going to take advantage of them. Once he restored their faith in Hutton, he was able to turn the office around. Nine months later he was back in New York, mission accomplished."

While he looked more like a Boy Scout than a broker, under the veneer of a fresh-scrubbed American lad lay a hungry and impatient ladder climber determined to reach the pinnacle of the business world. From the very start of his career, Ball (whose favorite expression is: "Average sucks") was repulsed by mediocrity and determined to rise above it in his own career. He would do it by devoting himself to his work and by earning the devotion of those who worked for him.

"George was wired into the broker's psyche," says a former Hutton broker who worked for Ball in the sixties. "He knew that in spite of all their macho chatter about writing sales tickets and making big bucks, they wanted more than money. Even as grown men with big incomes and big families of their own, they wanted someone on the job to pat them on the back and tell them how good they were. Hard as it is to believe, they were starved for attention and affection."

Ball recognized that by showering the brokers with attention and affection, he would win their undying loyalty. A loyalty he could use to advance his own career.

"Once when I brought in a particularly good piece of business, George, who was just a branch manager at the time, called me at home to tell me how well I'd done," the former broker recalls. "That may not sound like much, but no one had ever done it before and it felt good to be appreciated. From that day on, if George had asked me to walk the plank for him I would have done it. The man knew how to push your buttons."

When Bob Fomon arrived in Manhattan in 1970, George

Ball, then head of the New York region, found himself in an awkward position. Although he held a senior position in close proximity to top management, he was a strong Wellin ally and as such a symbol of the losing cause. With Wellin kicked upstairs and with his mentor Arthur Goldberg kicked out of the firm, Ball feared he'd be easy pickings for a vengeful Bob Fomon. As rumor had it, the new president would clean house and put his own team in place.

But it didn't happen that way.

"Over the years I'd spoken to George Ball a few times, but I'd never met him," Fomon recalls. "So when I got to New York, I didn't even know what he looked like. But that changed one morning when I made it a point to meet this emaciated young man who seemed to be the hardest worker in the office. Always first at his desk in the morning and last to leave at night, he was relentless."

Hooked into the Hutton scuttlebutt, Fomon learned quickly enough that Ball was the right man to lead his planned expansion and revitalization of the retail network. Having proven himself a Svengali of the sales force, Ball had a natural rapport with the brokers that Fomon had never had and didn't care to develop. As the president of E.F. Hutton & Co., Fomon's days would be reserved for governors, senators, statesmen, kings, queens, dukes, duchesses, and captains of industry. George Ball would take on the masses.

"Having Fomon and Ball out here for social events was a picture in contrasts," recalls a former West Coast branch manager. "Alone in the corner you had Fomon gulping scotches, talking to no one, looking like he was under house arrest in his own firm. Mixing with the brokers was painful for him and it showed. By his actions, his mannerisms, he was saying to the brokers: 'I'm too powerful, too high and mighty to be associated with the likes of you.' Having him out here was counterproductive.

"But as bad as Fomon was in the field, Ball was brilliant.

A master of small talk, he could work a cocktail party, mingling with the guests, flattering them, always having the right thing to say. He was the Fred Astaire of the corporate culture."

From the beginning Fomon relied on Ball's encyclopedic knowledge of the brokerage force. Facts and figures spewed out of him like printouts from the Hutton mainframe.

"Whenever Fomon needed to know something about some half-baked branch office in some godforsaken suburb, George had the answer—if not in his head, then in a memo pad in his breast pocket," says a former Hutton sales executive now with Shearson Lehman Hutton. "One time—and this really blew Bob out of his chair—Fomon asked George for the names and the payouts* of our top ten New York producers.

" 'Get back to me on Friday,' he said. Just as he turned to another matter, Ball started reeling off names and percentages.

" 'What the hell are you talking about?' Fomon blustered, convinced that Ball had gone off on some wild tangent.

" 'You asked for the names of our top ten guys, right?'

" 'Yes, but . . .'

" 'Well, I'm telling you. Would you prefer that I put it in writing?'

"From that moment on, Fomon knew he couldn't live without George Ball."

In the early days of the Fomon administration, the Ball/ Fomon relationship was a mutual admiration society. Awed and intoxicated by the CEO's power, Ball held Fomon on a pedestal.

"At this point in his career George took it as an article of faith that CEOs know everything," says a one-time Hutton sales manager. "He figured that somehow Bob was wired to God."

---

*These are the brokers' share of the commission dollars they generate.

For his part, Fomon found in Ball not only the diplomat who could charm the organization but also the trusted aide who could tend to day-to-day affairs while he mused about the global issues. Thus was born the Fomon-Ball team. As events would prove, it would be one of the great management duos in business history. While it lasted, it would propel the firm to new heights.

George Ball was the first to recognize that the Hutton mystique, a valuable sales tool for decades, could be used to mesmerize the sales force as well as the investing public. By promoting the image of the Hutton broker as Wall Street's elite, and by rewarding his men with the salary and perks to back it up, he created an esprit de corps that gave the account executives pride in their work and in their firm. No longer just salesmen sandwiched into tiny cubicles, they felt part of a team. The Hutton team. George Ball's team.

A monomaniac with a mission, Ball devoted himself to the field, focusing on the details of management that his predecessors considered trivial. Knowing that the little things build loyalty, he left no call unanswered, no request unserved.

"Whenever business took me to New York, I'd call on George," a former broker remembers. "That his calendar was always booked solid never stopped him from taking the time to see me. Whether I had an appointment or not, his door would be open."

Prior to Ball, the telephone had become an instrument of contention between headquarters and the field. Typically, when the brokers called, New York wasn't in. It was telephone tag, Hutton style, and it had built a wall of resentment between the Broadway boys and the retail ranks west of the Hudson River.

But Ball changed that. Making it known he was the brokers' friend in high places, he took calls he had no time to take and returned calls he had no time to return: all part of his campaign to prove to the field that when no one else would respond to their needs, "George would do it."

"I remember the time when one of our most talented bankers jumped ship to join another firm," recalls Rich Braugh. "Frustrated by Hutton's lack of support for investment banking, he'd complained to Fomon, only to have Bob tell him, 'If you want to leave, sayonara.'

"When I heard what Fomon had done, I got on the horn to George Ball, pleading with him not to let the banker go. Being out in high tech country, I needed good investment bankers to help take our clients public. Knowing how desperately I wanted the guy to stay, George went into action. Using that devastating charm of his, he convinced the banker not only to meet with him, but to leave the job he'd just started only a week before and return to Hutton. George made a personal plea and the guy reversed his career plans just like that."

Adds a former branch manager in the Midwest: "It didn't take long to believe that George could do the impossible. If you told me you saw him walk on water, I wouldn't have doubted it for a minute."

Ball won over Hutton's field force by being the headquarters ally they could turn to in a pinch. Whether it was an investment banker they needed back on the payroll or a commission cut they wanted restored, George would get it done.

But there was more to Ball than the devoted leader who rolled up his sleeves for his troops. If he won their minds with his can-do performance, he won their hearts with a slick campaign designed to make each big producer, each branch and regional manager, go to bed at night thinking that the boss was watching over them.

"George had a uncanny ability to remember everything about you," says a former Hutton account executive. "He charmed you, he flattered you, he made you feel special.

"A few years after meeting George for the first time, I bumped into him at a sales meeting. Because I was sure he wouldn't recognize me, I headed over to reintroduce myself. But there was no need for that. No sooner does George spot me than he's shaking my hand, saying, 'Hi, how's Betsy and the kids?'

"How's Betsy and the kids! The man hasn't seen me in three years and he remembers my wife's name. I was floored. And I was also moved. That was George's secret. He knew how to personalize business relationships. And you loved him for it."

The contrast with Bob Fomon's imperious personality made Ball all the more attractive.

"When you attended a meeting chaired by Bob Fomon, he'd think nothing of belittling you in front of fifty people, saying that the idea you presented was the dumbest fucking thing he'd ever heard," recalls the former account executive. "But George would never dream of doing that. He'd be gracious and diplomatic whether he agreed with you or not. And if he liked your idea, he'd jot off a handwritten note commending your good thinking. When you returned from a business trip certain everyone had forgotten just how brilliant you'd been, there was George's note sitting on top of your desk. He was amazing."

Adds former top broker Tony Malatino, "The man forgot nothing. When I thought that Bethlehem Steel was going to make a big move in the market, I called George, suggesting that Hutton take a big position in the stock. He passed on my advice, but six months later when the stock went through the roof, I crossed paths with George in an elevator. The first thing he says: 'Hey, Tony, we should have taken your tip on Bethlehem.'"

Ball's genius was in recognizing that the brokerage business is more than just numbers. Boil down the stocks and bonds and tax shelters and telephones and account statements, and you're left with a fundamental ingredient: people. Instinctively Ball knew that the real difference between the Huttons and the Merrills and Witters and Baches wasn't the size of their offices or the sizzle of their advertising, but the performance of their account executives. By creating a sales force that worked harder and smarter than the others, Ball knew that he could beat the competition in the battle for brokerage commissions.

He would do it with the carrot rather than the stick, motivating his brokers with sweetheart payouts, yes, but also with affection and attention from the boss.

It was all part of a master plan: Call it the Ball system of sales management. If George spotted his brokers on sight, if he asked about Betsy and the kids and all the other personal trivia that endeared him to the brokers, it was because he studied them the way other executives study balance sheets.

"When I first heard about George's uncanny ability to remember names, I was impressed," says Norm Epstein. "Very impressed. All those brokers and managers and wives and kids. The guy's a miracle worker, I thought.

"That's until I accompanied him on a sales meeting and saw just how he did it. About a half hour into our flight he removes this big chart from his briefcase and places it on his lap. There's about twenty mug shots of Hutton field guys arranged in rows with a few lines of copy under their faces.

"Looking over his shoulder, I could see that this is really a portable dossier. There's a thumbnail description of each guy he's going to meet, including—you guessed it—the wife's name and the kids' names.

"For the next hour or so George screws his head into the chart, studying and memorizing. He's like an IBM loading up on data. That evening he was greeting these people as if they were members of the family."

With Bob Fomon willingly washing his hands of salesmen

and with no one else in the post-Goldberg period able to challenge him for control, Ball slowly but inevitably tightened his grip on the brokerage business, building his own principality within the Hutton organization.

He could be a charmer, leading his men on the strength of his infectious smile and his flash-card flattery. But whenever his position or his ego was threatened, he was quick to bare his teeth. Aware that his peach-fuzz face and his little-boy stammer made him an easy target for fast-draw artists who would try to take on the boss, he dealt decisively with all comers.

"For some time, Hutton was having trouble with a branch office in New Orleans," Braugh recalls. "It was a promising market, but our performance there was anemic. Whatever the reason, we couldn't make things happen.

"Not until George put his mind to it.

"Taking things in his own hands, he dispatched a hotshot branch manager to take over the office. His man was terrific on the job. After years of dormancy he put us on the map in New Orleans. George loved him for it. Overnight he became Ball's fair-haired boy.

"But then he made a fatal mistake. He let it go to his head. He started to push George. Determined to parlay his success into a higher management post, he told George that he had to be promoted. It was a grand ultimatum: promote me or I'm out the door to Merrill Lynch.

"Ball never even waited for him to finish his monologue. He just canned him on the spot. The message was unmistakable: George Ball won't be held hostage by anyone."

While Ball pretended to run the retail ranks as a town hall democracy—the boys tell George and George gets it done—in many cases the election was rigged before the votes were cast.

"George would call these meetings where he'd throw out ideas and ask the group to come up with their own thoughts and strategies," says Rich Braugh. "Terrific. We'd all be part of the ultimate decision.

"But sometimes as the meetings progressed, I could tell that George had already made up his mind. He didn't really listen to the others, he just wanted the others to feel listened to."

In ruling over Hutton's brokers, Ball functioned more like a mafia don than a corporate executive. When you talked to George you talked not to the sales manager, which implied a purely business relationship, but to the godfather.

"It was all part of the Ball mystique. Mr. Nice Guy/Mr. Tough Guy," says a former retail executive who worked for Ball. "A dual image he worked hard to perfect. He wanted his people to like him, and he wanted them to fear him, too."

Still, whether you loved him or distrusted him, the fact remains that from the moment Bob Fomon laid his sword on George Ball's shoulder, a new era began at Hutton. The Camelot era. It would transform Hutton from a modest wire house, an also-ran in the brokerage business, into a Wall Street power.

"Bob Fomon put George Ball in charge of the retail system and it was magic from that day on," says the former West Coast branch manager. "Everything Hutton could or should have been over the years started coming together. We had a gutsy chief executive who was willing to make the big decisions, and we had a retail chief who could inspire us and who could make working at Hutton so rewarding that you hated to leave the office at night."

Chapter 8

"To those of us who worked there in the golden years, Hutton was our wife, and our wife was our mistress."
—*Norman Epstein*

In April 1970 the investment firm of Donaldson, Lufkin & Jenrette shocked the brokerage community by going public, shattering one of Wall Street's most sacred rules. Until D,L,J broke with tradition, offering 800,000 shares of its common stock to the public for $15 a share, Big Board rules forbade member firms from selling their stock to outsiders. The tradition of private ownership, in which most or all of the stock was held by the firms' partners and senior executives, was a lingering vestige of a simpler time when Wall Street brokerage houses were still run like exclusive men's clubs.

The change in the rules did not come easily. For eleven months Donaldson, Lufkin had maneuvered behind the scenes, begging, pleading, and cajoling the NYSE to lift its ban on public offerings.

"The traditionalists were up in arms over this," says Tom Lynch. "To their way of thinking, outside ownership was an unforgivable breach of etiquette and tradition. To hear them talk about it, it would be the end of civilization as we knew it."

But with a new breed of Wall Streeters moving into the

executive suites—men who recognized that worship of tradition would cripple their firms in the rough-and-tumble seventies—the heirlooms of management policy began to be replaced, like the gold pocket watches draped across the vests of the senior partners, with the signs of a new era.

As the *New York Times* said on the occasion of Donaldson's offering, "A door to Wall Street's private club suddenly will be open."

The break with tradition was based on a hard reality: Wall Street needed capital. With financial transactions growing in size and scope, and with the firms struggling to reorient themselves to a volatile and demanding marketplace, the demand for capital had suddenly mushroomed.

Selling stock had all the answers. Unlocking the door to Wall Street's private clubs would turn partners into instant millionaires and would provide the brokerage houses with huge capital infusions to modernize and computerize their back offices and to take bigger stakes in investment banking activities. If going public violated Wall Street lore, so what? It would make for a stronger industry.

The message was hardly lost on Bob Fomon. Although he had successfully shored up Hutton's capital in his first months of his tenure, these were only stopgap measures. Further infusions were needed to stabilize the firm's capital base and to bolster its competitive position. As long as Hutton remained privately owned, the firm was vulnerable to capital crises whenever longtime partners cashed in their chips and retired.

Donaldson, Lufkin's sellout to investors offered the ideal solution. Hutton would go public, too, replacing the insider's capital with permanent equity that would be impervious to the comings and goings of Hutton executives. And so in 1972 Hutton unlocked its own doors, selling 1,245,000 shares of stock at $23.50 each, raising $16 million for the firm and $12 million for the selling shareholders.

If the deal brought tears to Wall Street traditionalists, it brought only joy to Hutton's executive suite.

"For the partners with the big stock holdings, it was like Christmas," recalls a former executive in the syndication department, who, as a non-partner, had little to celebrate. "The night of the offering, a clique of big winners—including John Shad and Bob Fomon—met in Fomon's office for drinks before going out for dinner to whoop it up. When they asked me to join them for cocktails, I expected to see a group of buttoned-up executives quietly toasting each other on their good fortune. But the scene that greeted me when I walked into that room was right out of a movie. These pillars of the financial establishment were flipping one hundred dollar bills in the air, calling out heads or tails as the money floated to the floor. It was surreal.

"But the best was yet to come. When John Shad excused himself to go to the men's room, some of the other guys hatched a plan behind his back. They would call a game of poker, the main purpose being to cheat Shad out of his money. Because John was notoriously cheap and such a stuffed shirt, he was the perfect mark for a poker sting, Hutton style.

"It worked like a charm. By the time the game was over, Shad, who thought he'd run into the worst string of luck in his life, was fleeced for $10,000. To this day, the man who was Hutton's vice chairman, the same John Shad who would go on to become head of the Securities and Exchange Commission and ultimately U.S. Ambassador to the Netherlands, still has no inkling of what happened that night."

The decision to take Hutton public, and to consummate the transaction swiftly and effectively, was pure Fomon circa 1970s. That the move violated the long-cherished tradition of private ownership mattered not at all. To Fomon the maverick, opportunities were meant to be seized, without committees, studies, or long-winded reports. If the plan failed, he would take the heat. If it succeeded, he would earn the credit. Consensus had no place in Bob Fomon's culture.

At this point in Hutton's history, if it hadn't had a Bob Fomon it would have had to invent one. Coming as he did after decades of part-time CEOs who tended to their clients first, their management duties second, he was a new breed of leader whose style matched the temper of a more complex and competitive era. Time and again Fomon acted quickly and unilaterally, and time and again his instincts proved correct. Soon after he took Hutton public, the market for brokerage-house offerings collapsed, leaving the procrastinators dangling in the lurch. Had Fomon stalled, had he hedged his bets, the capital Hutton needed to ensure its independence and to stake its growth would have slipped through its fingers.

In the summer of 1973, nearly a year after its public offering, E.F. Hutton was stuck deep in a bear market that had clobbered its stock price from a high of $23.50 to $7.

Still, it was a fundamentally strong firm, now in its sixty-ninth consecutive year of profitability. Another key barometer of fiscal well-being, debt-to-capital ratio, stood at a respectable 6.6 to 1 as opposed to nearly 8 to 1 before the offering.*

Under operations czar Norm Epstein, the firm had begun to fine-tune its computerized systems, including the introduction of high speed data communications to all branch offices, being the first brokerage firm to install teletype model 40. Hutton had come a long way from the Rube Goldberg days of telegraph wires jerry-rigged into tin cigar boxes, but it was still very much a retail house, its brokerage commissions placing it among the top ten New York Stock Exchange firms.

*NYSE guidelines required firms to maintain minimum ratios of 15:1.

Under George Ball, who continued to widen his influence over the retail network, Hutton boasted 103 offices spread over 90 cities, 28 states, and 3 countries. A force of 1,500 account executives (out of 4,000 employees) served more than 300,000 customers in the U.S. and abroad. The individual investor continued to be the firm's bread-and-butter client, accounting for 70 percent of commissions.

Traditionally weak in investment banking, Hutton remained a sideline player, ranking 23rd among NYSE firms. But under John Shad's creative leadership, the curve was starting to rise. In 1972 Hutton had managed or co-managed 29 underwritings worth $667 million. Negotiated equity offerings were the fastest moving area, rising from $348 million in 1971 to $525 million in 1972.

The true mark of Shad's performance, measured by the growth of the firm's investment banking arm, was impressive. In the period from 1970 to 1972, investment banking fees nearly tripled from $9 to $25 million.

Retail commissions were also on the rise, with much of the growth spurred by acquisitions. Hutton had always been good at gobbling up smaller brokers and adding them to the retail network, and Ball and Fomon, who liked to play this game, were turning it into an art form. In the first half of 1973 two major acquisitions added twenty new offices to Hutton's retail map. In rapid succession the firm acquired the North Carolina-based R.S. Dickson, Powell, Kistler & Crawford, and the upstate brokerage concern of George D.B. Bonbright.

This frenetic deal-making was right up Fomon's alley. Being in the action, where the risks and the rewards were enormous and critical decisions could make or break the firm, was his element. Big moves. Big risks. Big rewards.

"When I think of Bob during that period," recalls a former aide, "I think of the officer in *Apocalypse Now* who looks over the Asian jungle and says, 'I love the smell of napalm in the morning.' That was Bob. The brokerage business was war, and he loved every minute of it."

For those who worked closely with him, it was clear by now that Fomon was not a traditional CEO. Though he sat atop a prestigious investment firm, drawing down a handsome salary and enjoying the perks of office that went with it, the rascal of the Campion School was still very much in evidence. And because he was still fresh and spontaneous, this irreverent side of his personality gave him a rakish charisma that bound his aides to him.

"When we were negotiating to take over the Bonbright firm, Fomon, Ball, Jerry Miller, and myself flew up to Rochester to have a first-hand look at the place," Norm Epstein recalls. "We arrived about midnight, just after a snowstorm, and it was bitterly cold. Rushing along the frozen tarmac, holding our topcoats tightly around our necks to stop the chill from seeping through, we were all beelining for the terminal building.

"All of us except Fomon. In the middle of this frozen tundra, he just up and starts a snowball fight. I mean, he's got this big snowbank that he's using like a munitions depot and he's firing serious snowballs at us. Soon we all forget about the cold and get into it. It was the last thing I expected to happen that night, but it was great fun.

"That's what I remember about Fomon in those days. He was unpredictable, and more often than not you loved him for it."

Already Hutton was taking on the personality of the man at the top. A split personality that could be infuriating and charming, cruel and caring, rational and bizarre. A personality that began to shape the firm's direction, basing its actions more on whims than on business plans or market factors.

In short, E.F. Hutton was becoming the cult of Bob Fomon.

Fomon did things the way Bob Fomon felt like doing things, whether anyone agreed with him or not. It was on this basis that Hutton's CEO took the biggest risk of his career, acquiring when no one else would the beleaguered brokerage firm of DuPont Walston Inc.

The story traces back to 1971, when Texas billionaire H. Ross Perot decided to do for Wall Street what he had done for the computer industry. A former IBM salesman, Perot had single-handedly built Electronic Data Services, a computer services company, into the success story of the 1960s.

In the process, Perot—who looked like a jockey and talked like a Bible salesman—had created a quasi-military culture complete with a battalion of clean-shaven, crew-cutted young zombies chosen because they pledged undying allegiance to their CEO. Armed with marching orders, the EDS corps of sales reps and computer consultants fanned out across the business landscape, helping thousands of corporations, institutions, and government agencies cope with the complexities of computerization.

Based on his maxim that computer users needed systems to bring to life their enormous investments in data-processing hardware—and on his ability to fashion a dedicated team to service those needs—Perot had built a modern-day giant. His EDS stock holdings alone were worth more than $1 billion.

But there was more to Perot than another businessman with a brainstorm. Infused with a can-do attitude that marked everything he did, the diminutive entrepreneur with the longhorn ears and a Texas twang was a flag-waving chauvinist whose patriotism was legendary. In one instance, he spent $2 million of his own money airlifting mail, medicine, and food to America's prisoners of war in North Vietnam. Later he would launch a daring mission to rescue EDS employees from among the Iranian hostages. If there was a challenge to be faced, old Ross would face it.

And so when "duty" called again, this time on Wall Street, Perot launched into battle, convinced he could do anything he set his mind on. He would learn otherwise. In the end, the adventure would cost him a big chunk of his fortune and, worse for a man who believed in his own press notices, would prove him only human.

Perot's star-crossed odyssey began in the dog days of 1971, when securities firms, suffering from bloated costs and antiquated operations, were dropping like flies. Faced with this crisis in capitalism, a Big Board vice chairman asked his good buddy Richard Nixon to pressure his good buddy Ross Perot into making an investment in capital-starved Wall Street—specifically in the wounded broker-age firm of DuPont Glore Forgan. With a number of once prominent firms, including Goodbody and Hayden Stone, already bankrupt or on the brink, the pillars of the Wall Street establishment feared that DuPont's collapse would have a domino effect, taking other brokers with it and, even worse, undermining what little was left of investor confidence. Although no one was admitting it openly, the fear was of a second market collapse in forty years.

It was in this crisis atmosphere that Perot, visions of banner headlines before his eyes—"Texas Miracle Worker Saves Wall Street"—heeded Nixon's call, buying DuPont and promptly merging it with another troubled firm, Walston & Co., to create a huge retail network second only to Merrill Lynch.

The publicity hoopla surrounding Perot's move (publicity he knew would follow the signing) and the enhancement of his image as "can-do Perot" figured into the decision to buy DuPont. But the move also reflected Perot's business and personal philosophy. According to H. Ross's Sunday-go-to-meetin' view of life, the intersection of Broad and Wall Streets was the Sodom and Gomorrah of the business world: an ungodly and immoral enclave where pampered brokers and executives squandered millions on costly perks and outdated systems. Into this den of iniquity Perot would introduce his good Christian culture, replacing Wall Street's potpourri of sinners with a corps of black-suited, white-shirted automatons.

"I am used to saying something once, in a whisper," Perot liked to say, "and having committed guys across the country go make it happen."

This discipline and clean living was at the core of Perot's strategy. By fielding brokers who were more interested in selling stocks than in driving around in limos or taking junkets to Bermuda, he would usher in a new era on Wall Street, turning its red ink into black, its cyclical performance into steady earnings.

But as Perot would discover, the approach that worked so well in the heartland could not be transplanted to Wall Street. Though H. Ross poured millions into the most modern systems and trading technology, the best brokers abandoned him, rushing headlong to the George Balls of the world who would treat them as prima donnas, not as enlisted men.

In short Perot's grand experiment failed. Although the wiry Texan kept believing that success was just around the corner, the red ink never turned to black. After investing $100 million in DuPont, Perot was ready to cut his losses. On January 21, 1974, the announcement came that DuPont Walston (as the merged entity was called) was placing its network of branch offices on the sales block.

The statement hardly sent Wall Street into a bidding war. With the market in the doldrums, and with a chorus of pessimists chanting that the industry's salad days were over (in part because commissions, long propped up by a fixed schedule, were now open to negotiation), a network of retail sales offices and the enormous expense that went with them was the last thing the big brokerage players wanted at the time. Reynolds Securities, Bache, Dean Witter, Paine Webber, and Hornblower & Weeks-Hemphill, Noyes (now defunct) quickly circled the corpse to pick off plum offices like the DuPont outpost in Beverly Hills, but just who, if anyone, would take on the bulk of the firm's offices was open to question.

Reflecting the skittishness of Wall Street's chieftains, Bache chairman John Leslie put it this way, "We're interested in a number of offices, but it's a very fluid situation." And Reynolds's president Bob Gardiner was equally indecisive, saying, "We're thinking and looking, but we haven't made any decisions."

Into this game of executive tiddlywinks stepped the gunslinger, Bob Fomon.

"The muckety mucks at the New York Stock Exchange were nervous about the fall of DuPont, so they called a meeting of the heads of all the big member firms," recalls Tom Lynch, who along with Norm Epstein accompanied Bob Fomon to the powwow. "All the CEOs were seated around this big oblong table listening to a presentation by Ed Lill, then a partner with Haskins Sells, DuPont's auditors.

"Lill's message is optimistic: the CPAs have checked out DuPont, found it to be a viable concern, and Haskins Sells is willing to bet its reputation on it. But not its money, which is precisely what the brokerage firms are being asked to do. And no matter what Lill says, they don't feel comfortable about it. So one by one they dance around the DuPont issue, saying they're afraid to acquire the firm because they don't want its liabilities, they fear its losses will mount, and blah, blah, blah.

"That's when Fomon, who's plainly turned off by this cry-baby act, grabs Norm and I, and says, 'Let's get the hell out of here.'"

Where does he want to go? Directly to Ross Perot's top man, Mort Myerson. The purpose? To make an offer for twenty-seven of the DuPont offices.

"Bob sits down with Myerson," Epstein recalls, "presents him with a list of DuPont offices, and says flat out, 'These are the ones we want. We're prepared to pay back value for the assets and the customers' accounts, and we're ready to act right now. Okay?'

"Myerson thought he was dreaming. After hearing all

the verbal hand wringing about why the firms couldn't take a gamble on DuPont, here's Fomon nonchalantly saying that he'll take about a quarter of the firm's offices and he'll do it without a dozen lawyers negotiating for him. Knowing a bird in the hand when he saw one, Myerson agreed to the deal on the spot.

"Soon after, Bob called a meeting of the Hutton board. With the directors assembled around him, he unveiled a map of Hutton's offices with an overlay of the DuPont branches we were acquiring. Ostensibly this was to convince the board that the deal was synergistic and worthy of their support.

"But it was a formality. Fomon had made the decision and no one was going to challenge him. As soon as the vote was taken, Mort Myerson, who'd been told by Bob what to expect, appeared in the boardroom. With that, drinks were passed around and toasts were made and Hutton had increased its retail strength by 30 percent.

"After that, other firms agreed to act, picking DuPont offices here and there. But it was Fomon who broke the ice and because of his bravado Hutton got the best of the DuPont branches. Every one of them turned out to be a winner. Overnight we were a much more substantial force in the business."

Actually, the DuPont acquisition was the product of teamwork, Bob Fomon and George Ball at their best. While the CEO was in front of the cameras, Ball was backstage pulling strings, making certain that when the boss strolled into Myerson's office, he would have the ammunition to strike a deal.

"Without telling anyone what he was up to, George hired some key people from the DuPont organization," Lynch recalls. "He wanted some of them for their brokerage production, but also because he knew they could identify the best offices and managers in the DuPont system. One senior guy we hired in Florida was particularly helpful. He had chapter and verse on all the DuPont offices, and he told George which ones to go after and which ones to avoid.

"Just to cover his bets, George had his own branch managers visit with their counterparts at DuPont, getting the inside scoop on their operations and seeing if the best of the lot wanted to work for Hutton. By the time George had completed his research, we had a road map leading us to DuPont's premier offices. When Fomon gave his list to Myerson, there was no guesswork involved. We knew where the treasure was buried."

Fomon's strength as a leader was also his weakness. As he put his stamp on the firm, he did so more as a monarch than as a chief executive, one whose power was so absolute that it would never be challenged in his own kingdom. It was with this in mind that Fomon surrounded himself with a menagerie of cronies and yes men who would become the managers and directors of E.F. Hutton and who would flatter the king and insulate him from the real world. For the most part, those allowed into Fomon's inner sanctum were there to entertain the monarch, not to challenge him or to help shape his decisions.

Hutton's board of directors, to which he theoretically answered, was composed entirely of insiders, all of whom reported to Fomon as corporate employees. The members included San Francisco vice-president Bob Bacon, George Ball, Charles and Gordon Crary, syndication chief John Daly, Norm Epstein, Jim Gahan, Houston regional vice-president Mike Judd, attorney Tom Rae, John Shad, Dallas regional vice-president Bob Wigley, Tom Lynch, and John Latshaw.

As one insider put it, "Bob loved to sit there and play God. If we were in a meeting and the vote was 9 to 0 before he voted, he'd say, 'Now it's 9 to 1 and the 1 wins because my vote counts more than all the rest.' "

What's more he surrounded himself with people who

knew nothing of brokerage at all. When Hutton had gone public, Fomon used the occasion to bring in a famous face, not as a valued addition to the management team but as a celebrity who would add stature to his entourage.

"In 1972, I got this call from a Robert Fomon, who introduced himself as the head of my father's company," recalls Dina Merrill. "He said that the firm was going public, and that he would take it as an honor if my children and I would join him on the floor of the New York Stock Exchange to cut the first ticker tape.

"Apparently, Bob liked the idea of bringing a Hutton back into the firm. The sense of history, of continuity, appealed to him. Later, when he asked me to join the board, I was pleased to accept. It seemed like a natural evolution in the history of the Hutton firm and the Hutton family."

But to Fomon, who had begun collecting English art and antiques, Dina was just another collectible. Having a wealthy heiress with society-page pedigree and a movie star husband (Cliff Robertson) in his menagerie added nicely to his prestige.

Beyond the status appeal, Fomon believed that in bringing Dina into his camp, and ultimately making her a board member, he would be assuring himself of another ally in the ranks.

"Bob's request that I become involved with the company really took me by surprise," Dina says. "I told him so. I said, 'I'm not a businesswoman at all. I'm an actress.' And he said that's okay. 'You can learn this the same way you learn a script.'"

Chapter 9

"Everyone else in his position decorated their staid offices with burl-framed sailing prints, globes of the world, and leatherbound libraries, but Bob Fomon made his office home to a goddamn parrot. A big, dumb bird—Alexander he called it—that just sat there all day cackling 'Bobby, Bobby.'

"Let me tell you, this was no sweet little pet. It was a prehistoric beast that cracked butternuts in its mouth and walked around the executive suite jumping on tables and grabbing people's arms with its beak. Everyone detested that damn macaw. Everyone but Fomon. The more people hated it, the more he adored it."

—Norman Epstein

If there was doubt in anyone's mind that Bob Fomon considered himself and the firm of E.F. Hutton to be one and the same, the DuPont blitz put an end to that. By year-end 1974 the man who had lucked into office viewed the firm as his private domain, to do with as he pleased. The one-time rebel was awed and infatuated by power. Power that led him to thumb his nose at the world.

Recalls another former Hutton executive, one who remains a close friend of Fomon: "Bob would go to 21 Club with these beautiful young girls, and would sit there with his hand on their knees. When I told him, 'Don't do that, Bob. Not in public. It's not becoming of Hutton's CEO,' he'd say, 'Mind your own business. I do what I want to do.' "

In line with his imperious view of his corporate chairmanship, Fomon began to surround himself with an eclectic entourage of hangers-on whose only denominator was that they could curry favor for the CEO. Increasingly he wanted friends who could do his bidding for him, whether that meant gaining access to Manhattan society or building bridges to Europe's royal families.

It was with the latter in mind that Fomon forged a liaison with Henry Mortimer, introduced to him by their mutual friend, Sylvan Coleman. For Fomon it was love at first sight.

A passionate Anglophile, Mortimer dressed in expensive English suits, and played the nobleman to the hilt, tucking lace doilies into his sleeve as he sipped his tea, pinky finger hanging gracefully in midair. Fomon ate it up.

Born to a wealthy and established New York family, Mortimer had the right social connections—connections Fomon wanted for himself. It was on this basis that they teamed up, with Henry serving as Hutton's broker to society. As part of his unofficial duties, Mortimer would sponsor Fomon's entrée into the right circles in New York, Southhampton, and London. More than anyone else, he emerged as Fomon's social guru.

In a story that's pure Mortimer, he choreographed a black-tie dinner introducing Bob Fomon to a British aristocrat visiting New York on a business trip. Because the Brit was bringing along a clique of associates, Mortimer decided to balance the table with a handful of Fomon's senior executives.

While the Hutton group was in the dining room waiting for the guests to arrive, Jerry Miller noticed from the table plan that he'd be seated next to a Mr. Marquand.

"Who's this Marquand guy?" Miller asked Mortimer in

an impatient tone that revealed his distaste for the whole affair. At this point he was concerned that he'd have to spend the evening small talking with a Mortimer clone.

"Is he interesting?" Miller asked. "Is he a good conversationalist?"

Repulsed by Miller's bourgeois query, Mortimer answered through his nose, "I can only assure you that he'll be rich—and important."

While Mortimer pollinated Fomon's social ties, another member of the CEO's entourage, Andre Backar, delivered political clout. A prominent broker with Evans & Co. before Fomon hired him to work as a deal maker for Hutton, Backar was like a private-sector Kissinger: a man with a mysterious ability to reach across national borders to get things done.

"Andre was just the kind of guy Fomon loved to befriend—affluent, glamorous, wired into the international jet set," says Norm Epstein. "They met as neighbors in the U.N. Plaza (a fashionable building where Fomon bought his first apartment in New York) and hit it off famously. To Fomon, Andre was a passport to international clout and prominence. He introduced Bob to a Who's Who of business leaders, power brokers, and deal makers.

"Understand, Backar wasn't just a name dropper. He had an uncanny ability to pull strings anywhere in the world. Some years ago my wife and I decided to go to Mexico. We wanted to stay at Las Brisas, but because we called only days before our scheduled departure from New York, the place was booked.

"When I happened to mention to Bob Fomon that we'd been locked out of our first choice, he suggested that I give Andre a call. I was certain it was a dead end, but what the hell, there was nothing to lose so I called Andre to see what he could do.

"What he could do! What couldn't he do? Twenty minutes after my call, the secretary to Mexico's ambassador in the U.S. is on the line with confirmed reservations to Las Brisas.

"On another occasion, my mother-in-law, a South African who was visiting the United States by way of Canada, lost her visa and couldn't get from Montreal to New York. She was frantic, my wife was frantic, and although I pleaded with everyone at the embassies in New York, Washington, and Canada, my efforts vanished in the black hole of international bureaucracy.

"Then it struck me to call on Andre for help. Not that I was really sure he could do anything. Hotel reservations are one thing, but whisking people through national borders is a feat of a higher magnitude. But what the hell, I wasn't getting anywhere on my own.

"How could I have doubted Backar? Within two hours of my call, officials from the U.S. embassy were at my mother-in-law's side in Montreal, arranging the documents to clear her through to New York. She was with us the next day. The man was awesome."

Another ranking member of the Fomon entourage, Dick Jones, had first befriended Fomon when they were young men in Los Angeles: Fomon working his way through Hutton and Jones running Mitchum, Jones & Templeton, a prominent regional brokerage firm founded by his father. The friendship hit high gear when both served on the Pacific Stock Exchange, Fomon as a board member and Jones as chairman. (Fomon would later succeed Jones as chairman.)

"It was then that we became quite close," Fomon recalls. "When Dick's company went kaput, he approached me about buying it, but I didn't see a match there. So I suggested instead that he approach Paine Webber. They made a deal and Dick stayed with Mitchum for three years after the merger."

Ultimately he would come to New York, where Fomon
hired him to bring institutional business into the firm. As a
director of the General Telephone Company and chairman
of its pension investment committee, he was said to have
top contacts with prominent money managers—men whose
business he could win for Hutton. Though he served officially as a high-level account executive, the scuttlebutt around
Hutton was that he was paid, and paid lavishly, mostly to
keep Bob Fomon company.

"Dick had one of the biggest expense accounts in the
firm," says a former Hutton vice president and director.
"Because Bob enjoyed his friendship, Dick lived like royalty. Everyone at Hutton knew it and resented it.

"I remember the time Dick showed up for lunch in the
Hutton dining room. For Jones to eat with the common
folk was an event. So when Tom Rae saw him, he blurted
out, 'Hey, Dick, what's wrong? The Concorde broken?' "

To the hardworking executives who made Hutton run,
and who did it for modest wages by Wall Street standards,
the idea of Jones living off the fat of the land rubbed many
the wrong way. But Fomon the monarch paid no attention.

"One time when I did a big trade, Bob said, 'Put Dick
Jones's account number on it,' " says the former director.
"When I asked why, he said, 'I need to generate some
commissions so that at the end of the year when the board
bitches about his expense account and his salary, I can
show that he generated all these commissions.' When I
said, 'Bob, he didn't have a thing to do with it, it's a house
account and I'm not giving him credit for it,' he said, 'Oh
come on, put it down so I can show him he generated a
million dollars in revenues and everyone won't yell at me.'

"I told Bob to go find the money some other place."

Though he'd risen to the pinnacle of a Wall Street institution, Bob Fomon was still a wide-eyed Appleton farm
boy, a sucker for smooth-talkers in handmade suits. And

none were smoother than the Italian charm boy Guisseppe Tome.*

"When Bob first met Tome, the Italian was running the overseas brokerage offices for Bache & Co.," recalls Tom Lynch, who pegged Tome from the start, thinking him a two-bit gigolo hiding behind a Marcello Mastroianni accent. "At the time, Hutton had a minor presence overseas. Sylvan Coleman had opened a small office in Zurich, mostly for institutional sales, and we had a one-man investment banking operation in Paris plus a modest London office. Things remained on a small scale until Tome had the grand idea of christening a big Hutton brokerage network in Europe with—you guessed it—Guisseppe Tome as the ruling prince."

Suave and debonair, Tome had the essential credentials to join the Fomon inner circle: he could slip seamlessly into a clique of aristocrats. He had friends in high places, homes in Rome and Paris, and a ski chalet in the Alps.

When a charmer like Tome talked, Fomon listened. The same man who had the cool self-confidence to take over Hutton as a dark horse and put his stamp on the firm went gaga in the company of glamorous people. In their company he was a wealthy sugar daddy who would use his position to bankroll their dreams.

"I told Bob to stay away from Europe—that it had been nothing but a drain on Bache—but with Tome pouring on the charm, he wasn't listening to me," Lynch says. "So he embarked on a major adventure, opening offices in Geneva, Lugano, Germany, Amsterdam, and Greece and putting Tome in charge of them. I kept saying, 'Bob, don't do it. It's a headache. You'll spend so much money and have so many problems that you'll never make a profit there.'"

---

*Convicted for securities laws violations, Tome is now a fugitive from U.S. justice.

But it wasn't a profit Fomon was after as much as the chance to hobnob with dukes and duchesses. To the grand snob Fomon had become, things American (including his domestic brokerage system) were bourgeois, Ozzie and Harriet dull, things European were intoxicating, Rolls Royce elegant.

Fomon's infatuation with the Continent deflected his attention from Hutton's main theater of operations to a little sideshow across the Atlantic. As he drifted away from New York, following his social itinerary wherever it carried him, he began neglecting the company he was paid to run. For his sycophants to be happy, that mattered more than Hutton's bottom line.

"When one of the senior people in my department returned from a European fact-finding trip, he informed me that some of Tome's senior people were engaging in strange bookkeeping transactions for foreign currencies," recalls Norm Epstein. "He said, 'Look how stupid these guys are, they're using single-entry bookkeeping, thus failing to convert their transactions from one currency to another.'

"Naturally, the report shocked me, but I said nothing at first. Instead, I went home to reflect on it. I asked myself, 'Who am I dealing with?' And I had to answer that 'who' I was dealing with wasn't 'stupid.' And so I tried to figure out why they were doing what looked on the surface like an ignorant maneuver. And then the answer jumped out at me. Company rules forbade trading in currencies. To get around this, they were trading in Eurobonds, and covering their trail by failing to convert from dollars to the Eurobonds. To confirm my suspicion I went back over each transaction and found that my hunch was right. They were out to break company rules.

"With the evidence in hand, I went to Fomon and told him that something was afoul in our European operations and that we'd have to do something about it. There were three options: first, to fire the fuckers right off the bat; second, to tell Tome—who was responsible for supervising these guys—that we were onto them, that they'd have to cease and desist and that if they did it one more time we'd shoot them down; or third, we could play dumb, pretending we knew nothing about their scheme.

"Naturally Fomon opted for the play-dumb option. Confronting his friend Tome was the last thing he wanted to do. Tome took him hunting. Tome took him partying. Tome introduced him to the right people. Who the fuck cared what he was doing with the company's money? The king had to be served."

But for Epstein, widely regarded as the conscience of Hutton, playing dumb was an option in theory only. No way this grizzled bear from New York was going to play "hear no evil, see no evil" with an Italian con man. Because all of Hutton, Fomon included, believed that Norm could "nuke" the back office were he so provoked, the CEO had no choice but to limit his pickings from options one and two.

"Faced with my ultimatum that he take some meaningful action, Bob chose option two and so we flew to Switzerland to drop the bombshell on Tome and his senior guys that the gig was up.

"We met for lunch at this fabulous restaurant near Hutton's office in old Geneva. Right away you know these guys are piling up the expense account because the waiter leads us to the best table in the house. And damn if it doesn't have a plaque with their names engraved on it.

"Right from the start, Fomon tries to sidestep the issue at hand. He talks about Europe, about Tome's wine cellar, about every subject in the small-talk encyclopedia. But I hadn't flown all the way to Geneva for that. So after a half hour of inane chatter, I break the ice, telling them what we'd discovered, when they break into a chorus of the old

'Would we do something like that?' routine. But I'm not
about to let them get away with that. Instead I lunge into a
full explanation of what I'd found—the single-entry bookkeeping, etc.—and they just sit there tongue-tied, dying to
retaliate but knowing it's a lost cause.

"For a minute or two we all just stared at each other in
silence. It was the first time in his life that Tome had
nothing to say. Then, his wheels spinning, he opted to
admit it all and let his charm carry him through. Flat out he
says, 'You guys are right. That's what we were doing. We
promise to be good boys and never do it again.' And that
was it. Period. Fomon just turned the conversation back to
the wine cellar. He felt a great load lift from his shoulders.
Not because we'd acted against a violation of company
rules, but because he hadn't come to blows with Tome.
The party invitations would not be interrupted. The hunting trips would go on."

By the fifth year of his tenure, Bob Fomon had come to
believe that the seventy-year-old firm of E.F. Hutton &
Co. was greater than any abuse he could heap on it. He
could plunder the company, lavishing perks on himself and
his entourage, and his excesses would simply be recouped
by the army of brokers he despised. So what if he squandered millions here and there? So what if his cronies did
the same?

"When people were cheating the firm, if they were
Fomon's friends, the order came down to ignore it," charges
Paul Bagley. "We called these people the 'untouchables.'
No matter what kind of infractions we discovered, including cheating on expense accounts, we were told to cover
them up. The long and short of it is that Fomon started
creating a wasteful, arrogant, and immoral culture.

"I remember when he started running around the world
with Saudi financier Adnan Khashoggi, jet-setting from

Africa to Paris, to Morocco. Bob kept saying that Khashoggi was going to become the firm's biggest client. The fact that Khashoggi failed to pay us fees never dissuaded Fomon. No sir. Instead he did more deals with Khashoggi, like placing capital with such oil ventures as American Completion Development Viking Petroleum, which are now the subject of multimillion-dollar lawsuits. When Bob started to combine his friendships with deal making, the firm started going downhill on a very slippery slope that cost us tens of millions of dollars."

"Fomon and his top executives were in a swoon over Khashoggi," Backar recalls. "At one time, they were considering doing a joint venture with Khashoggi. When George Ball asked me what I thought of that, I said it would be an outrage to align the Hutton name with Khashoggi. George said he agreed and asked for my support on the matter.

"Although I didn't think I'd carry much weight on this one, I told Fomon what I thought of it. I said before we do a deal with Khashoggi, let's see what he really has. Let's look at his bank accounts and his other assets and see if there's much substance behind the glamorous facade. Well, I guess they must have had second thoughts, because the joint venture never came off. But a lot of the men at the top of Hutton were still taken with Adnan."

While Hutton cried out for a management structure that would shoulder the burden of its growth—growth Fomon himself engineered—and prepare it for the challenges of the decade ahead, the king was in his sandbox playing with his toys, shielding his friends, buying whatever his heart desired. He even viewed the company chef as a personal caterer.

"When some of the top executives wanted to have breakfast meetings in the Hutton dining room, we asked the chef to come in early," recalls Humbert Powell.

" 'No way,' Bob said. 'He doesn't want to get up that

early. He comes out to help me in Southampton and I don't want to lose him. He likes his schedule the way it is now. That's how we'll have to leave it.'

"I said, 'Bob, who's running this place, Alfonso or you? The way it is now, the goddamn chef is telling us how we should run our dining room.

" 'Maybe we should put him on the board and let him run the firm.' "

But Fomon was deaf to it all. What had started as intuitive brilliance had turned into conspicuous arrogance that began to rub people the wrong way. Arrogance that was taking the fun out of working at Hutton.

Chapter 10

"Bob ran Hutton as if it were some kind of Chinese menu, where you could pick one from column A, one from column B, and what you didn't want to manage you could leave to others. He thought that the company existed for the express purpose of Bob Fomon's pleasure."
—Former member of Hutton board of directors

Although Fomon was spending more and more of his time indulging himself in the spoils of his office, he could still muster an active interest in the glamour side of the business. When he put his mind to it, the vision, entrepreneurial instincts, and rakish charm to get things done were still in evidence.

And so he decided that Hutton should become a major force in public finance. This function, which raises capital for state and local governments through the sale of tax-exempt bonds, had emerged as a hot market on Wall Street, earning prodigious profits for the leaders in the field. Profits Hutton hardly shared in. Considering the firm's ranking as forty-fourth among securities firms in public finance, it was a virtual nonentity. A fact of life Bob Fomon intended to change.

Going for the quick kill that had become his trademark, he launched a secret assault on top-ranked Blyth, East-

111

man, Dillon, making a bold bid for its public finance stars James Lopp III, Richard Locke, and Scott Pierce.

Considered by their peers to be among the best in the business, this trio was an anomaly in the Lone Ranger canyons of Wall Street. They functioned as a team, bringing a mix of talents: Lopp the creative whiz, Locke the administrator, and Pierce the marketer. This synergistic union had raised billions in debt financings, contributing substantially to Blyth's coffers.

But in that success were born the seeds of conflict. Convinced that their contribution to the firm's bottom line entitled them to a bigger share of the profits than the poorly performing retail brokerage division, the three musketeers demanded a dual bonus for key numbers of the public finance department: 10 percent of the department's profits plus 15 percent of the firm's aggregate earnings.

Judged purely on its merits, the demand was not unreasonable. Securities firms have always been structured as meritocracies. Partners who generate the most business earn the most. It's as much a tradition as silk braces and Hermes ties.

But in 1975 Blyth, Eastman was hardly basking in tradition. The product of a recent merger between Blyth & Co. and Eastman, Dillon, the firm was divided by rival cliques that split the partnership into warring camps. In this contentious environment the "brethren" were not about to let a small band of prima donnas cut a larger piece of the earnings pie. The dual bonus demand was rejected. If that defied the spirit of a meritocracy, so be it.

The rejection left the three musketeers fuming, a situation tailor-made for Bob Fomon. Learning through Hutton's public finance staffers that Blyth was vulnerable to a talent raid, he arranged a meeting with Dick Locke.

"Bob instructed Bill Victor, the head of Hutton's public finance operations, to get me in to meet with him at Fomon's office," Locke recalls. "So Billy called me up and asked me to lunch. I told him I couldn't leave Blyth at that point because it was in such dire shape. So I wasn't interested in going to Hutton at the time.

"When Victor reported back to Fomon, Bob said, 'I didn't ask if he was interested in Hutton, I told you to get him over here.' "

Soon after, a meeting was arranged, with Fomon telling Locke of his interest in making Hutton a power in public finance and offering him the equivalent of a blank check: the chance to run his own show, building the revamped department from scratch. Although intrigued by the offer, Locke felt that if he left Blyth, it should be as a team, with the three musketeers moving together.

But that idea faced a roadblock in the name of Jim Lopp. A tall, swaggering Missourian turned out in hand-tailored suits, Lopp feared that Hutton's lack of stature in public finance would sabotage the new effort from the start. If the team was going to move, he argued, it should be a step up to a Merrill Lynch or one of the other established powers in tax-exempts.

"Dick Locke had a series of meetings with Bob Fomon, from which he would always emerge enthusiastic about the Hutton offer and about our prospects there," Lopp recalls. "And each time he'd try to get me to share his enthusiasm by insisting that I meet with Fomon and hear what the guy had to say.

"But I didn't see any reason to do that. Hutton had nothing to offer but a poor image in public finance that we'd have to overcome just to get back to peg one.

"It was an open-and-shut case. I wasn't going to work for Bob Fomon no matter what he said."

When word of Lopp's intransigence reached Fomon, the man who'd grown accustomed to having his own way pressed the issue harder. He turned his behind-the-scenes recruitment drive from Locke to Lopp.

"Bob kept calling, asking me to meet with him, and I

kept calling him back and saying no, no, no," Lopp recalls.
"At that point I wasn't even certain I'd leave Blyth. All I
knew was that if I did, it wouldn't be to join Hutton."

But then in April 1975, the door opened a bit. After
another bloody confrontation with his partners, Lopp decided that he would indeed be leaving Blyth.

"It was then that I agreed to meet Bob at his office.
Only to listen. My objections to Hutton were as strong as
ever.

"But then something happened that I hadn't expected. I
found myself liking this Fomon guy very much. Coming
from such an intensely political environment at Blyth, I
found Bob's candor and imagination immensely refreshing.
I thought to myself: 'This is a terrific guy. I want to be his
friend.'

"But I still didn't want to work for him. My affection for
Bob didn't change the fact that Hutton was zero in the tax-
exempt area. I told Bob that, but he refused to accept it."

Instead the former bad boy of the Campion School turned
on the charm.

"Bob would call every two weeks, always with the same
line," Lopp recalls. " 'What are you doing Friday night?'

"When I'd say, 'Nothing,' he'd say, 'Yes, you are, you're
coming to my house for dinner.'

"At the time Bob and Sharon* lived in this grand place in
Greenwich, Connecticut. It was a marvelous house, and
Sharon, who was a delightful hostess, knew how to make
you feel at home. So against my better judgment I'd drive
out for dinner. We'd talk and drink well into the evening,
and then Bob would set his trap again.

" 'What are you doing Saturday night?' he'd ask.

"Yes, I'd wind up there Saturday, too, and after we'd
drink and talk through the evening, he'd say, 'What are
you doing for Sunday brunch?'

*A former Miss America, Sharon Kay Ritchie was Fomon's second wife.

"After a few months of this, he started breaking down my resistance. I thought I might have to go with him just to save my liver."

By winning over the gregarious Lopp, Fomon would be bringing the three musketeers into the Hutton fold. Still, he wasn't taking any chances. Much as he did with Lopp, Fomon started to woo Scott Pierce.

"It was a Friday night in June of '75 when Bob Fomon called me at home and asked, 'What are you doing tonight?' When I said that my wife and I were hosting a dinner party, he said he was sorry to hear that because he'd wanted us to be his guests for dinner. We exchanged some pleasantries and hung up.

"But a few hours later, he called back and asked, 'What are you doing Saturday night?' When I told him we had an engagement Saturday night as well, he said, 'Fine, thank you, maybe another time.' With that I thought I'd heard the last of Mr. Fomon. But an hour later there was a call again, and that now familiar voice on the end of the line.

" 'What are you doing Sunday night?'

"At this point I knew he wouldn't give up. So I told my wife, 'We'd better accept or he'll call at three in the morning.' "

Throughout the summer the three musketeers seesawed among Blyth and Hutton and the Merrill Lynches of the world. We should leave; we shouldn't leave. We should go into business for ourselves; we should go with Hutton; we should go with anyone but Hutton. All the while Fomon kept wining and dining his prey, tempting them with the kind of carte blanche offers they wouldn't get anywhere else on the Street.

Determined to decide the issue once and for all, the partners met at Dick Locke's Pocono retreat, spending the long Labor Day weekend rehashing the issues they'd hashed out a hundred times before. As they debated among themselves, a majority of two began to emerge. Locke and

Lopp, who'd grown bitter over Blyth's internal politics and the effect it had on their stature, voted to accept Bob Fomon's challenge, taking their talents (and hopefully some of their clients) to E.F. Hutton. Scott Pierce preferred to stay put, but having committed to majority rule, agreed to join his colleagues.

Snaring the dynamic trio proved to be another coup for corporate-raiding Bob Fomon. In two years Locke, Lopp, and Pierce would transform Hutton from a perennial cellar dweller in public finance to the hottest house on the Street, rapidly rising through the ranks to the number two spot. Clients on the magnitude of DuPont, U.S. Steel, Conoco, which had never before considered Hutton worthy of their business, came into the Hutton camp, corralled by super salesman Lopp and his endless stream of creative financing strategies.

As the department rolled along, it became a power unto itself. The three musketeers claimed the credit for its success, but behind the scenes, Bob Fomon continued to play a critical role.

"Time after time we made millions of dollars for the firm because Bob Fomon was willing to take risks," Pierce recalls. "Risks others in his position would consider imprudent and would refuse to accept.

"I remember the time Congress pulled the plug on our single-family housing bonds, which enabled municipalities to create single-family housing for their citizens. The instruments had been very successful until a change in the law said this was not a legitimate purpose for issuing tax-exempt bonds. Still, we had a window of opportunity to issue the single-families before the law changed. But because the bonds couldn't be rated in time, that involved quite a bit of risk.

"So when we asked Fomon for the authority to underwrite a half billion dollars worth of the bonds, we weren't sure how he'd react. But we shouldn't have doubted him.

After listening to the pros and cons, he said to go for it. He was willing to trust our instincts that we could make money on the offering. And we did. Bob made a gutsy decision and Hutton gained from it."

Because he saw glory in dealing with the Exxons and the U.S. Steels of the world, because he always fancied himself an investment banker, Fomon extended himself to public finance the way he never did to retail. In behavior that was positively shocking for King Fomon, he would even come down from the royal roost to mingle with underlings.

"When we were recruiting young college kids fresh out of Harvard and Wharton to join our department, Bob would get a table at 21 Club and regale them with visions of Hutton as a great and glorious firm that under his leadership was getting ever greater and ever more glorious," recalls Lopp, who became one of Fomon's closest friends and advisers. "He'd sit there with those recruits, wooing them and charming them until the small hours of the night.

"Once the kids came on board, Bob kept an active interest in them. He knew everyone by name. He followed their careers. He took an interest in everything they did. By the time I left Hutton we had hundreds of people in public finance and Bob knew each one's salary within five hundred dollars."

But ask Fomon to name Hutton's top ten retail producers and the CEO went blank. When it came to the messy business of brokers, and branch managers, and one-on-one with John Q. Public, Fomon left it all to Ball.

"If something caught his fancy, like playing the role of roving ambassador in Europe or building the public finance area," says a long-time Fomon friend, "then he threw himself into it with great zest. But if something bored him, or worse yet, if he thought it pedestrian, he treated it like a stepchild.

"Once I was hearing a grumbling from the field that the chief executive was a phantom in his own company, that his own branch managers never saw him and they took it as an insult. Thinking this was a fence Bob should mend, I suggested that he attend a regional sales meeting scheduled for Phoenix the following week. But when I told him the sales force needed a show of support from the boss, he looked at me curiously and said, 'I can't. Don't you know I have dinner plans?' "

With the board of directors stacked with cronies and pushovers, there was no one on board to force Fomon to live up to his management obligations.

"Hutton's 'board of directors' was a misnomer," says a former senior vice president. "It should have been called a 'board of protectors.' That should come as no surprise when you consider that Bob stacked the board with a menagerie of old buddies, bootlickers, and assorted freeloaders who wouldn't think of challenging him because he held the key to their promotions, salaries, and expense accounts. Except for a few principled guys like Epstein and Miller who spoke their minds, most of the directors shut up and played dead.

"It got to the point where the board functioned like a rubber-stamping machine. Fomon wants to enter a new business? Like that, the stamp comes down: 'APPROVED.' Fomon wants to create a new department? Like that, the stamp comes down: 'APPROVED.' Fomon wants to throw out ten million on some European adventure? Like that, the stamp comes down: 'APPROVED.'

"The issues weren't even decided at the board level. Fomon's modus operandi was to work behind the scenes, cornering people in their offices, twisting their arms or whatever it took to get their support. When the board met, he would present his latest scheme as a fait accompli. No discussions. No votes.

"In a typical case, I'm in Bob's office one day discussing

a series of matters when he leans across his desk and whispers to me, 'You're going on vacation for two weeks, right?'

" 'Right, Bob, I'm leaving tomorrow.'

"I'm wondering why this innocuous conversation should be couched in whispers. But he continues:

" 'I have to clue you in on something. I don't want you reading about it in the papers and going crazy that I did a deal while you were gone.'

" 'A deal? Going crazy?' Now I'm starting to get nervous. Fomon's up to something. 'What are you talking about, Bob?'

" 'The board doesn't know it yet,' Fomon continues, 'but I picked Goldman Sachs to run the $200 million convertible offering.'

" 'What? Goldman Sachs? Why are they running it? We're a public company. Why don't we run it?'

" 'They know more about it. They came over here, they made a pitch, they'd be right for this.'

" 'Who did they make the pitch to, Bob?'

" 'To me.'

" 'And to who else, Bob?'

" 'No one else. No one even knows they were here.'

" 'That's wonderful, Bob. You're the chairman of a public company and you're pulling the strings on a $200 million convertible offering without telling anyone. What makes you so sure the board's going to approve this?'

"Fomon looks at me as if I'm speaking in some kind of foreign tongue. Then he answers, this time with an indignant shriek, 'Fuck the board, I've decided on my own. That's all the approval we need.' "

Tom Lynch admits that the board meetings were more a formality than an independent review of management's plans and performance. "Bob would get it in his mind what he wanted to do and then he'd get on the phone, calling this one, calling that one, arranging things so that he'd have his way with little or no interference. If the matter required board approval, I would bring it up at the next meeting, not as a subject for discussion, but as something to be ratified. That's the way it was presented. You can vote on the issue, but the only acceptable vote is a vote in favor of the chairman's motion."

"When you look at the fall of Hutton, you can't point a finger at someone and say, 'He did it,' " says Norm Epstein. "But you can point a finger and say, 'He could have prevented it.' And the guy you have to point that finger at is Bob Fomon.

"Why? Because he wasn't paying attention. Because toward the end of the seventies, he didn't seem to give a shit. He let the firm, except for the retail part that George Ball had under his control, run itself."

The securities business had changed, but Fomon was too busy playing king to notice. Whereas in the past he could make moves on the fly and quickly turn the firm around, things had become too complicated for that. For Hutton to survive as a leading-edge firm, it required a kind of discipline, analysis, and painstaking research and development that wasn't there.

"With a snap of his fingers, Fomon could have corrected this," Epstein says. "All he had to do was say to his managers: 'I want completed staff work. I want to know in advance what's going to happen in your departments. I want to understand the economic life cycles of our products and their profitability. I want to understand how we get in and out of key markets, and minor markets. I want to have a harmony out there. I want our functions to interrelate. I want this to be an integrated firm.' But he did none of that and Hutton suffered terribly for it."

Beginning in the late seventies, the size and pace of the securities industry began accelerating like never before. Between 1978 and 1980 alone, Hutton's revenues doubled from about $500 million to more than a billion. This was six times the $84 million the firm had generated the year Fomon had come to power.

"The Bob Fomon of the late seventies and eighties wasn't that much different from the one who had emerged as a dark horse a decade before," Epstein continues. "More arrogant, yes, but he was still decisive, still the fastest draw in the West. But that was no longer the ticket to success.

"I'd say to him, 'Bob, I need a new computer system for the back office.' He'd say, 'Get it.' But shit, you can't just 'get it.' You have to understand why I want it. You have to understand the costs, the implications, how it fits into the rest of the firm. But Bob didn't bother himself with any of that."

Part of the problem was that Fomon was so successful as a builder and securer of his own power that there was no one in his inner circle to force him to see the new realities and to pressure him to act on them. Tom Lynch, one of Fomon's closest advisers, couldn't do it. Many considered him over his head as chief financial officer. General counsel Tom Rae, another of Fomon's aides, couldn't do it. Staffers thought he had his hands full performing as a lawyer. Warren Law, the Harvard professor Fomon had hired as Hutton's first outside director, couldn't do it. His home was in the classroom. Henry Mortimer, the boss's passport to the Southampton social circuit, couldn't do it. He was too busy arranging black-tie dinners with foreign dignitaries.

"At Fomon's board meetings you could draw a line down the table," says Hum Powell. "On one side sat all the people beholden to Bob. On the other, you had the rest of us who wanted to hold him accountable. The problem is, we were badly outnumbered. Jerry Miller asked Bob to get a vote-counting machine so that we could at least tally the ayes and the nays, giving us a better chance of having our way if we could manage to carry an issue. But naturally Bob preferred to do it his way. He'd say everyone who agrees with me raise your hands. But before anyone had time to count the vote, he'd slam his fist on the table and say, 'I told you we'd win.'

"That's the way he ran his meetings."

"With no one to balance Fomon, there were vacuums all over the firm," Epstein adds. "A vacuum in compensation, in risk management, in allocating the firm's assets, in investment banking. It got to the point where you couldn't turn around without running into a vacuum. You were sucked from vacuum to vacuum."

The dearth of leadership took a heavy toll on the corporate finance department, where internal cliques battled one another for power. By refusing to mediate between them, Bob Fomon allowed the feuds to fester.

"Much of the antagonism in the department stemmed from John Shad's personality," Bagley says. "He was always nitpicking, backbiting, being adversarial. Whenever someone presented an idea at a meeting, John believed he had a responsibility to go after it hammer and tong. If a concept came through the crucible of a John Shad interrogation, then—maybe then—he would consider it worth its salt.

"But for those on the other end of the firing line, the Shad treatment could be humiliating, and it led to deep-seated resentment.

"Also Shad's focus in serving his own investment banking clients led to bloody battles with the syndicate department led by John Daly. When Daly proposed a strategy for underwriting a Shad client, Shad would push for more, better, faster—even if this ran contrary to the syndicate's interests. When the syndicate people proposed that a convertible bond coupon be priced at 7-1/4, Shad would fire back, 'Let's try 6-1/2.' Because the lower price meant lower profits for the syndicate department, Daly resisted, but Shad was relentless, constantly pushing people to the line.

"Not once did Fomon try to referee these disputes for the good of the firm. Not once did he try to get Daly and Shad and Powell and equity trading chief Bill Dunn to work together. No, that would have meant managing, and that's something Bob Fomon refused to do. He would rule, but he wouldn't manage. He would look for the flash-in-the-pan scheme, he would abuse people, but he wouldn't manage. To Bob Fomon, running a company had nothing to do with managing it. You just took what you wanted and let others worry about the rest."

But no one else was empowered to fill the gap. In the wake of Fomon's neglect, a management vacuum sucked up the firm's talents, resources, and energies. While his banking departments were bludgeoning each another, senior executives watched from the sidelines as the Salomon Brothers and the Goldman Sachs of the world responded to a changing marketplace, building coordinated firms with discipline and harmony between the various services and disciplines. As such, they gained an enormous advantage in investment banking.

"By 1980 the big boys had invaded our market, but we had done nothing to encroach on theirs," Bagley says. "On every public offering we were chasing, we were running into the likes of Goldman and Salomon. Five years before they wouldn't have bothered themselves with the mid-sized IPOs that were our meat and potatoes, but now they were dispatching teams of bankers to get them. And they were beating us at our own game. We lost the initial public offering for the mail-order firm of William Sonoma because Goldman Sachs came in fifteen points above us in their multiple indications. Because they were integrated and well managed, they were able to promise the client more. Naturally, they got the business.

"While our competitors were creating modern invest-

ment banking firms, we were bogged down in these inter-
necine wars with each department trying to puff up its own
position without regard for what that meant for the firm as
a cohesive unit.

"As the man at the top, that was Fomon's job. But it's a
job he wasn't doing. Instead he was partying with his band
of sycophants, doing hare-brained deals that never made a
dime. He'd force losers into the Hutton organization and
they in turn would force the good people out.

"In the end we were left with nothing. Under Fomon the
managerial organization turned to mush. All it would take
was a crisis to destroy the company."

By the early 1980s that crisis wasn't far off.

Chapter 11

"George, what are we supposed to do? Should we bunt, squeeze, or swing for the seats? You're the only one with the game plan, George, the only one who knows how to run this place. You can't leave, George. You just can't."

—Humbert Powell

In early 1982, the firm was stunned by a surprise announcement: George Ball, the most beloved man in the organization, was leaving E.F. Hutton.

To the men and women hawking the stocks and bonds and mutual funds, to the account executives who were the traditional backbone of the firm, Robert Fomon was only a name in the annual report, someone who courted counts in the capitals of Europe.

"In their view, George Ball, elected Hutton's president in 1977, was 'the' boss. That view Ball had worked hard to perpetrate.

"George insisted that the big producers and the managers in the field report directly to him and to him alone," recalls Bruce Tuthill, once Hutton's top-ranked account executive. "It was a flat management structure. If you had a problem, you called George and he responded to it. If you didn't like one of the Hutton ads you saw on TV, you'd get on the phone with George. If you didn't like one of our new products, you'd get on the phone with George. You'd say this sucks or that sucks and if George thought your gripe was legitimate he'd get it rectified. Time after time you reached out to George, and time after time he reached back."

Under George the Great the retail system was a benevolent autocracy. If there were decisions to be made, if there were battles to be fought, George would do it. It had all started when he had still been a branch manager in New York.

"One time the brokers were complaining that our research director was preparing stock analyses that did no one any good but the research director," says a former Hutton regional vice-president. "Unless investors could read the reports and buy stocks on the basis of what they said, the research was useless. Fish wrapping.

"That was precisely what we had under the ivory-tower research chief, whose writing was so befogged by academics and analytical self-flagellation that it was impossible for the layman to decipher what he was saying. When George heard the brokers' complaints about this, he went directly to the research director, telling him that his product was out of touch with the marketplace. Well, this guy happened to have twenty years of experience on the Street and the last thing he was going to do was cave in because some pipsqueak sales manager comes barging into his office demanding that he change the way he'd been working for two decades. Instead he threw fire at fire, telling Ball, 'If you don't like what I do, tough shit. I report to Sylvan Coleman, not to you. Get lost.'

"But George Ball was never the 'get lost' type. So he did the research director one better, going straight to Coleman himself, arguing that if research reports didn't earn the faith of investors or brokers or anyone else but other research directors, they weren't worth the paper they're printed on. And Coleman agreed. Changes would be made. Bottom line? George Ball put his stature on the line—a defeat at this stage of his career would have been costly—and he won. With flags waving and bugles blaring, he returned to his troops the conquering hero.

"It's always hard to pin things to a specific date and say, 'Yes, that's when everything changed.' But gradually, the brokers began to look to George as their protector. It's a feeling that intensified as he assumed more power and ultimately the Hutton presidency. The producers were dependent on George and he liked it just that way, thank you."

So did Bob Fomon. With Ball running the messy business of retail, Fomon could sit atop a brokerage firm without dirtying himself with the brokers. Having George in charge meant he could cavort on the Continent or in the mansions of Southampton, hobnobbing with the Tomes and the Khashoggis of the world.

But unbeknownst to both men, Fomon and Ball had been laboring under false assumptions. Ball had assumed that as the heir apparent, he would be elected chief executive officer, succeeding Fomon after a reasonable term in office, perhaps ten years. At that point Fomon would serve out his years as chairman, à la his mentor Al Jack: a well-paid but powerless figurehead.

Fomon's assumption, equally naive, was that Ball would be content to remain as president. With that kind of permanence, Fomon could cede the retail system to his second in command, certain that George would always be there to keep the machine humming. The chief executive didn't have to run the business. His proxy would do it for him. Hadn't they always functioned like a well-oiled "older brother, younger brother" team? Older brother set the policy and younger brother executed it?

In truth, Fomon was hardly the sort anyone would want as a brother. A proud, imperious man, he resented Ball's competence. That he relied on George was one thing; that the world knew about it was something else. To camouflage his dependence, he had abused Ball almost from the beginning—verbally lashing him before secretaries, sales managers, and senior officers of the company.

"Sometime in the early seventies Bob Fomon called a meeting to discuss Hutton's expansion in the mid-Atlantic," says a former Hutton branch manager. "Because I was visiting the New York office, George Ball thought it might be valuable to have my thoughts on the matter.

"I was pleased to attend the meeting, mostly to see firsthand the chemistry between Fomon and Ball. From what I'd heard, they were an extraordinary team. Two remarkable executives sewn together by affection as well as by pride and ambition.

"But shit, what I saw was an embarrassment. From the minute he strolled into the meeting—twenty minutes late, no excuses—Fomon started ridiculing everything George said. When Ball suggested that we enter the new market not in piecemeal fashion but by christening three offices at once, Fomon raised his hands in the air like an evangelist preacher silencing his congregation. Gaining everyone's attention, he pointed to Ball and said, 'George here just came up with the dumbest idea I've ever heard.' "

Fomon's tantrums were outbursts of a man who had risen to power unexpectedly and was so taken by his position that he was compelled to flaunt it. "Bob would denigrate everyone episodically," says a former Ball confidant. "It was his way of proving how important he was. His title, his position, his power—none of that was enough. He had to rub it in people's faces.

"And with George there was another dynamic at work. Because Bob knew that Ball was the only one in the firm who could outshine him, he consciously humiliated him in front of others. To dirty-trick Fomon—the man was always the Richard Nixon of Wall Street—making Ball look small made Bob look big. So he'd shout at George in

earshot of other executives, 'Who asked for your opinion?
Who asked to see you? Go back to your office.' "

In private, Fomon was a different man, stroking Ball and
supporting the very proposals he ridiculed in public. Because he needed Ball, and because deep down he admired
and respected him, he gave his alter ego great leeway in
running the brokerage business. For this reason he assumed that Ball would forgive the outbursts, the scoldings,
the humiliating abuse that would echo through the Hutton
hallways and provide fodder for gossip around the typing
pool.

Though Ball never retaliated openly, neither did he forget. Instead, in the quiet of his office, where he would
retreat after the infamous tirades, he made a pact with
himself to get revenge on Fomon.

It was a pact he was now honoring.

To the brokerage team he'd built over the years, and
who had come to see him as the father figure, George's
leaving was like the Dodgers leaving Brooklyn. Even hard-
boiled executives with decades of experience in corporate
musical chairs felt saddened and betrayed. They simply
refused to accept Ball's decision.

"The day George left, I walked down the hall with him,
down the elevator, and to his car," Humbert Powell recalls. "All the while I'm telling him he can't go. I said,
'George, we're in the World Series, in the bottom of the
ninth inning with the bases loaded, and you walk out of the
stadium. George, how can the coach leave in the bottom of
the ninth inning? You've been talking teamwork all the
way, and the team has been with you all the way, and all of
a sudden you're waving good-bye.' "

With his handwritten memos and thoughtful comments
and pervasive presence, George Ball had accomplished
something unique for Hutton and something rare on Wall

Street. He had established an emotional bond with his people. To the brokers wedged into their claustrophobic cubicles, the branch and regional managers above them, and even to the staff executives at One Chase Plaza, George was the glue that held the firm together. They adored him.

And now the leader was moving across the street to head up Prudential-Bache Securities, a Hutton competitor. Say it ain't so, George.

"George had always insisted that Hutton was a family as much as a firm," recalls Jerry Miller. "Whenever one of his brokers or executives left for another firm, he'd rant and rave, calling them traitors. Just because someone is offering you a bigger paycheck or a fancier title, he'd say, that's no reason to leave your family. Only greedy sons of bitches would do that.

"That's why it came as such a shock that George was leaving. The way he lambasted others for doing that, you just assumed he'd stay at Mother Hutton until they had to carry him out."

Why did George Ball leave E.F. Hutton at the height of his career?

The answer has to do with power and pride, with resentment and revenge. Yes, George Ball was Bob Fomon's heir apparent, but like the vice-president of the United States, his proximity to power was misleading. As long as Bob Fomon remained CEO, Ball would be a perennial number two. With little else in his life besides Hutton, fifty-seven-year-old Bob Fomon was hardly a candidate for retirement.

This fact of life Bob Fomon, always jealous of his rank, had driven home ruthlessly, and did it by abusing the only real threat to his power.

"I remember a time in the fall of 1981 when I was in Fomon's office shooting the breeze with Fomon and Tom Lynch," recalls a former executive in the syndication department. "In comes George Ball to ask Fomon when he's going to release the quarterly earnings report. A simple question, which as the company's president he had every reason to inquire about. But Bob doesn't see it that way. 'Hey, I run this place, not you,' he says, 'I'll decide when to release the earnings. You go back and run retail like a good little boy.'

"Jesus Christ, Ball is our president and Fomon's treating him like that. 'Go back and run retail like a good little boy!' You don't talk to the company president that way."

As the years passed, though, Ball's tolerance for Fomon's arbitrary attacks had worn thin. Resentment began to boil to the surface, born not only of the shabby treatment he suffered, but increasingly because he began to feel superior to Fomon.

"George was in the office every morning at seven," recalls Tom Lynch. "He was a workhorse. He wouldn't go home until seven in the evening and he'd take a satchel of work home with him. But Fomon, on the other hand, would come in at ten and read the newspaper. He wouldn't answer the phone and he wouldn't read his mail. After a while he wasn't doing much of anything. He was leaving the management of the firm to Ball. He'd never say that publicly—his ego wouldn't allow it—but that's exactly what he was doing and no one knew that better than George."

If Ball had started out as Bob Fomon's "kid brother," time, talent, and experience had changed that. By the early eighties Ball believed that he had come to surpass Fomon in managerial skills and leadership qualities. It was then that Ball started hearing voices in his head. Associates say that he wondered, "If I'm better than Fomon, why the hell am I working for him? If I know he's not going to retire for years, why am I waiting dutifully in line? If I'm as good as I think I am, why don't I go out and prove it? Not here, but at another company, as a CEO in my own right."

And so when a recruiter at the executive search firm of Russell Reynolds called Ball in the spring of 1982, offering him the chance to head up Prudential-Bache, it was as if someone had been hearing those voices in his head. Yes, he would accept the offer, and just like that all the years of preaching about allegiance and family would be tossed out like a worthless stock.

But as one peels away the layers of Ball's complex and intimate relationship with Hutton, it becomes apparent that his departure was more than a naked play for power or revenge. The very concept of family that George Ball fathered during his extraordinary tenure at the firm may have forced him to leave. The fact is, he had created a monster and that monster was suddenly turning on him.

"By setting himself up as the godfather of the retail network, by insisting that everyone come directly to him and that he alone would solve their problems, George was weaving himself a spider's web of tangled relationships that would ultimately choke him," says Rich Braugh. "His weakness was that he didn't want to delegate. In the end, the need to control everyone and everything was doing him in.

"You have to understand, George didn't operate by the book. He cut deals with dozens and dozens of his people. That's how he retained top producers and managers. The cards and letters and phone calls weren't enough. George did much of his managing by handing out sweetheart deals."

For example, the day a broker becomes a branch manager, he is supposed to give up most of his personal production in exchange for a ten percent cut of the office's net profits. In theory, he helps his brokers to earn more and shares in their success through the override.

But human nature being what it is, some managers always want more. They want to keep their personal production as well as the override. They would lobby Ball for this, and if they were valuable enough and persistent enough, Ball would often cut deals with them.

"Branch managers had all sorts of different deals," says a former regional vice-president. "One branch manager could produce all he wanted and get paid for it in addition to his override, while another would have a cap on production, say $10,000, plus the override. George decided who got what and when they got it."

Ball's showering brokers with special concessions took its toll on Hutton. By making them the most pampered lot on Wall Street, he created an army of brokers so used to having their way that once the markets changed and belts had to be tightened, Hutton found itself incapable of change.

"Hutton's industry position was one of a full-service retail firm characterized by very productive brokers on the retail side and virtually nothing of an institutional presence," says former Salomon Brothers partner Kendrick Wilson, III, who served as Hutton's investment banker before becoming its executive vice-president in the spring of 1987. "Ball was the chief architect of this and it worked as long as the market allowed it—as long as investors believed they were getting value added for the high commissions.

"Under George Ball it was an article of faith that strong commissionwould cover bloated costs. And so under him the firm's expenses were out of control. Every product had a product coordinator. Everyone had an override. Hutton was a great trough and everyone was dipping into it.

"Hutton's position as a high-end retail producer, which had been a strength through the 1970s, became a liability in the eighties. The competition diversified—Shearson bought Lehman Brothers and Merrill Lynch became an investment banking house—but Hutton stayed the same. And it would pay a steep price for this.

"Even after the times no longer allowed reckless spending, Hutton kept on doing it. The field had become so spoiled that the inmates were running the asylum."

* * *

For King Fomon, the impact of George Ball's resignation sunk in slowly, like a shocking telegram in the night. "I'll never forget the image of a glassy-eyed Bob Fomon straggling into my office, saying of all things that George was really great, that Pru-Bache was lucky to get him, and that the least we could do was to host a first-class send-off for him," recalls Norm Epstein.

"He's talking about a real bash—black tie, bands, a night to remember. But just as he finished painting a picture of the extravaganza, he stops in midstream, staring in utter silence at the ceiling. That was the moment of truth, the first time he realized what George had done. His second in command had deserted him.

"It was then that his mood swung 180 degrees. When I saw him the next day he looked pale, ghostly, bereaved, as if all the blood had been drawn from his face. Feeling sorry for him, I put together an impromptu condolence committee to call on him. That evening Jerry Miller, Dick Locke, and myself sat in Fomon's office till midnight, consoling him, assuring him that he'd overcome the loss. I remember Miller saying, 'Hey, Bob, don't worry, we'll support you. We'll get you through this.' When I think back on it now, it was like a wake."

For those who had come to pay their condolences, the gesture was more than an act of charity. Even the hand holders needed reassurance that E.F. Hutton could survive without George Ball. Knowing that Fomon was trading on past glory and that Ball, for all of his excesses, had been a strong and inspiring leader, they feared that his departure would leave the firm rudderless, turning in circles.

To brace themselves for the future, and to rouse their collective spirits, the Hutton men turned on Ball, vilified him, transformed his image from that of a departed hero to a deserter. United against this common villain, they could chant the battle cry of revenge to snap them out of their depression.

No one shouted louder than Fomon. The chance to retaliate against Ball served as an emotional elixir, lifting his spirits and breathing new life into the old man. Suddenly the gunslinger had returned. George Ball had struck him and he was determined to strike back.

He would do it by proving to the world that he was just as good as George. He could inspire and flatter the brokers, he could drink with them and chew the fat with them, he could remember to send his best to Betsy and the kids. With the legend-making machine already establishing Ball as one of a kind, and an irreplaceable leader, Fomon felt the need to reassert himself and prove to the field that he could out-Ball Ball.

"But first he had to do something he hadn't done for ages—come out of his dark office and mingle with the brokers," says Scott Pierce. "He had to spread the message that the firm wouldn't self-destruct without George. Bob Fomon could lead them just as well. Bob Fomon didn't have three heads.

"Bob was determined to succeed at this. His resolve grew by the day. Not only had Ball abandoned him, but to rub salt on a wound, he started picking off our top AE's. When Ball left, his faithful followers claimed he'd never raid Hutton. But raid he did. In 1982 he took 72 of our AE's, many of them heavy hitters. That's what George was after: the big producers that every brokerage firm prizes."

To counterattack, Fomon launched a two-pronged offensive. Operating out of New York headquarters, the CEO presided over a damage-control force that called key brokers around the country, assuring them that Hutton had survived the great San Francisco earthquake, two world wars, a market crash, and a depression—and that it would surely survive the loss of George Ball.

This was designed to steady the firm, to boost morale and to prevent further defections. But for those at the front line of the damage-control effort, the message from the commander in chief was a mixed one. Yes, Fomon wanted revenge on Ball, and yes, he wanted to prove himself as much a field marshal as his former president, but he wasn't up to the task. The defects in his personality and the arrogance that had turned the brokers off to him years ago would surface during this critical period, making a mockery of his efforts.

"Right after George left, Bob asked me to come to New York to do damage control," recalls a prominent retail executive whose influence and credibility with the other brokers made him valuable to Fomon. "So I stayed in New York for a couple of weeks, calling brokers, holding hands, assuring everyone that there was life after George Ball.

"The program was a good idea, but it needed strong leadership and Fomon failed to provide it.

"One evening during the damage-control mission Bob invited me to his apartment for a drink. Well, with Bob Fomon there was no such thing as 'a drink.' The guy was a varsity boozer. There he was downing one after another and there I was trying to keep up. Well, it's getting later and later and we're drinking more and more, and suddenly I get that horrible sensation that a bottle of scotch is coming back up my throat with my breakfast, lunch, and dinner not far behind. I just made it to the bathroom. Gee, I must have spent an hour in there, and when I returned all pale and wobbly-legged, Bob just poured me another one. He'd probably downed two or three drinks while I was busy puking my brains out, and I guess he thought I needed a chance to catch up.

"People say the way the man drank was his business, and maybe they have a point. But after spending that night with Bob I knew one thing: you can't put it away to the extent that he did and wake up the next morning functioning well. Not as a chief executive. Not in a crisis period."

In phase two of his ill-fated counterattack, Fomon took his "We don't need George Ball" dog-and-pony show on the road, making the rounds to the firm's sales regions. Try as he might to create the image of "Bob Fomon, regular guy," his lack of experience with the field and his lifelong disdain for the men and women who toiled in it showed through wherever he went. King Fomon was too accustomed to the Adnan Khashoggi's of the world, to the Guisseppe Tome's and the dukes and duchesses of God knows where, to know how to relate to the common folk. He'd written them off three decades before in Los Angeles.

"When Mr. Fomon visited us, he suggested that we have dinner in the best place in town," says a former Hutton branch manager who met with Fomon during the damage-control campaign. "The idea, he said, was to talk business, to see how headquarters could make life easier for us. It would be a real working dinner.

"But when we get to the restaurant, Fomon starts picking the menu apart. He's mumbling, cursing, having a real fit. Why? Seems the place wasn't up to Manhattan standards. No snails or oysters Rockefeller or whatever the hell he wanted. 'What the fuck am I going to eat?' he complains.

"This nonsense goes on for fifteen minutes. Then, just when he appears to be calming down, he asks for the wine list and goes apeshit over that, too. The problem? They have no Bordeaux, or they had the wrong year or I don't know what had his ass in a frenzy, but he was really off the wall. When someone suggested that he have a Bud and forget the whole thing, he looked at them as if they suggested he drink a glass of urine.

"At one point he did calm down—I think someone found something he liked—but by that time the cause was lost.

No one listened to a thing he said. We knew the guy had nothing in common with us.

"Maybe we worked for the same firm, but we lived in two different worlds."

Although George Ball's departure stirred Fomon's sense of bravado, whatever magic he'd brought to the job more than a decade before had been lost to the shuttling from black-tie party to black-tie party, from liquor bottle to liquor bottle.

To those who watched Fomon close up, it was as clear as a margin call that he could no longer run the business. Mr. Decisive, Mr. Buck Stops Here, had lost it.

Ball had become Hutton's leader in so many ways that the extent of Fomon's deterioration as a CEO was not fully recognized until he tried to lead the firm once again. The confidence that had once been his strong suit had disappeared. Now, when the company needed another Harry Truman, it was stuck with a waffler.

"George Ball's empty office became a symbol of Fomon's ineptitude," says Hum Powell. "He was afraid of leaving the presidency vacant—God knows he was learning the hard way that he couldn't run the firm singlehandedly—but he was also reluctant to make a choice for fear that would alienate the others. So he did nothing, and as you can imagine, that was disastrous.

"While Bob was twiddling his thumbs, the place was out of control. Everyone and his mother was vying for George's job. A day or two after George left, the candidates started crawling out of the woodwork in waves.

"It began with John Latshaw, who shows up in New York telling Bob, 'I know you're having problems, right? I know you need a president, right? I'm your man.'

"Then Peter Muratore, George's right-hand man, who ran products and markets, suggested that he move into

Ball's office so that he could be close to Fomon, to bounce new product ideas off of him.

"I said, 'Bob, you've got to make a decision. We've got to get a president in here. Everyone is going to be wandering in.' Sure enough, the next day Lopp decides to have his office repainted. He suggested that he should move into George's office until it's done. The way I figured it, he was going to tell the painter to paint one brush stroke a day."

"I kept trying to prompt Fomon to act. I said, 'Bob, everyone's going to spend the next six months fighting to get into that goddamned office. Everyone is tossing their hat in the ring. You can't let this kind of thing go on. Either wall up the office or put someone in there.'

"His answer? 'I've talked to some people and it's better to leave it open.'

"Leave it open! 'Why?' I asked. 'We know everyone in this place. What do you think, someone is going to come out a rat hole in six months and suddenly be our savior. Make a decision, Bob.' "

But he couldn't. The man who had once been the gutsiest leader on Wall Street was now frozen in place.

The worst, though, was still to come. On the evening of August 9, 1983, Bob Fomon's obsession with the liquor bottle caught up with him.

It all began on a night like any other for Bob Fomon. Accompanied by his son Bobby, Jr., the CEO had been holding court at Mexican Restaurant, downing his usual bucket brigade of booze, in this case Margaritas. Just what happened next Fomon says he can't recall. But putting the pieces together, it's likely the events occurred as follows.

With the chairman of the board barely able to sit up in his seat, it was time to cut the night short. Though Fomon protested that he was "fine, just fine," he was deposited in a limousine and whisked away to his 70th Street co-op, just steps away from Central Park. Here the chief executive of E.F. Hutton & Co., his hair in wild disarray, his custom-made English suit as wrinkled as an old sheet, staggered to the elevator and up to his ninth-floor apartment, cluttered with enough nineteenth-century English furniture, embroidered throw pillows, antique brass andirons, and collector's bric-a-brac to fill a Sotheby's catalogue.

Stumbling through the grand rooms, Fomon wobbled into the bedroom and lurched for the mattress, overcome by the need for sleep. Missing his target, his full weight slammed into the side of the bed and knocked him to the floor. Dizzy, disoriented, shocked by a knifing pain in his ribs, he groped for the side of the bed and, summoning all of his strength, hoisted himself onto the mattress.

Deciding to undress before he blacked out, he stood up on the mattress (he dared not leave the bed again) and proceeded to drop his trousers. Reaching down to slide the pants from his legs, he felt the floor spring up to slam him in the face. Lying unconscious, he was a drunken stumblebum alone in his million-dollar co-op.

Aroused from his alcoholic stupor by an excruciating pain in his right leg, Fomon tried to raise himself from the floor but found himself unable to budge. Frightened, he wondered if he'd be left there to die.

From this point on, Fomon's memory of the incident returns. He recalls thinking of the telephone. Crawling on his soft, flabby gut to the night table, where the phone was perched, he dialed the one person he was used to calling in emergencies, his former wife Sharon Ritchie. Though the marriage had fallen victim to Fomon's neglect, they had remained on friendly terms. Now Fomon was reaching out to her.

"Sharon, Sharon, you have to help me. I've broken my leg. You have to help me."

Ritchie, who had seen her share of late-night Fomon fiascos, wasn't responding to her former husband's SOS.

According to Fomon, she said, "Oh, Bob, go back to bed. You didn't break your leg."

"Sharon, listen to me. Something's really wrong. I'm nearly paralyzed. I can't move. I—"

"Bob, take two aspirin and go to bed. You'll forget this ever happened in the morning."

"No, Sharon, you don't understand, I—"

Click.

For the first time in his life, Bob Fomon realized how alone he was. With hundreds of "friends" dotting the social circuit from Manhattan to Southampton to London and Geneva, and with thousands of employees reporting to him as the chairman of the venerable E.F. Hutton & Co., he couldn't think of a single friend who would care enough to rescue him from his pain and disgrace in the wee hours of the night.

Clinging to consciousness, Fomon struggled to come up with a name, any name.

Just when he thought he would faint from the searing pain in his leg, he thought of a savior. "I knew that one of my investment bankers, Red Jahncke, lived nearby, so I thought he would come to my aid. And when I called, he responded immediately, rushing to my apartment, trying to comfort me, and getting on the phone to my doctor. He wasn't in, but the service promised to track him down quickly.

"But it wasn't quick enough. I was in excruciating pain— pain so bad I was hoping I'd pass out again. The seconds crawled by like hours. The wait was interminable.

"Finally the doctor called. He questioned me about my condition and asked if I could wait until morning to see him. He said he didn't want some hospital resident getting his hands on me. But hell, I couldn't wait another hour, much less the rest of the night. The pain was unbearable. I wanted to scream, but I didn't have the energy.

"The doctor called an ambulance and they brought a

stretcher up to my apartment. They had a hell of a time getting me on it. When I asked, 'Why didn't you bring a stretcher with a lift, like one of those garbage truck things?' the attendants said, 'We would have, but when we were using that contraption to get someone with cerebral palsy onto the stretcher, we got her caught up in the lift and broke her leg.' That's when I thought, 'Oh shit, and I'm putting myself in their hands!'

"But I had no choice. It was either go with them, or die of pain on the floor."

In minutes Lord Fomon was wheeled into the emergency room at New York Hospital, his leg rolled under an X-ray machine, his wrinkled suit replaced by a battle green hospital gown that barely covered his groin. When the pictures were pinned to the lightbox the verdict was announced: he had suffered compound fractures. It was even worse than it sounded. Clamped into a plaster cast, the lord and master of E.F. Hutton & Co. would be relegated to bed for six weeks. The booze, the philandering, the late-night carousing, had finally caught up with him.

"At first Bob thought he could rise above the accident," says Norm Epstein, "that all he'd have to do was to turn his bedroom into an office. And he gave it a good try. He hooked himself into telephones, held staff meetings at bedside, played the role of the wounded general operating from a field hospital.

"But being immobilized like that started to get to him. He felt helpless, impotent, and terribly ashamed at the rumors that swirled around the office. Rumors that he'd crippled himself in some kinky sexual episode. In any case, the frustration of being chained to his bed and out of the action took a heavy toll. Lying there in his bathrobe, he looked like a beaten man."

Six weeks after his drunken tumble, Bob Fomon was sufficiently recovered to return to active duty. But the man who limped back to work was not the same man who had marched out six weeks before.

"The pain and frustration of that broken leg crushed Bob Fomon's spirit," recalls consultant Neal Eldridge, who worked with the CEO on his return to the office. "He talked without the usual braggadocio. He gave orders without the swaggering, macho style that had become his trademark. He kind of took up space where before he had dominated it.

"It was as if the old Bob Fomon had disappeared and was replaced by an imposter."

Chapter 12

"Branch managers are the most important people in a brokerage office because they represent the firm to the public. They are Mr. Hutton, Mr. Shearson, Mr. Paine Webber. Once Hutton's executives lost sight of that, the firm lost the great secret of its success."

—A former Hutton retail executive

Shortly before he left his "family" to take over Prudential-Bache, George Ball had drastically reshuffled Hutton's executive ranks, turning what had been a management free-for-all into ten semi-autonomous operating divisions, each responsible for a key aspect of the firm's business from retail brokerage to equity trading. With each division headed by a senior officer running his department on a day-to-day basis, the management bottleneck that had built up around Ball would break up. As a result, the old partnership mentality that had held a hammerlock on Hutton's internal structure would give way to more decentralized, corporate-style governance.

It was a dramatic change.

After years of jealously guarding his power—power he enhanced by creating the image of an omnipresent force—George Ball finally delegated some of his authority to others. Or at least that's how it appeared on the surface. But what was he really up to?

144

Although the divisional setup he engineered before leaving Hutton was grounded in good management science, Ball added a mysterious twist. Rather than selecting the most experienced executives to command the operating divisions, in two critical areas he picked apparent misfits.

Scott Pierce was one. Tall and slender, with boardroom good looks right out of a Hart, Shaffner & Marx ad, Pierce was Hutton's Mr. Congeniality. Possessed of a soft-spoken, easygoing style and a genuine sense of fairness, he was a dolphin in a school of barracudas. Most everyone liked Scottie.

And most everyone thought he would be the worst guy to run retail. Having built his career in public finance for seventeen years at G.H. Walker & Co. before moving on to Blyth, Eastman, Dillon and then to Hutton, he was a virtual stranger to the retail system. On the personality side, he lacked the cunning, the steel, the manipulative ability to charm and inspire and hold together thousands of prima donna brokers and branch managers. The good-guy personality, the Eagle Scout sense of honor and fair play that made him so popular in the headquarters environment would work against him in Hutton's retail system, where lies and cons and under-the-table deals were as much a part of the culture as a phony smile and a promise that a bull market was just around the corner.

But it was into this snake pit that Ball cast Scott Pierce, naming him national sales manager, a post that he himself had held for a decade and was now relinquishing, ostensibly, to concentrate on the global issues facing Hutton's president. But why choose this unlikely successor? And in the process, why leapfrog the one man most qualified to take over retail, Jerry Miller?

A cigar-chomping, arm-waving motor mouth from the streets of Queens who lived and breathed the retail system and who had risen through the ranks from sales trainee to account executive to branch manager and regional vice-president, Miller was the natural choice to succeed Ball as head of sales.

But here, too, George threw a curve into the works, exiling Miller to equity trading, a function he knew even less about than Pierce knew about retail.

Why take men who'd devoted entire careers to mastering complex facets of the securities business, only to move them to foreign turf where they would have to learn on the job, with millions of dollars of the firm's money riding on their actions?

Though Ball claims he did it simply to round out his senior executives, exposing them to radically different parts of the business, others see an ulterior motive. They suspect that Ball, always a ferocious competitor, acted to weaken the firm he knew would soon be his competitor at Prudential-Bache.

"To George, every competition is war," says a former high-ranking Hutton retail executive. "That's the way he plays squash, that's the way he plays tennis, that's the way he plays business. Because he knew he'd be raiding Hutton's account executives, and because he knew Jerry Miller had the most credibility with the brokers he was after, he put Miller in a cubbyhole where he couldn't use that credibility to keep the men from jumping ship.

"What was Jerry going to say to the producers who'd been wooed by George? 'Stay with Hutton and work for me?' No way, Jose. Ball had already taken care of that. Jerry would have to say, 'Stay with Hutton and work for Scott Pierce.' But shit, that was like saying 'Stay with Hutton and work for the one guy in Hutton who knows diddlysquat about retail.' "

No one knew that better than Scott Pierce himself. "When I was offered the job of running retail, I accepted it on the assumption that George would still be president and that he would work with me as I eased into the new role. But no sooner had I moved over to retail than George was gone. I was left out there all alone and I was furious about it. I felt that George was the image of the firm, the heir apparent. As such he had a fiduciary responsibility to the firm and to its employees. It would have been okay for him to leave for a career in politics or another business, but to go to Pru-Bache . . .

"I knew the retail force was worried about having me in charge without George there. I began to hear the rumblings immediately. So within weeks I met with Fomon and tendered my resignation. I said, 'There's a lot of concern out there and I don't disagree with that. I'm going to resign.'

"But Bob just stared at me in cold silence. That was his way of saying, 'Forget it, buddy. You're on the job.' "

After Ball's departure, Bob Fomon had the opportunity to flip-flop Pierce and Miller, restoring each to their rightful positions, the former as a public finance chief and the latter as retail czar. With that one stroke Fomon would have done much to regain the confidence of the retail forces, which viewed Pierce as an interloper and a wimp.

"George's management style had been very hands-on," says a former Hutton retail executive. "He'd write to people, call them on their birthdays, attend their weddings and baptisms. He was very good at the touchy, feely type of stuff. And most important, he believed that the securities business began and ended with the guys who got on the phones with the clients.

"But Scottie came from a different direction. He'd been groomed in one of those mysterious back rooms the brokers knew little about. They didn't think—and correctly so—that he could empathize with them, and they resented having him as a boss."

With the retail forces pampered and spoiled by Ball for a decade, the hope in the brokerage ranks was to find another sugar daddy who respected their importance and was willing to pay through the nose to keep them at their phones dialing for dollars. Had they been asked to pick their own replacement for Ball, the votes would have gone to Jerry Miller.

"Scottie's a hell of a nice guy," says Hutton's former top broker Tony Malatino. "The kind of guy you like to have over for dinner or to play a round of golf with. He'd make a good prime minister.

"But we needed a hands-on guy, an aggressive guy who could go out and make things happen for the retail system. That was Jerry Miller. He was like a bulldog on a pork chop. He'd go on the attack for us, and that's what we wanted."

But Fomon refused to act.

"Pierce and Miller were wrong for their positions—everyone knew that," says Hum Powell. "In fact, they came to Bob and said they wanted to change jobs. But Fomon wouldn't hear of it. He was afraid, for some off-the-wall reason, that the move would make him look bad.

"I said, 'Bob, I don't care how you'll look. We've got to run a firm.' But it didn't do any good. He was deaf to it all."

Worse than that, he was deaf, dumb, and blind. In his next move, he aggravated an already tense state of affairs, proving that whatever instincts he once had for savvy strategies and enlightened appointments were long gone. In announcing his choice to replace George Ball as president, he would select two men both widely viewed as "the last guys you'd want to run the firm."

On December 15, 1983, Bob Fomon named Scott Pierce as president of E.F. Hutton, Inc., and chief financial officer Tom Lynch as president of E.F. Hutton Group, the holding company for Hutton's subsidiaries.

The move, which had been brewing for months, pissed off everyone: brokers, branch managers, regional vice-presidents, traders, investment bankers.

"For Tom Lynch, who was a Fomon crony, to be made president of Hutton Group—well, that was an abomination," says Norm Epstein. "That's the opinion I expressed at the December board meeting when Bob nominated Lynch. I said, 'This is an outrage. You can't make this man president.'

Epstein, always outspoken, was expressing a sentiment widely held throughout Hutton's executive hierarchy: that Tom Lynch, though a savvy and intelligent man who knew the firm perhaps better than anyone else, was not a field marshall, not the kind of hands-on manager who could go out and lead the firm. The power that he wielded, and it was considerable, came from his skill as an infighter, as a shadowy figure who would manipulate Fomon and in turn could force his will on the firm.

"If you wanted to do a deal with E.F. Hutton & Company and Tom Lynch didn't agree with it, chances were very slim that you could get that deal done," Epstein says. "And if you got into a shootout with Lynch on an issue—on any issue at all—you found yourself with bullet holes in your chest. Those were battles you didn't win. Not with Lynch. I wasn't denying that Tom had power. I was just denying that he was the right man to run the firm.

"Fomon was incensed. How dare I question his choice. But I wasn't going to sit back on this one. No, I fought him at that meeting, eyeball to eyeball, for thirty-five minutes. You know how long that is in a board meeting? After twenty minutes Fomon looked at his watch and said, 'You've got fifteen more minutes.'

" 'Fifteen more minutes?' I said. 'How the hell can you watch the clock when we're discussing the nomination of a new president? We need someone to run this organization on a day-to-day basis and Tom Lynch, goddamn it, isn't the one.'

"But protest as I did, Fomon was set on having his

trusty buddy in office and nothing was going to stop him. So he railroaded the election, and by the end of the day we had Lynch as president."

Lynch's coronation was another case of Fomon surrounding himself with a longtime corporate ally. He was chosen not because he would fill the management vacuum, but because he was no threat to the CEO's power. It was another case of Fomon serving himself rather than the firm.

"Lynch's was a thinly veiled strategy designed to block a more popular succession," Epstein says. "Throughout the firm there was wide sentiment for a new generation of leader—a Dick Locke or a Jerry Miller—to become president, but Fomon wanted none of that. He wouldn't tolerate anyone with a power base of his own."

Although Hutton executives saw this, their anger was tempered by the knowledge that the group presidency was little more than a titular post. Because Fomon sat atop the holding company as chairman, Lynch had little power beyond his ability to influence the boss (a power he had held before he was made president). So save for Epstein's outbursts, the objections against Lynch were subdued.

But the election of Pierce as president unleashed a fire storm. To the brokers and branch managers, it was a slap in the face. The same "wimp" who had been thrust upon them as sales manager was now being elevated to the job George Ball had shaped in his own image. To the guys in the claustrophobic cubicles, the guys on the phones hawking the stocks and the bonds and mutual funds that brought in the great bulk of Hutton's revenues, it was a sure sign that the power in the firm had shifted away from the field and back to the bankers in New York. No one was more upset by Pierce's rise to power than Jerry Miller, and no one had more of a right to be. Were it not for an ugly Hutton tradition, the presidency would have been his.

In the months leading up to Pierce's coronation, influential brokers and field managers had called Fomon to lobby on Miller's behalf. The points they made were valid and convincing: to retain its retail strength, Hutton needed another George Ball—a powerful field marshal, cheerleader, and ombudsman.

Although the lobbying swayed Fomon, who believed that Miller was the best man for the job, the CEO accepted the counsel of old Hutton hands—graying senior partners in Los Angeles, San Francisco, and the Southwest—who secretly rejected Miller for the same reason his mentor Arthur Goldberg had never made it to the top: he was a Jew.

The euphemism for all of this bigoted blackballing was that Fomon couldn't "sell Miller" west of the Hudson River.

"Throughout the firm, Miller was considered a tough New Yorker," says Fomon, who now admits that his appointment of Pierce over Miller may have been a watershed in the decline of Hutton. "I didn't think he would sell nationally."

Hearing through the internal rumor mill that Fomon was on the verge of anointing Pierce, Miller stormed in to see him. A six-foot plus mass of kinetic energy, he was boiling, red faced, struggling to control his temper. "What the hell is going on here?" he blurts.

"What do you mean?" Fomon asks, knowing full well what he means.

"I hear you're going to name Scott Pierce as president."

Miller hopes against hope that Fomon will deny it.

"Well, we don't have many alternatives."

"No alternatives?" Miller responds. "Guess who. Guess who."

Fomon picks up on the not-so-subtle hint and crushes it. "Well, you're an alternative. But as good as you are, there are *some people* who would not be happy with you."

Miller is pissed.

"Hey, don't you think there are some people unhappy with you being chairman? Some people are going to be unhappy no matter who you name as president. What you have to do is select the best person and let him worry about handling the others. I can do it. I can sell myself."

But Fomon was a stone wall. Once again the idea of having a man who takes off for Yom Kippur assuming the presidency of Edward Francis Hutton's WASP legacy was like replacing the national Christmas tree with a menorah on the White House lawn.

But the question remained: why Pierce? Was it because the soft-spoken Pierce would never challenge the king on critical issues? Yes. And was it because Pierce would never pose a threat to Fomon's power? Yes. And was it because Pierce with his distinguished all-American looks fit the mold of Hutton president? Yes. But there was also another factor, a top-secret objective known inside Hutton as the "Bush connection."

According to this school of thought, the only thing Fomon really liked about Scott Pierce is that he was George Bush's brother-in-law. Considering his obsession with power and the "right people," Fomon loved the idea of using Pierce to wangle his way into the Reagan administration. Or better yet, into a Bush administration.

"Even then Fomon could figure out that George Bush had a good shot at becoming president someday," says a retail VP who worked closely with Fomon in the post-Ball damage-control program. "He liked to fantasize about Bush becoming president of the United States while his brother-in-law was president of E.F. Hutton. What a happy coincidence. He'd do anything to make it happen.

"You have to understand Bob Fomon. He'd sell Hutton down the river just to get invited to the White House."

As much as Fomon touted his new president in public, behind the scenes he worried that Pierce didn't have what it took. It was a lurking suspicion that dated back to the day George Ball had made Pierce head of retail.

"In early 1982, Hutton vice-president Paul Hines called me saying that Bob Fomon wanted to see me about an assignment," says Neal Eldridge, then a management consultant with the Big Eight accounting firm of Touche Ross. "He said it had something to do with tutoring a new executive at Hutton. Since my specialty is in helping newly appointed senior officers with organizational development and business focus, I was interested in exploring the engagement.

"So I went to visit Bob Fomon. That was an experience. He was unlike any other chief executive I'd ever met. No sooner had I entered his office than he made it clear he wasn't expecting me to be a woman, and he wasn't going to be diplomatic about it. 'Neal Eldridge?' he says. 'You're Neal Eldridge?'

"And that wasn't all. Fomon struck me as really weird. He paced up, down, and sideways. He was staccato in his speech. The man was bundles of nervous energy.

"When he finally got down to the reason for calling me in, he said, 'Go figure out who the hell Scott Pierce is, because I'm not sure he can do the job.' "

As part of her consulting technique, Eldridge takes "executive snapshots," assessing a manager's strengths and weaknesses and sizing up his ability to perform in a position. It didn't take Eldridge long to come up with a picture that in a well-run corporation would be grounds for a swift demotion. She found Pierce to be lacking conviction and decisiveness.

But when Eldridge presented her thumbs-down findings on Pierce, Fomon preferred to shoot the messenger rather than cure the problem. In an ugly confrontation he cursed Eldridge out, calling her "a bitch, a bitch, a bitch," and routed her from his office. That was his way of dealing with the issue that his handpicked president was the wrong man for the post. A fact even Pierce himself may have recognized.

"Right after Pierce took office, Hutton held this big sales conference at a country club in Traverse City, Michigan," says a former Midwest regional manager. "Scott gets up to speak and we're all waiting for this fire-and-brimstone speech, where he'll surprise us, showing that he really can lead and motivate.

"But no way. He's the nicest guy in the world but he didn't have it in him to lead the sales force. He's trying to be positive but he's coming from such a weak position, from such a lack of self-confidence, that it comes off sounding negative.

" 'This company is so strong,' he says, 'it has such a strong culture, that I couldn't fuck it up if I wanted to.' "

Today there are those who will take issue with that.

Blaming Pierce for "fucking up" Hutton is a case of pointing at the most visible target, but there's no doubt that things began to slide under his tenure. As George Ball knew instinctively, a sales organization runs on men and money and organization, but it also runs on pride and ego and esprit de corps and under Pierce these qualities were lacking. As a carpetbagger in the retail ranks, as a play-it-by-the-book executive in a free-wheeling culture, he couldn't win the respect, affection, or allegiance of his men, who continued to lobby for his replacement.

Fomon couldn't ignore it. Faced with a growing mutiny in the ranks, the CEO came up with the bright idea of bringing in regional vice-president Bob Witt, one of his few friends in the sales organization, to serve under Pierce as executive vice-president in charge of retail.

A big, square-shouldered man who looks more like a farm boy turned fullback than a brokerage executive, Witt's career with Hutton traced back to 1960, when he started out as an account executive trainee in the Los Angeles office and where he first met Bob Fomon. Displaying a flair for management, he rose to become an L.A. branch office manager in 1964, and in 1969 he was assigned to Boston to launch the firm's Northeast region. It was then that he became a vice-president and regional director.

A fiercely ambitious man, Witt yearned to rise above his regional duties and move to headquarters to help run the firm beside Bob Fomon, with whom he'd remained close. Witt's chance came when Fomon asked him to leave New England (where he had achieved impressive results) to replace retired regional vice-president Mike Judd as head of the Houston-based South Central region. Though far from the caliber of move Witt was daydreaming about, he accepted the offer with a string attached: that Houston would be his launching pad to New York. His next move, Fomon promised, would be to headquarters.

So when the SOS went out for a retail Svengali to assist the floundering Pierce, Fomon gave Witt a call.

"On paper, the idea looked good," says a former Hutton retail executive now with Shearson Lehman Hutton. "Teaming up Pierce and Witt would give Pierce the opportunity to play the global role while Witt worked the sales function day to day. Theoretically, it would be a balanced team, one that would make everyone happy."

But the so-called team was doomed from the start. The moment Witt rolled into New York, egos erupted. For his part, Pierce resented having Witt thrust upon him like a savior from the South. If Fomon had cut a deal to bring Witt to New York, how far did the deal go? Would Pierce be a figurehead? Would Witt detour the president, reporting directly to the CEO? Did Witt want to be president himself? Plagued by uncertainties, Pierce saw Witt as a threat.

From Witt's perspective, the call to New York signaled

his rise to the pinnacle of Hutton power. Serving as Pierce's second in command was all right for starters, but he hoped to proceed beyond that. Someday, perhaps, Pierce's job would be his.

With the "teammates" eyeing each other nervously, a battle for power was inevitable.

"Pierce and Witt started fighting each other over positions, policy, marketing—just about everything," says Eldridge, who was still working with Pierce when Witt came on the scene. "At one point, about six months after Witt had taken over retail, I took Pierce and Witt and the regional VPs to a retreat at Troutbeck in upstate New York.

"Troutbeck is one of those woodsy conference centers with streams and ponds and working fireplaces. The tranquil environment is supposed to disarm the participants, getting them to loosen their ties, to seek compromise and harmony."

But it didn't work here. To Witt and Pierce the script was the same: only the stage had changed.

"The tension in the room was so thick it felt like you were walking through barbed wire," Eldridge recalls. "All day long Witt and Pierce were jockeying for position, power, dominance. The animosity between them started before the meeting and continued after it, poisoning everything they did together."

If the specter of retailing's top two executives battling each other wasn't enough to demoralize Hutton's sales force (now numbering 6,600 account executives), many of the brokers and field executives were turned off by Witt's personality and by his management style.

"Bob Witt never understood why he was disliked by the field," says Rich Braugh. "To this day he probably doesn't understand. But to anyone who really understood Hutton's retail system, it was abundantly clear.

"Under George Ball the firm worked on a conceptual

framework. George inspired us. He told us how successful we could be and then he'd motivate us to achieve that success.

"But Witt was never articulate. He'd hold a meeting and say, 'You're all a great bunch of guys.' Well, that's not what we wanted to hear. We wanted to know about changes in the securities industry and what we had to do to respond to them. Witt never told us that."

Ever since Hutton had been founded, the account executive had been king. As long as retail generated the lion's share of the revenues, it had to be that way. Under Ball, brokers were treated not as serfs or lowlifes, the way King Fomon saw them, but as valued members of the corporation.

"When George wanted to lower payouts he'd be diplomatic about it, saying, 'I've got to get costs down so that margins will improve, and when margins improve, I'll take care of you,' " Braugh says. "George made you think that your earnings would go from $100,000 to $90,000 and then to $150,000."

But Witt was seen as steamrolling the Hutton culture. As many of the brokers saw it, his was a macho management style. Me boss, you employee.

"You can take that attitude in a bureaucratic type culture, but not in a Hutton," Braugh adds. "That's because we never were a bureaucracy. We were trained to think independently. When Witt told you to do something, his attitude was 'Do it because I told you to do it.' That never worked at Hutton. Tradition had it that you gave people a voice in decisions. You didn't ram things down their throats."

Led by two unpopular leaders, the Hutton field force began to lose the pride, the camaraderie, the Camelot spirit that had made it so effective over the years. In the process the firm's most valuable asset, its sales organization, was beginning a long but inevitable decline for which

Fomon deserved much of the blame. His imperious view of corporate governance had detached him from the middle American breadbasket of the Hutton organization—from the brokers and the branch managers in Michigan and Ohio and Illinois, from Ed Hutton's heartland. To Lord Fomon, management was a Hollywood set, a casting call, a matter of picking the best face, the best pedigree for the role.

"Fomon was disappointed in the way the field responded to Pierce," Lynch says. "It ruined his plans, especially the secret plan to have Pierce succeed him as CEO.

"As far as Bob was concerned, Scottie was his logical successor. He made a fine appearance, he spoke well—and his sister just happened to be married to the person who could well be the next president of the United States."

Chapter 13

"That building was more to Fomon than a mountain of glass and granite. It represented the culmination of his career. It was his monument to the world."

—*Jerry Miller*

By the end of 1984, E.F. Hutton was an accident waiting to happen.

Everywhere you looked, there were gathering clouds. The neglect, the incompetence, the arrogance, the conceit, the Concordes to Paris, the civil wars, the booze, the lack of planning, the cronyism—it was all coming home to roost. Hutton's sales force, long the envy of Wall Street, had turned surly and contemptuous. With passions boiling to the surface, there was talk of lynching Pierce and Fomon in the air.

So too was the management vacuum catching up with Hutton, sucking people and profits into it. Without a strong institutional presence, the firm was watching its traditional markets shrink. The firm's 1984 annual report admitted: "Since mid-1983, the market has been dominated by institutional trading, while retail activity has declined." But nothing was done to reposition Hutton.

On the corporate finance side, where for years it was said that Fomon would make his real mark, there was hardly anything to brag about. Jim Lopp, whom Fomon had put in charge of the function, appeared to some to be more interested in launching his own business than in running Hutton's.

"Jim decided to devote himself to creating a company for himself," says Paul Bagley, and he spent the last two years at Hutton starting up Financial Security Assurance, a firm insuring corporate debt. All with Bob Fomon's full knowledge and acquiescence.

"It was the kind of situation where everybody in investment banking knew that Jim wasn't long for this world as soon as he had put FSA together."

Even worse was Fomon's favoritism toward the department's salary scale. Hutton's corporate finance department was hardly setting Wall Street on its ear, but that didn't stop executives in the department from demanding and winning enormous salaries. For example, in 1984 Jim Lopp earned $262,461 in salary and an $800,000 bonus, for a grand total of $1,062,461. At the same time Jerry Miller was earning a relatively modest $665,000.

"Hutton's compensation system, if you can call it that, was run like a combination beauty contest and tug-of-war," Neal Eldridge recalls. "The way it worked, Bob Fomon would go down the list of executives, giving the biggest raises and bonuses to the people he liked most. Then when the word leaked out about the fat deals some of the good old boys were getting, others would burst into his office, screaming, 'If so-and-so got a million, I want a million too.' If they created enough of a furor, they'd get it. It was the squeaky-wheel system of corporate compensation. And because a lot of the guys in corporate finance were closest to Fomon, they got the most money. Which royally pissed off everyone else in the firm."

Eldridge warned Fomon that it was no way to run a railroad. With a good deal of pleading and arm-twisting she convinced him to commission the consulting firm of Handy Associates to design a formal compensation plan linking salary to performance. But when compensation time rolled around again, Fomon reverted to his old system of whoever squeaked the loudest got the most money.

"Under Bob Fomon, management had come to a standstill," Eldridge says. "The firm's growth had outstripped his ability to manage it. He was in over his head, still doing things the old way as if he could defy all the changes in the marketplace and get away with it.

"In every attempt I made to update his practices, and bring some management discipline to the organization, he fought me tooth and nail. In the end, ego or jealousy or cronyism won out.

"I remember telling Bob that we needed more structure in the organization. There were seventeen senior executives reporting to him and that was too many. So I suggested that we divide the firm into two main divisions, retail and capital markets, and appoint heads of each to run them semi-autonomously. There would also be an executive committee on top of them.

"Bob nixed the idea. Why? He claimed it was too difficult to structure, but that was nonsense. The real obstacle was his friend Tom Lynch, who saw the new setup as a threat to his power. Under the crazy-quilt system they had in place, Lynch would sit down with Bob and make decisions with him. But with the structure I recommended, the executive committee would claim that role. Because Lynch feared he'd lose his power, he vetoed the idea and Fomon went along with him."

Lynch's influence over Fomon was extraordinary. A sloppy, remote, even distant man, he hardly seemed on the surface like a power broker. But for years he was the second most powerful figure in Hutton: a power that stemmed from his relationship with Fomon.

"Bob liked Lynch's cool, aloof demeanor," recalls Neal Eldridge. "He saw strength in it. And so he came to rely on Tom, to confide in him and to vest him with considerable power. A power Tom never hesitated to use. If he didn't like what someone said or did, he'd cut them down at the knees. Just like that."

With Hutton's costs mushrooming out of control, the financial statements cried out for a tough-minded manager with a sharp pencil. Tops on the list of emergencies, the brokers' payout structure needed immediate pruning. For decades Hutton had paid its account executives two to ten percentage points more than the Merrills and Shearsons and Paine Webbers. This indulgence became unacceptable in an increasingly competitive and cost-conscious marketplace.

But this was the hottest of potatoes. With many of the account executives hopelessly spoiled by a decade of George Ball's largess, demanding wholesale cuts in their commissions seemed like a sure way to turn a rumbling in the ranks into a mass exodus.

Certainly Fomon wasn't going to take the lead. Savings, reductions, budgets—the words were foreign to his management lexicon. For a fifty-nine-year-old corporate mogul who'd spent his career leasing private jets, padding the payroll with cronies, and housing pets in company apartments, austerity would hardly sound the theme for the last years of his reign. Instead he would go out with a flourish, one that would saddle the firm with a $100 million white elephant, sinking it into financial quicksand from which it would never recover.

It all began when Fomon, contemplating his mortality, decided that Hutton needed a new home that would serve as his legacy.

"It was in 1983 when Bob first told me that he wanted to move the firm up to midtown," recalls Norm Epstein. "He said it so casually that I thought it was a passing thought, a daydream. 'Wouldn't it be nice to get out of these dreary downtown surroundings and into a posh new building on the Upper East Side?' Okay, daydream over, let's get back to work. We were hardly in a position for that kind of expense.

"But I saw quickly enough that it wasn't a daydream. Fomon wasn't 'going back to work.' No, sir, he was serious about moving. More than that, he was obsessed with it. All of a sudden the move, the move, that was all he would talk about."

This wouldn't be just any move. Bob Fomon was dreaming of a grand edifice, a Buckingham Palace of office buildings. As the dream took shape over the following months, Fomon commissioned developer Gerald Hines to build a thirty-story glass-and-pink granite structure on a vacant lot on West 52nd Street. From the beginning Fomon announced that money was no object. Award-winning architect Kevin Roche was hired. Truckloads of marble were ordered. Plans were drawn for twelve corner offices per floor, many with dramatic views of the Manhattan skyline. There were nine private dining rooms with state-of-the-art kitchen facilities, a health club, a private art collection, toilets fit for kings. It would be a corporate palace.

And it would cost a fortune. In a deal that clearly favored the developers, Hutton signed a lease on May 9, 1984, calling for the rental of 600,000 square feet at more than $50 a square foot, totaling $30 million a year. Leasehold improvements, including the private dining rooms and the marble slabs and museum lighting Fomon wanted to spotlight his art collection, totaled $100 million. All of this grotesque indulgence was being squandered at a time when Hutton needed to cut back.

"Bob couched his extravagance in the idea that the industry was moving uptown," Epstein recalls. "He said that First Boston, Paine Webber, and a lot of our clients were already there, and that it was the wave of the future. But it was all bullshit. Bob Fomon simply wanted a monument, a permanent symbol of the man who'd built it.

"But we couldn't afford that kind of self-indulgence. I

said, 'Bob, we just can't afford it. If you told me that we were creating a building uptown that we would own, I'd bite the bullet and say okay, we're sacrificing the short-term for the long-term. But you're telling me that we'll have no equity in this building. We'll have nothing except the obligation to pay an enormous rent that will more than double our costs and will escalate over time. Bob, this is the worst deal I've ever heard of.'

"But I wasn't getting through. Fomon didn't give a shit about the deal. It was the carpeting and paintings and bathrooms that he doted on. If it cost a king's ransom to get the best, so be it."

"At a time when the shit was really hitting the fan, when we were having all sorts of financial and image problems, Fomon was in his own little world, playing Donald Trump," says a former Hutton senior vice-president in the firm's retail operation. "All of his attention was focused on a monstrosity of an office building he was putting up on West 52nd Street.

"It was during this time that I got a frantic call from Bob to come see him. Because it sounded urgent, I dropped everything and rushed to his office.

"No sooner did I get through the door than he waved an accusing finger at me.

" 'Gotcha!' he said.

"Gotcha? Got what? I had no idea of what he was talking about, but naturally with the boss worked up over something, I was concerned. 'You got me? What are you talking about, Bob?'

"His eyes darting as if he'd uncovered some kind of embezzlement, he pointed at a blueprint spread across his desk. 'There it is,' he said. 'Right before your eyes. Try to explain that. Just try.'

"I looked at where he was pointing—it was a rendering of one of the floors my staff would occupy in the new building— and for the life of me I didn't know what he was all lathered up about.

" 'Bob, you're pointing at a floor plan. What's the problem?'

" 'What's the problem?' he shrieks. 'What's the problem? The problem, asshole, is that you approved a men's room with only four urinals up there when you'll need at least six.'

"Four urinals? Six urinals? I couldn't believe my ears. More than that, I couldn't believe the CEO of the firm had been reduced to this. Trying to calm him down, I tried a little humor. 'Trust me, Bob, four urinals are enough. My guys are too busy to piss.'

"But to Bob Fomon, this was no laughing matter. 'Go ahead, make light of this. But don't blame me when you build it your way and there's a goddamn line outside the men's room door.'

"Talk about an edifice complex. To Bob Fomon that building was going to be his legacy to the world. It had to be perfect."

As part of Fomon's feudal blueprint, the lord and master of Hutton Castle would be housed in a huge office suite while the peons (meaning everyone else) would be relegated to broom closets.

"Bob had fallen in love with the European concept of shoehorning executives into tiny spaces that could hardly be called offices, and then sprinkling the floors with conference rooms," recalls Jerry Miller. "The theory being that with all those conference rooms scattered about, the staff didn't need big offices. He'd seen this at Goldman Sachs and at some of our British clients, and he wanted to give his building the same 'international quality.' That's how he put it.

"But I put it another way. I couldn't see putting up a $100-million-dollar colossus only to force the senior people into closets. When I got wind of his plan, I told him flat out: 'There's no way I'm sitting in a ten-by-twelve crawlspace. If I'm going to be in an office for fifteen hours a day, it's going to look like an office.

"We battled about this endlessly. When he saw that I wasn't relenting, he agreed to give the senior executives decent-sized offices. But there was a string attached. In exchange he wanted me to tell my vice-presidents that they couldn't have offices. They should sit on the trading floor and use conference rooms when they need them. When I told him I wouldn't strip my top people of their offices, he didn't answer, so I thought he'd backed off.

"But the next day I'm walking by his office when I catch a glimpse of one of my senior people talking with Bob. Because this guy rarely spoke to Fomon directly, I had a hunch it was about the office thing. So I asked if I could sit in on the meeting, and without waiting for an answer I took a seat next to my man. That's when Fomon picks up where he'd left off, trying to talk the guy out of an office. Well, the guy's not buying Fomon's pitch and, as I make it abundantly clear, neither am I.

"That's all Fomon had to hear. He launched into a world-class cursing, screaming rage that led to his throwing us out of his office. He was berserk, out of control. My guy, who'd never seen Fomon in his natural habitat, asked, with this horrified look on his face, 'Is he always like this?' "

Humbert Powell was, as usual, succinct in his observation: "I told Bob as he was making the final plans to occupy the new building: 'You move uptown into that fortress and it's going to be your tombstone.' "

To others, most notably the field force, the new building was a monument to his incompetence, his extravagance, his willingness to squander the profits of the firm. In time it would become another rallying point in the gathering retail mutiny.

In mid-1984 Bob Fomon had a last chance to relinquish his position as the firm's CEO and depart in dignity. Though he was already viewed as a lush, a womanizer, an arrogant elitist who'd squandered much of the firm's fortune, had he voluntarily retired, the decency of the act would have earned a ground swell of goodwill. In short order his sins would have been forgiven. Like Richard Nixon, who had risen from the ashes of Watergate to a second coming as an elder statesman, with time Bob Fomon would have been remembered as the great leader who took Hutton from revenues of $85 million to $2.8 billion. His portrait in oils would have hung beside those of his patrician predecessors: Hutton, Loeb, Cutten, Coleman.

It was an opportunity he failed to seize. As a lonely man with little in his life besides E.F. Hutton, he would never step down. As Morgan Stanley partner Fred Whittlemore puts it: "He enjoyed playing chairman too much to give it up."

Still, the realization that Fomon had passed his peak had struck his closest cronies. Even those who were indebted to him, and who had no inclination to rout him from office, recognized the need to bring new blood into the executive suite, if not to replace the monarch, then to help him manage.

It was in this spirit of complementing rather than replacing Fomon that longtime friend and Hutton vice-president Dick Jones arranged a top-secret meeting between Fomon and a highly touted Wall Street executive Robert Rittereiser, then a senior executive with arch rival Merrill Lynch.

Jones, who had wide contacts throughout the financial community, considered the Merrill executive to be the ideal candidate to round out Fomon's sharp edges and to ultimately succeed him as CEO. With an Eagle Scout image and a reputation as a strong administrator, he was everything the firm seemed to need but lacked in the Bob Fomon of the 1980s.

Working behind the scenes, Jones set up a rendezvous at Fomon's apartment. Both men agreed to the meeting, but approached each other warily, unsure if the other was there to talk or to spy. They had met several times before on business matters, but this was the first time they would be talking secretly.

Fomon broke the ice almost immediately:

"Look, Bob, it's no secret why I've invited you here tonight. I've heard impressive things about you. With your talents and experience, I think you could make a valuable contribution to E.F. Hutton & Co."

Rittereiser, who'd suspected that an offer was in the making, wanted to know what Fomon had in mind. "What kind of contribution are you referring to?"

"In a senior management position."

"I'm flattered by that, Bob, very flattered. But let me ask you, when you say 'a senior management position,' how senior do you mean?"

Fomon didn't have to think for a moment. "President of the firm."

"And you would be . . . ?"

"CEO."

"So what you're saying is that you're offering me the number two spot."

"Yes, for now. And I hope you'll consider it."

In agreeing to the clandestine tête-à-tête, both men had ulterior motives. Rittereiser loved the idea of being sought after by a CEO of a Wall Street competitor. As a former stickball player from the streets of Manhattan's Yorktown section, he felt like a bonus baby talking contract with the Yankees and basked in the glory of it.

But nothing else. At this point Rittereiser believed he was in the running to succeed Bill Schreyer, whose health had remained a question mark ever since he'd undergone triple-bypass surgery. With the dream of running Merrill apparently within reach, he was hardly about to accept Hutton's offer. To a man with his grand designs, Hutton was small potatoes.

If Rittereiser toyed with Fomon, the lord of E.F. Hutton returned the favor. In telling Rittereiser that he would be number two "for now," Fomon was holding out the subtle promise that he would soon succeed him as Hutton's CEO. But Fomon had no intention of ceding his throne to anyone.

In fact, the offer to hire Rittereiser was little more than a PR ploy. In landing Merrill's best-known Boy Scout, Fomon would be outdrawing a competitor (shades of the old gunslinger) and would be proving to the Hutton staff, to the field, to the press, and to the world that he was a responsible corporate chieftain paving the way for a smooth and orderly succession.

It was a charade.

"I was sitting with Bob in his office one night, watching him work his way through a bottle of scotch, when he volunteered that he'd met with this guy Rittereiser from Merrill Lynch," says a former senior vice-president and one-time confidant. "Well, I'd heard of Ritt, and knowing that he was pretty high up the Merrill Lynch ladder, I figured there was a high-level shuffle in the works.

"But when I inquired about it, I could see that Bobby boy wasn't taking it very seriously. He had this smirk on his face. With Bob that was always a sure sign that he was setting a trap.

"And another thing. He kept calling Rittereiser 'a nice fellow.' That was a dead giveaway. In Bob Fomon parlance, 'nice fellow' was a euphemism for 'wimp.' "

In short, the Two Bobs dated and danced and went home alone, certain that their brief courtship was over before it began. Little did they know that in less than a year they would be united in corporate marriage. A marriage that would wreck their careers as well as the eighty-one-year-old firm they were paid to run.

Chapter 14

"Just like that, business dried up. Accounts stopped returning calls. Those who did call wouldn't buy or bought less. They were taking their business to brokers who weren't criminals."

—Clarence Catallo

To the American public, E.F. Hutton & Co. was best known as the firm behind the familiar television commercials "When E.F. Hutton talks, people listen."

Created by advertising agency Benton & Bowles, the commercials made a compelling statement: when a firm with the knowledge, experience, and stature of E.F. Hutton imparts its wisdom to the world, everything else stops in its tracks. The spotlight is on us and no one else.

But Lord, how that message could backfire. When Hutton uttered a single word in May 1985, it discovered how the same spotlight that had served it so well could come to destroy it. The word was "guilty." The crime was check kiting.

It had all started a few years back, on a bleak winter day in February 1982. E.F. Hutton's deputy assistant general counsel Lorin Schechter had been busy at work on what figured to be a routine day when the company's cashier, Bob Ross, informed him of a curious call. For some ungodly reason, a deputy superintendent of the New York

State Banking Commission had asked to meet with representatives of the company to discuss, as he put it, "some questions we have about Hutton's banking practices."

A graduate of NYU Law School who viewed his role as the corporation's first line of defense against the outside world, Schechter was perplexed. State officials had questions about Hutton's banking practices, but what kind of questions? Which practice could they be referring to? And why would the deputy chief of the state banking authority want to question a lawyer for E.F. Hutton? Hutton wasn't even a bank.

The more Schechter tried to piece the puzzle together, the more he came up a blank. At this point the government wasn't talking. The matter would have to remain a mystery until Schechter, accompanied by Bob Ross and Hutton's internal money manager, Thomas Morley, showed up for a February 10 meeting at the banking commission's World Trade Center offices.

From the moment he entered, Schechter knew the problem was more serious than he'd feared. Hoping to face an aging bureaucrat propped behind a government-issue steel desk, he was instead ushered into the commission's boardroom and seated opposite a dozen government officials, including an assistant general counsel from the Federal Reserve Board. No one was smiling. No one was making small talk.

As the officials opened the meeting, they explained that in the course of a routine investigation of Manufacturers Hanover bank, a computer model of Hutton's accounts with the bank had revealed a large amount of uncleared funds. Apparently this had led them to look closer at Hutton's banking practices. That was the purpose of the meeting. After a series of questions about Hutton's methods of depositing and drawing out money from its national network of bank accounts, the Federal Reserve attorney popped the $64,000 question:

"Are you familiar with the Genovese County Bank in LeRoy, New York?"

Schecter was bewildered. Why should he know anything about the Genovese County Bank? Or about LeRoy, New York?

An official leaned across the table, answering slowly and deliberately, "You should know about the Genovese Bank in LeRoy, New York, because that's where your company bounced $20 million in checks."

Hutton bounced $20 million in checks? How did that happen? Was it an innocent mistake? A clerical oversight? That seemed unlikely. The Federal Reserve Board doesn't call you in for that.

As the examiners charged, there was evidence there that Hutton had engaged in "pinwheeling" (also called "chaining"), a process whereby a company shifts uncleared funds from one account to another for the purpose of creating artificial balances and then drawing on those funds before they are available to the company. There was also evidence that Hutton had engaged in massive overdrafting, writing checks far in excess of balances and then seeking to cover the withdrawals with other checks before the funds cleared.

Determined to get at the root of the matter, the banking examiners ordered the Hutton executives to look into the matter. Schechter promised they would.

It didn't take him long to discover that there was indeed a problem.

On his return to the office that same day, Schecter made some calls around the firm and found that there were indeed pinwheels and overdrafts. That much he knew. What he didn't know at that point was if Hutton was guilty of criminal activity.

In May 1982 the check-kiting inquiry took another shocking turn as Hutton received a grand jury subpoena ordering the firm to deliver an avalanche of checks, bank statements, and financial documents. Although Hutton had launched an internal inquiry and ceased the pinwheeling practices in the hope that the matter was history, it was only first beginning to surface. What had started out as a minor inquiry had turned into a full-scale investigation conducted by the Justice Department.

In the beginning, Hutton's longtime outside counsel, the law firm of Cahill, Gordon & Reindel, took the matter lightly, thinking they could bully lead government attorney Albert Murray into dropping the case. They lectured the government on the principles of cash management—an attempt to frame Hutton's checking practices as acceptable by industry standards—failed to return phone calls from government lawyers, and then tried to play hardball by filing a blizzard of legal documents. All of them backfired, only hardening the resolve of the Justice Department's fraud section chief to pursue the matter vigorously.

Through the course of the investigation, the government found that Hutton had engaged in a series of schemes designed to manipulate the banking system, both to create interest income from inflated balances and to benefit from an artificially created float by drawing down funds in excess of actual bank balances. To accomplish this, Hutton's branch offices used a bag of tricks such as keeping accounts in remote banks known to be slow in clearing checks, kiting checks from one account to another in order to draw on checks before they cleared, and intentionally writing checks far in excess of actual balances.

The scheme was pervasive and of an extraordinary magnitude. In the chaining or pinwheeling tactic, branch managers conspired to pass checks sideways through banks in their areas before sending them on to Hutton's regional or national accounts. This created the illusion of local bank balances, thus producing interest income for the branches. "It got to the point where the New York office would transfer funds to Tucson and Tucson would transfer it to Chicago—all without any business purpose," Lynch says. "The idea was to create movement that would in turn create artificial balances."

Overdrafting was even more outrageous. Branches would draw down enormous sums without any regard for their actual bank balances. On some days overdrafts exceeded $1 billion— money the branches then invested for their gain. Hutton's Alexandria, Virginia, branch deposited $34 million in the United Virginia Bank in 1981, but withdrew $640 million during the period. Typically, the branches would appear to cover the shortfall with newly deposited checks, which would take days to clear. In the meantime, the branches would have use of the money.

Hutton had clearly crossed the threshold of aggressive cash management and had forayed into the danger zone of corporate fraud. The quest for interest income inside Hutton had become so obsessive that in one case the participants at a Midwest branch managers' meeting were handed out envelopes of play money. The fake cash was meant to underline just how much the interest ploys could add to their incomes.

Culpability for Hutton's fraudulent practices extended from the retail brokerage executives, who created incentives and inducements for maximizing interest income, to the headquarters officers, who allowed, through acquiescence or oversight, the fraud to be committed.

No one knew this better than the men responsible. With word leaking out that the government was building a strong case against a long list of senior officers, panic was spreading through the halls of Hutton. Most ominous, rumors were flying of individual indictments. A court battle appeared to be lurking, one that could put Hutton's top management behind bars.

It was at this point that a frantic management started

searching for a deal, a plea bargain, any way to end the threat of criminal action.

With this in mind, Cahill, Gordon & Reindel concocted what seemed at the time like a winning strategy: in exchange for a guarantee of executive immunity protecting Hutton's officers, the firm would plead guilty to charges of mail and wire fraud.

Cahill's senior litigator, Thomas Curnin, presented the plan to the board, arguing forcefully for its approval. Going to trial, he warned in a fiery monologue that lasted for nearly an hour, would take years of agonizing and highly publicized legal maneuvers, would generate a tidal wave of scandalous press coverage, and would expose Hutton executives to prosecution.

"He reminded us that a brokerage firm must have the confidence of its customers," recalls Scott Pierce, "and that being tied up in criminal proceedings would jeopardize that confidence to such a degree that it could seriously impair our ability to do business. He didn't say we'd lose in court, just that the publicity we'd get for being there would be abhorrent.

"And the board bought his argument. Although Peter Ueberroth* wondered aloud if this was a wise move, and Tom Rae reminded us that we were licensed to do business in fifty states and that a felony plea could have serious repercussions with state officials, there was no serious objection to Curnin's strategy. It passed the board unanimously."

Behind the scenes, Curnin had tried to change the government's charges, and in turn Hutton's plea, from criminal to civil law. But it was a deal the feds refused to make. Faced with this intransigence, he believed the next best approach was to plead guilty to the criminal charges, thus avoiding an ugly trial.

Ueberroth joined the board in 1984.

In theory, the strategy was sound. As a corporation finds itself caught in an illegal or unethical act and is swept up in controversy and subject to hostile reporting, admitting its sins and promising never to repeat them is the best way to diffuse the scandal. It's a lesson learned from the errors of Watergate. With this in mind, Fomon believed he was acting appropriately by accepting Curnin's plea-bargain strategy and ending the siege.

But Fomon and Curnin and the entire Hutton board had misjudged a critical factor. As the plea bargain was structured, Hutton would pay a $2 million fine (FN plus $750,000 in government fees). A financial hardship? Certainly not. But because the maximum penalty for mail and wire fraud was $1,000 per count, to accept responsibility for the full $2 million, Hutton would have to plead guilty to 2,000 counts of fraud.

For a corporation that lives and dies on its credibility, that has fiduciary responsibility for its customers' life savings, to say "guilty, guilty, guilty" two thousand times proved to be disastrous. The way the world saw it, a prestigious brokerage firm was saying, "The *F* in our name stands for fraud."

"Within hours of the guilty plea, swarms of newspaper reporters were over us like waves of killer bees," recalls Paul Bagley. "And why not? We gave them the story of a lifetime: 'Major Securities Firm Admits to 2,000 Counts of Fraud!' They treated it as the crime of the century.

"And the reporters had a disturbing question: Why weren't any of Hutton's executives indicted? Why is no one being held accountable for this massive fraud? How can you have a crime without criminals?"

This question the press pursued vigorously, digging up every sordid detail of the chaining and overdrafting and the pressure within the Hutton culture to maximize interest income. For every layer that was stripped away, another more damaging revelation was dredged to the surface. If the courts wouldn't treat Hutton as a criminal, the press would. And it did so relentlessly, fueling and expanding the story day after day, week after week.

By mid-May Hutton was in a state of siege. Fomon's bite-the-bullet strategy had blown up in the firm's face like a faulty grenade. Forget the lawyer's counsel. Forget the PR firm's assurances. The headlines weren't going away.

"For two months after the plea was announced, there wasn't a day that went by that Hutton wasn't excoriated in the press," Bagley says. "Every form of business and general journalism got in on the act. The *New York Times,* the *Wall Street Journal,* local dailies across the nation—they all had a field day.

"Once I checked the Dow Jones News Service to find that our scandal had gotten three times the coverage of Union Carbide's Bhopal disaster—and they killed hundreds of people. The Hutton's story had become filler. Editors would say, 'Look, there's room on page one today. Let's take another shot at Hutton.'

"And the assault wouldn't stop. It snowballed beyond management's ability to handle it. They were faced with a crisis they couldn't contain."

The crisis extended beyond the corporate headquarters to the firm's power train—its brokerage network—where the impact was immediate.

"For years I'd gone to work each morning ready to take on the world," says Clarence Catallo. "But that changed dramatically after the guilty plea. Suddenly I found myself tiptoeing into the office and gingerly, very gingerly, opening the daily newspaper to see if we'd been accused of another crime. And there was usually some devastating article about Hutton and this or that banking practice, this or that branch office. After weeks and months of these stories, it looked like we were up to our eyeballs in crime.

"Clients believed that. Instead of managing their portfolios, I had to spend my time defending the company to people who'd trusted us for decades, for lifetimes. And no matter what I said, I couldn't convince everyone that the firm wasn't dishonest.

"On any given day, half the firm's brokers were on the phones giving their clients Hutton's side of the story. They weren't selling. They were spending their time explaining and defending and justifying. It was damage control on a massive scale, and no one was getting paid for it."

Executives who'd been with Hutton for their entire careers found decades of goodwill blown away by a single incident. "Pleading guilty was a disaster—and everything that followed after it was worse," says a long-time manager in the Southwest. "You'd spent your whole life living ethically, and suddenly people assumed you were a crook. No matter what you did, they lumped you together with crooks, and nothing you could say would talk them out of it. To those of us who cared about our reputation, it was a tragedy."

The impact of the guilty plea reached deep into the bowels of Hutton, damaging every aspect of the firm's business.

"The day before the guilty plea was made, we had registered Silver Screen Partners, a big tax shelter program for Disney Studios," recalls Paul Bagley. "As soon as they heard what we'd done, the Disney executives called a meeting to see if they wanted to proceed with Hutton doing the deal. Fortunately for us, Disney president Frank Welles called after the meeting saying, 'At a time like this, you learn who your friends are. We're going with you.'

"But just as we dodged one bullet, another one whistled by. That's when the second wave of bad news made the headlines. It seemed that our law firm, Cahill Gordon, had failed to notify the fifty states that the offering was effective with the SEC and that we were starting to sell it. So once the deal was in progress, we got calls from some of the states saying that we were in violation of the law. It was just a technical error, but some of the state officials made us jump through hoops, including giving those who'd already invested in the partnership the chance to bail out. Newspapers across the country jumped on the story.

"Coming when it did, Cahill Gordon's mistake was more than an oversight. It was a fiasco. For all of those who might have given us the benefit of the doubt before, this confirmed their suspicions: Hutton does whatever it pleases. Hutton breaks the law at will. Hutton is an outlaw."

The toll also extended to public finance—which quickly plummeted from second place to seventh in the ranks. And because it pleaded guilty to a felony, Hutton was automatically barred from operating as a broker dealer in all fifty states—unless the states chose to waive that harsh penalty.

"We had to negotiate with the securities commissioners in all the states and it became an incredible mess," recalls Tom Rae. "In states where we had no banking relationships at all, commissioners would say, 'Pay us a $50,000 fine.' When I'd object on the grounds that we had no bank activities there, they'd say, 'We know, but because of all the bad publicity, we have to show that we're doing something to punish Hutton.'

"In other cases, securities commissioners would call up and say, 'You paid that other state $50,000 and you only paid us $25,000, so we want $25,000 more.' And in the end, we'd have to pay. We really had no choice."

Even Hutton's mergers and acquisitions business, which had just begun to produce meaningful revenues, collapsed under the weight of the guilty plea.

Only a year before, Jim Lopp had decided to cash in on the M&A binge that was sweeping Wall Street, earning hundreds of millions in profit for the Drexel Burnhams of the world. Recruiting talented merchant banker Daniel Good, Lopp and Fomon gave their new executive a mandate: put Hutton on the M&A map. Blessed with a free hand from top management, Good used Hutton's capital and good name to succeed beyond the most optimistic projections. By the spring of 1985 Hutton's fledgling M&A department boasted thirty employees and revenues of $40 million.

Good's team was on a roll. When Rockwell International acquired Allen-Bradley Co. for $1.7 billion, Hutton was the investment banker, pocketing a $7 million fee for its efforts. And when Atlanta's favorite son, Ted Turner, launched his highly publicized pursuit of CBS, he hired Hutton to represent him. In the process Good earned $10 million—the largest investment banking fee in the firm's history.

But just when Good believed he was on the verge of building a major M&A practice, just when Fomon—always enamored of investment banking—believed he'd engineered another Locke/Lopp/Pierce miracle, the bottom fell out.

"Fomon liked to stop by my office all the time to tell me how well I was doing," Good recalls. "He took great pleasure in our success. But on the morning of May 2, 1985, he reversed his usual practice, inviting me to stop by his office instead.

"The call was surprising; the tone of his voice was tenuous, wary. That's when he told me about the plea agreement we'd be announcing the following day. In the same breath he told me not to worry, that he'd set up a good public-relations program, and that the matter would be history in a couple of weeks. I said, 'Okay, if you've figured out a way to solve the problem, there's nothing to worry about.'

"Nothing to worry about? Nothing to worry about! After the plea Hutton's name was hammered in the press. Clients who had been calling me regularly just stopped, like that. Those who did call wanted to talk about the F matter, about Hutton the convicted felon. We were tainted. We couldn't do business."

Clients weren't the only problem. Recruiting became a nightmare. With the firm being brandished by the press, talented bankers refused to show up for interviews, fearing that their reputation would be tainted by Hutton's. That they would be joining a firm on the verge of disaster. Their instincts were good. With business turning down sharply and aggregate expenses continuing to go through the roof, Hutton's capital position was deteriorating. The cash pipeline, which had been open full spigot to Good's department, was suddenly choked off.

"The timing couldn't have been worse," Good recalls. "The trend was for investment firms to act as merchant banks, putting their own money into deals. But we couldn't do that. We were hamstrung by the lack of capital. Combine that with the recruiting roadblock and growing client resistance, and it became painfully apparent that the success we'd achieved before the plea could not be sustained."

Facing the inevitable, Good left Hutton for Shearson Lehman. With his departure Hutton's M&A boomlet was over almost as soon as it began.

Only after the guilty plea had been made and the terrible fallout from it had rained down on Hutton did disturbing news filter back to top management. Cahill, Gordon, which had started off trying to bluff the government lawyers, had been bluffed themselves.

As it turned out, the threat to indict Hutton executives—which had started the stampede toward settlement—was mostly a scare tactic. Government officials admitted secretly among themselves that a trial would be long, arduous, and expensive, and would have only a fifty percent chance of winning convictions. They would much prefer a settlement, one they believed they could engineer by frightening Hutton executives into thinking they could be held personally liable.

As a Justice Department lawyer would later acknowledge, the specter of individual prosecutions was part of a plan to "force the company to sit down and bargain with me. It was like playing hardball."*

Frustrated by the scandal enveloping him, Bob Fomon cursed and tilted against the papers all over the country who'd picked up on the F matter. Behind every headline, behind every client loss, Fomon saw a demon lurking in the shadows.

"During this period I had to see Bob on urgent business pertaining to a big deal we were involved in," says a former Hutton vice-president in the corporate finance department. "As I walked down the hall toward his office, I could hear a banging noise, as if a workman was hammering a nail into a wall. That's what I thought it was until I saw that it was Bob himself kicking and flailing at a chair. Yes, the chief executive of a Wall Street institution was in his office kicking and flailing at a chair.

"When I asked him, 'Bob, what's wrong?' he mumbled some gobbledygook about the *New York Times* and do-gooder attorneys general and how he'd had it up to here with them. It was clear that the checking matter had taken its toll on him, that he'd crossed the breaking point, and was dealing with it the only way he knew how to: by kicking an inanimate object."

Fomon's troubles were starting to overtake him. With the bad leg and the booze and the knowledge that he'd erred in copping the guilty plea weighing on him terribly, and with mild strokes he'd suffered in December 1984 and again in August 1985, he looked like he was dying.

"He gave the appearance of being a sick man," recalls Dan Good. "He looked pale and withdrawn. You left him wondering just how he was functioning."

The answer is "not very well." When he wasn't kicking furniture or engaging in flights of fantasy over his emerging

New York Times, April 9, 1986.

monument on Fifty-second Street, he was acting irrational in other ways.

In one episode, Fomon force-fed an executive into Hutton's corporate finance department. The move was made, staffers were convinced, as a favor to one of Fomon's former girlfriends (from his single days), who was married to the executive.

"Fomon had arranged a series of interviews for the guy with everyone up and down the chain of command," recalls a former VP of corporate finance. "Everyone who met the guy thought he was a disaster area and swore he'd never be part of our firm. The guy was inept. He'd been fired by another firm. He'd been looking for a job for a year. He gave as references people who, when you talked to them, broke out in laughter. Clients would call up and say, 'If you send that guy out here again, you're not going to have us as a client.' That's what we were dealing with.

"When the interviews were concluded, one of the senior executives came into my office and said Bob had been putting a lot of pressure on him to hire the guy, but there's no way he was going to do it. But an hour later he returned, full of chagrin, saying we had to give this guy another series of interviews.

"So the guy was interviewed extensively again, this time with the investment banking executives committee, and they too rejected him. Incompetent, they said.

"So what happened? The verdict was reported to Fomon and Fomon hired him anyway. That's the kind of animal house Hutton had become."

As word spread through Hutton that Fomon was straggling into the office, later and later, at ten or eleven and that he was force-feeding people into responsible positions, resentment over his lack of leadership grew intense. As the father of the guilty plea, he was held personally accountable for the firm's precipitous slide.

If Fomon had truly cared for the firm of E.F. Hutton, he

would have resigned at this point. Not as a departing hero, as would have been the case at other critical junctures, but as a leader accepting responsibility for his sins. With this one move he would have engineered a symbolic house-cleaning, shifting attention away from Hutton the institution and onto Fomon the man. If the press had been handed its scapegoat, the incriminating headlines would have lost their punch.

Scott Pierce saw it that way. Meeting secretly with the CEO in July 1985, Hutton's president, a beleaguered man in his own right, advised Fomon to resign.

"I saw it as a symbolic move. He'd go to the press, admit that we should have had stronger internal controls, and accept responsibility for his failure to implement them. In effect, he'd sacrifice himself for the sake of the firm.

"But Bob wouldn't hear of it. Resigning would be an admission of guilt, and he didn't feel guilty."

Chapter 15

"With Rittereiser there was always a reason for inaction. For example, he disliked Norm Epstein. Their joint backgrounds in operations clashed from day one. So I tried to get Rittereiser to fire Epstein immediately. But he wouldn't do it. Bob Fomon worried that if Norm left, the whole back office would fold. So Ritt listened to that. And because Jerry Miller and Epstein were close, he worried that firing Norm would upset Jerry. And so he gave in to that. The point is, he wouldn't say, 'I'm president. Here's what I want to do. I'm going to do it and make it work.' Instead he'd just let things drift."

—Neal Eldridge

Bob Fomon was determined to cling to power. In the spring of 1985, he launched a dual strategy for diffusing the F matter and for silencing his critics both inside and outside the firm. It was a carefully calculated effort to establish himself as a fair-minded and responsive chief executive. Just as everyone was writing him off as a stubborn, egocentric monarch, he would prove them wrong.

In act one of his two-part drama Fomon commissioned a renowned jurist, former attorney general Griffin Bell, to serve as the grand inquisitor on the checking scandal. Judge Bell—then a senior partner with the prestigious Atlanta law firm of King & Spalding—would investigate the F matter, reporting back to management on how it happened, who bore responsibility, and what controls should be put in place to prevent a repeat performance.

By selecting a prominent member of the legal community to investigate the scandal and by pledging in advance to heed the recommendations of Judge Bell's report, Fomon was assuming the role of the righteous chief executive repulsed by the scandal and determined to root out the evil that produced it. On May 17, 1985, Bell commenced his investigation. He would report his findings to the Hutton board on September 4.

On a second front, Fomon—who was under enormous pressure to recruit a new president untainted by the scandal—began negotiating again with Merrill Lynch's Bob Rittereiser. A lot had changed since the first meeting a year before. Ritt's mentor, former Merrill chairman Roger Birk, had taken early retirement, leaving his protegé in the lurch. Without a rabbi to escort him through the ranks, Rittereiser recognized that his dream of becoming Merrill's CEO would remain just that. Though he'd met secretly with Fomon several times over the year, it wasn't until the outlook at Merrill soured that he was willing to take Fomon's courtship seriously.

By this time Fomon was also prepared to make a deal. As much as his previous offer was meant to be rejected ("Don't blame me," he could tell the world, "I offered him the job"), now he truly wanted Rittereiser to accept the presidency. Not because he wanted the outsider to run the firm, but because he believed Ritt's choirboy reputation would advance the image of a reborn Hutton.

"In recruiting Rittereiser, Fomon hoped to be putting a lightning rod in place," Bagley says. "All the slings and arrows that had been directed at the CEO could now be deflected to the new guy. One with the image, whether he deserved it or not, of someone who could address Hutton's problems and get us moving again. At this point Fomon knew that was the only way to save himself."

On June 3, 1985, Robert P. Rittereiser became Hutton's president.

In little more than two years, he would take a troubled but salvageable firm and lead it straight into the grave.

Bob Rittereiser came to Hutton on the wings of angels. Touted as the great white hope whose whistle-clean ethics and administrative brilliance would turn around the troubled firm, he was greeted with a standing ovation in and out of the firm.

Referring to Ritt's appointment, respected Wall Street analyst Joel Rosenthal wrote of Hutton in the *New York Times*: "Their reputation was somewhat tarnished by the cash management scandal, and they are bringing in someone to run the company who has nothing to do with it and has an outstanding reputation on his own."

Even hard-boiled Huttonites felt a renewed sense of hope when Ritt became president of Hutton Group, joining the newly created office of the chairman that also included Fomon as CEO, Tom Lynch as vice chairman of Hutton Group, and Pierce as president of Hutton, Inc.

"When Ritt came in, there was a widespread feeling of euphoria," says Paul Bagley. "People thought, jeez, we've finally got a professional manager who'll take charge of this place and get it straightened out."

An up-from-the-streets New Yorker, Rittereiser had grown up in a working-class family given to hard work and clean living. The son of a truck driver, whose work often took him away from home, young Robert was influenced mostly by his mother—a housewife from the old school who recognized the value of education and who prodded her children (three boys and a girl) to rise above their blue-collar caste.

It was a lesson Robert learned well. Like many young men seeking fortune in the Eisenhower fifties, Rittereiser's divining rod directed him to Wall Street. Starting out in 1958 as a

Merrill Lynch margin clerk, he worked his way through the Merrill organization, ultimately coming under the wing of Roger Birk, who shepherded him through the executive hierarchy. By the time he left Merrill, he'd served as both chief financial officer and head of administration.

Although Ritt had performed well in the land of the bull, he was for the most part a back-office functionary, no more capable of running E.F. Hutton than Hutton's own back-office guru, Norm Epstein. Focused as he was on computer systems and cash-flow analyses and product-profitability studies, he had little experience for the role of corporate maestro. Yes, he was a pleasant man with a Norman Rockwell smile and yes, he was Gerry Ford clean to Bob Fomon's Dick Nixon, but Hutton needed more than that. It needed a commander-in-chief, a Lee Iacocca, who could take charge, leading, inspiring, and integrating the firm's component parts from retail brokerage to corporate finance, from administration to accounting. And it needed someone who could do it quickly and decisively, without studies, committees, and endless procrastination.

Nothing in Rittereiser's experience prepared him for that. He was a Merrill Lynch man through and through, and a Merrill Lynch man couldn't run E.F. Hutton.

"At Merrill Lynch, systems were king," says a former Rittereiser colleague. "There was a way of doing things, a corporate bible, that everyone followed *or else*. There was structure, clear lines of authority, and committees, committees, committees. No one was bigger than the organization and everyone, even the senior officers, worshiped it. It was a consensus style of management: you made decisions as part of a team.

"Well, if there was a polar opposite of that, a wild and wooly zoo where everyone had his own agenda, that was Hutton. What rules there were were meant to be broken. The corporate structure—hell, it's a joke to call it that—was more like a free-for-all. And teamwork in the Hutton culture was considered sissy stuff. The guy in charge made the decisions, and he made them by himself or he wasn't in charge for long. Bob Rittereiser never realized how shockingly different it would be to operate in this environment."

When word first leaked out that Bob Rittereiser had agreed to join E.F. Hutton, the company's stock shot up $1.50 on the news. Like the Hutton people, who greeted his arrival like the second coming, Wall Street investors apparently believed the hype that Rittereiser was an emerging Wall Street superstar about to demonstrate his true potential as a brokerage president. Out from under Merrill's bureaucracy, acting as his own man, he would be magnificent.

Rarely has a man been so misjudged. In assuming the role of Hutton's president, Rittereiser acted not like a seasoned executive finally rising to his high-water rank, but instead like a freshly minted MBA who'd just walked out of business school with his head full of esoteric concepts and theories.

In the very first weeks it became apparent that he was so accustomed to the Merrill Lynch consensus-style bureaucracy that he had trouble making decisions on his own.

"Soon after Rittereiser became president in June 1985 he called me, saying Bob Fomon thought I could help him get acclimated at Hutton," says consultant Neal Eldridge. "Because I'd been on the outs with Fomon, the referral surprised me. 'Bob tells me you're objective and that you would be a good person to bounce ideas off,' Rittereiser said. If Fomon was willing to forgive and forget, so was I.

"When I met Ritt, he told me his first priority was to restructure the senior executive staff. By this time he'd already met with the officers and compiled a list of names, complete with comments that were quite perceptive. For someone who'd only just met these people, I thought he was very good at judging what made people tick.

"That was the good part. The bad part was that he couldn't go beyond that point. When he saw the need to fire people, to demote them, or strip them of authority, he froze in place. You could tell from the start that he was a mediator, not a decision maker.

"Personally, he was a delightful man. But as an executive he was the most frustrating person I'd ever worked with. A hundred times more frustrating than Bob Fomon."

To some, Rittereiser's paralysis stemmed from fear. Fear of crossing an internal power group, of angering another executive, of antagonizing the board of directors. He seemed to fear that an unpopular move would come back to haunt him. Forces within Hutton would plot against him to rout the new president from office. Rather than taking control of the organization, he feared it.

"Ritt used to talk in terms of movie analogies," Eldridge says. "*The Godfather* was his favorite. He kept referring to the tollbooth scene. Because I didn't know what he was talking about, I rented the movie, watching it carefully for clues. Still, I was bewildered. All I could think of was that he saw himself as a target."

A month after Rittereiser assumed the presidency, the long simmering mutiny in the sales force bubbled over the top.

Bruce Tuthill, one of Hutton's premier producers and an outspoken member of the field force, called Bob Fomon to tell him—not ask him—that he would have to hold an emergency meeting with a contingent of top-ranking account executives. According to Tuthill, Hutton's brokerage force was in danger of self-destructing. The AE's were in a stinking mood, and something had to be done post haste. Because retail brokerage accounted for 85 percent of Hutton's revenues, the situation was serious, if not dire.

The brokers had a long list of gripes. The new headquarters building known around Hutton as "Fomon's last erection" had tempers flaring. With the firm's earnings on the skids (at a time when the rest of Wall Street was performing well), their chairman squandering millions on a high-rise ego trip rubbed the wrong way. Adding insult to injury, word spread throughout the field that headquarters had suffered major losses in fixed-income trading.

"Knowing that we were making money on the retail side but that some geniuses in New York were pissing it away just didn't go down well," says Tony Malatino. "At first we were bewildered that management could let this happen. When they let it continue, we got cross-eyed. And when they let it get worse and worse, we got incensed. And we weren't willing to sit on the sidelines any longer. We were determined to take action ourselves."

The budding vigilantism owed much of its bite to the brokers' distaste for the Fomon/Pierce/Witt trio. Without an executive whom they could look to as a regular guy who acted as their whip in the firm, the top producers felt disenfranchised. The eighty-one-year-old firm that had always been theirs was slipping away.

They were determined to get it back. Their vehicle would be the Director's Advisory Council (DAC), an elite group of successful Hutton brokers launched years before by George Ball. In theory, the DAC was meant to keep the Hutton board informed of the brokers' thinking and lobby for changes on their behalf. But to this point the council had been little more than an atta-boy sales club lavishing black-tie dinner dances and other perks on its members. This toothless role Tuthill, Malatino, et al. were about to change. They started with the phone call to Fomon.

His back against the wall, the CEO agreed to a meeting between management and the DAC. The face-off, held at the Parker Meridien, a glitzy faux French hotel on Manhattan's West Side, proved divisive from the start. The moment the producers were escorted into the same room with Fomon and Witt, sparks flew. This wasn't a meeting, it was a lynching, and many of the brokers wanted their necks in a noose.

Pierce was also high on the brokers' shit list. Sensing this, "Scottie"—who was in Europe on a "business trip" (others called it a vacation)—decided to stay put in spite of a frantic call from Witt informing him of the impending meeting and asking that he return to play host. Pierce, who knew a shark tank when he saw one, said, "You can handle it, Bob. You don't need me."

What Witt needed was a bodyguard.

As the meeting opened, Bob Fomon had this "Why am I forced to mingle with the common folks" look on his puss. Launching into a song and dance about the trauma of the F matter, he presented a melodramatic monologue of his heroic efforts to rescue the firm from its PR fiasco.

But there was little patience in the hall for check-kiting talk. The problems ran deeper than that. Bruce Tuthill broke the ice: "The situation in the field is critical. The firm is running out of time. Key brokers are preparing to leave and entire offices are ready to defect. Our Chicago office is having such an exodus that a Hutton broker interviewing at Shearson had to wait in a room for five minutes so that he wouldn't come face-to-face with his colleagues also applying there."

Tony Malatino picked up the torch, charging that top management was so out of touch that "it doesn't know how critical the situation is."

Quickly cries for blood filled the room.

"The sales force is in a suicidal mood," a producer charged. "We cannot wait. *We must let someone go at this point.*"

Fomon saw the writing on the wall. Let someone go? The CEO tried to stem the tide. "It would hurt us to fire one person this week and one person next week, et cetera. The press would just love it."

But to no avail.

Voices rang from the floor:

"The field needs someone in retail to call everyday. Not Fomon. Not Pierce. Not Rittereiser."

"We are now dealing with emotion, not facts. Everyone is scared to death."

"Our brokers are ready to bolt and our customers are concerned. The field has lost pride. We need something . . . we must listen to our troops."

"I'd like to know why we pleaded guilty in the first place. That's the question most asked by the account executives."

"We need a retail-oriented person at the head. Nobody represents retail."

"We need somebody removed."

It was then that Bob Fomon asked the question the DAC had been waiting for. It startled them just the same: "What do you want me to do, fire Witt?"

The room fell silent, a piercing kind of silence that carried an unmistakable message: yes, they wanted heads to roll.

And they wanted to remind Fomon of a better time, a Camelot time, a time when happiness rained on the kingdom. A time when George Ball presided. Three years after his departure, Ball's ghost was still very much in evidence, complicating Hutton's internal politics, recalling a standard his successors could not duplicate.

A voice from the room:

"We need a representative. Someone there for us. There never was a question with George Ball. If they, the brokers, feel that can be put in place, a lot of problems will be solved."

They wanted a strong and sympathetic leader popular with the field. At this point Jerry Miller was the hands-down favorite. Still presiding over equity trading, where Ball had exiled him before departing to run Pru-Bache, Miller was dreaming of returning to the central nervous system of E.F. Hutton.

By using the DAC meeting as a platform to appoint Miller as the head of the field, Fomon would have diffused much of the anger and demonstrated that he could be responsive to the field.

But Baron Fomon had a different response.

He simply turned around and left the meeting. He walked out. It was as if he couldn't be bothered with these lowly stockbrokers and their petty whining. Oh, he mumbled pitiful excuses about previous engagements, but the fact is he wanted out.

"When I told Bob we had to have the meeting he agreed to it because he thought he could smooth the problems over," Tuthill recalls. "He would give the producers a few drinks, say a few nice words, and we'd all be pacified. But the issues ran deeper than that and Fomon couldn't deal with it."

"You knew that no matter what his title said, Fomon was no longer our leader," says one of the senior brokers in attendance. "Not only had he walked out on us—imagine the gall of that—but when he returned later that evening, he was drunk and incoherent. A pitiful figure. Watching him, you knew that Hutton had a power vacuum of crisis proportions."

That vacuum Rittereiser, attending his first big powwow with the troops, jumped in to fill. As a consensus politician, he saw an opportunity to establish his presence in the firm by befriending the sales force and in the process building a power base of his own.

Taking the floor, he tried his hand at cheerleading. It was a surreal performance, complete with his mysterious movie analogies. As was often the case with "Rittspeak" Rittereiser, his message was perplexing.

"I believe this company has the best chance to be the champion in the investment services business. I believe that relative to Merrill Lynch, American Express, Prudential-Bache. I believe this is the place to be.

"Remember *Cool Hand Luke*? The point of the whole story is Paul Newman was a wise guy escaping from prison for the fourteenth time in a row and the warden actually liked him; however, as he was lying dead with the dogs sniffing at him, the warden with the mirror sunglasses said, 'What we have here is a failure to communicate.'

"We have to deal with this right now. We have a failure to communicate as well as we can or should. The time has come to treat each other with the same intelligence and respect we would an idiot in the street."

The DAC had flown to New York to accomplish two major goals: to vent their collective spleen at management and to demand a greater role in running the firm. Specifically, they wanted representation on the Hutton Inc. board, a demand Rittereiser was more than happy to support.*

Seizing an opportunity to win over the producers and fill the power vacuum that was so evident, Rittereiser put on a one-man campaign for good guy of the year.

"I will add to my operating committee people from this group, so as Bob Fomon leads us through, we can get some work done. Strategic performance systems. Restore confidence, communication.

"I'll add to the advisory group. We'll enter 1986 with a brand-new attitude. A series of changes will evolve. Move forward, move on. We all have great respect for the field. We must restore the confidence of the people—changes are needed."

The brokerage war veterans had heard it all before, but Rittereiser would get the benefit of the doubt. At this point he was their only hope.

---

*By August, brokers John Wood and Bruce Tuthill would be appointed to the board.

Chapter 16

"We do not hold Fomon, Chairman and Chief Executive Officer, responsible for failing to detect and terminate the improper overdrafting and other abusive practices which occurred at Hutton. Our justification is a matter of proper corporate governance. A corporate officer is, in the performance of his duty and functions, entitled to rely on the decisions, judgments, and performance of other officers and employees of the company if the officer believes that such decisions, judgments, or performance are within the professional or other competence of such officer or employee."
—Bell Report, page 171

On September 4, 1985, the eagerly awaited Griffin Bell report on the F matter was released, fanning the fires of the still-smoldering scandal it was supposed to extinguish.

The Bell Report—a massive document replete with 183 pages of text and hundreds of pages of letters, printouts, and interoffice memos—painted a picture of a poorly managed and poorly controlled firm. Its weak board had failed to control the Hutton companies, its culture had permitted overdrafts, and its employees had violated acceptable conduct.

The introduction of overdrafting as part of the drawdown sheet on the cash-management system was an expression of a Hutton policy to accept overdrafting as a

196

means of doing business. Once embodied as part of the system, overdrafting on an unregulated basis was in place. Prudent management, however, required that some mechanism be established at the same time that the overdrafting principle was adopted to make certain that abuses did not result from overdrafting. Such mechanisms should also have insured that overdrafting that did not have any relationship to an economic transaction would not become part of the Hutton way of doing business with banks.

No such mechanism was established, however, and we did not find any evidence of an internal or external auditing of a type that would have discovered overdrafting. Instead, overdrafting became tantamount to a *loose cannon* fired at will by a minority of Hutton employees in a position to overdraft.

Just as the F matter story began to recede from the headlines, the Bell Report surfaced, bringing the swarms of reporters back to fortress Hutton.

"You had to see this Bell Report," says a former Hutton broker now with Shearson. "It's bigger than the Manhattan telephone book, and it's filled with pages and pages rehashing all the things we'd done wrong, pointing fingers at every mistake we'd ever made, regurgitating all the charges and complaints, describing in sickening detail how Hutton supposedly ripped off the world. And it gets personal, naming names, saying this one's responsible for this and that one's responsible for that. If our competitors on the Street had written the script, they couldn't have done a better job.

"Fomon was an ass for hiring Bell, for paying millions of dollars to air our dirty laundry. What did he hope to accomplish? To prove to the feds and the press that he was Dick Tracy crusading against corporate misconduct? Bullshit. The guy was a master of misconduct. Morality?

He never believed in it. But somehow he thought this report was going to come out and it was going to make him look like Mother Teresa for commissioning it."

It never happened. With the *New York Times* and the *Wall Street Journal* and *Business Week* and every other newspaper or magazine now jumping all over the story, Hutton's phone banks lit up like the aurora borealis. Once again the brokers were in the hot seat, accosted by angry clients who wondered how the good name of E.F. Hutton & Co. could be so hopelessly mired in corporate scandal. Once again there were the stinging questions and provocative headlines:

"HUTTON'S TOP OFFICIALS WERE RESPONSIBLE FOR FAILURE TO DETECT FRAUD"
"PLACING THE BLAME AT E.F. HUTTON"
"HUTTON'S REPORT ON CHECK OVERDRAFTING IMPLICATES ABOUT A DOZEN EMPLOYEES"
"A VERDICT: BELL NAMES NAMES"

In substance the Bell Report was the kind of weak tea one might expect from a sponsored study, former attorney general or not. Yes, Hutton was guilty of overdrafting and yes, there were loose cannons, but when it came to fixing blame for these transgressions, the good judge absolved most of the senior officers, meting out his harshest words for six branch managers, a regional manager, and the firm's money manager. Judge Bell, whose law firm did substantial legal work for Hutton and regarded the firm as a valued client, found Bob Fomon and George Ball (CEO and president during the 1981–82 period when the banking transactions were conducted) free of culpability.

That the buck is supposed to stop at the CEO's desk was discounted by Judge Bell. Based on the rationale in Bell's report, Fomon could say, "I've appointed subordinates to manage the affairs of my company. With that my responsibility ends. I can turn my back and let the inmates run the asylum."

Describing George Ball's role in the checking scandal, Judge Bell notes his role in creating a culture that fostered it, but then excuses Ball on the same grounds that absolved Bob Fomon.

> The peculiar management structure of Hutton placed no responsibility on Ball as president for finance, accounting, operations, or legal and compliance, nor did the vice-presidents of these divisions report to him. He was in effect an executive sales manager . . .
>
> As a sales manager, he constantly exhorted the regional vice-presidents and branch managers to earn more through sales and through better interest earnings. His goal was to promote interest earning by chastising those who were below the average and thus seeing to it that the average was being constantly raised. This added to the Hutton overdraft culture. We do not find that Ball had operational responsibility to control interest improprieties or to create and supervise internal audit controls over them. Ball did have the responsibility as a senior corporate officer to report improprieties in overdrafting or gaps in accounting controls once he was put on notice. There is no substantial evidence that he was put on notice as to any gaps or lapses in accounting controls. The overdraft interest data showing aberrations did not constitute sufficient notice of overdrafting problems.
>
> (Bell Report, pages 94–95)

What complicity Bell found in the executive suite was focused on general counsel Tom Rae and chief financial officer Tom Lynch.

According to Bell, Rae's sin is that he failed to properly manage the delivery of documents subpoenaed by the government. This referred primarily to eighteen documents left behind by George Ball when he left Hutton for Pru-Bache.

A final subpoena dated March 5, 1985, was directed to Robert Fomon as Chairman of the Board of Hutton and to the "Custodian of the Records." This subpoena sought specifically all correspondence, memoranda, and other documents relating to Hutton's cash-management policies and banking practices.

On March 19, 1985, Rae forwarded a memorandum to all regional vice-presidents, all regional operations managers, and all branch managers advising that Hutton was "required by federal authorities" to produce all documents specified in the 1985 subpoena. The memorandum explicitly notified the field personnel that they were required to conduct a new search of all pertinent branch and regional files as well as a search of any personal and private files. Each of the field personnel was required to certify in writing that all such documents had been collected and forwarded directly to Robert Brunton of the Hutton legal department. An example of the required certification was attached to the memorandum.

Although certain documents were produced by Hutton from files maintained by Hutton executives, it does not appear that any systematic search was made with respect to files maintained at the Hutton headquarters.

(Bell Report, page 151)

Hutton's failure to systematically search executive files in response to the 1985 subpoena cannot be excused. Here again, Hutton's failure of compliance stemmed from incompetence in approach.

(Bell Report, page 154)

Although Rae supervised the delivery of seven million documents, so many that they could not be photocopied, his feet were held to the fire for failing to achieve one hundred percent compliance. In doing so, Bell holds Rae accountable to the buck-stopping principle that he chooses to ignore in his findings on Fomon and Ball.

As has been noted in the subpoena problem portion of this report, the responsibility to respond to the subpoenas rested on Rae as general counsel. This problem and the failure, not Rae's personally but his responsibility, to collect and provide all documents to the Department of Justice in its investigation cannot go unnoticed. Most were produced, but not all. This, coupled with the failure to require internal financial auditing which would have included cash management, leads to the conclusion that the Legal and Compliance Division of Hutton left something to be desired. Rae, as general counsel, bears responsibility for this although we specifically note that Rae was not involved in the activities that gave rise to the plea. (Bell report, page 173)

As one of the scapegoats in the Bell Report, Rae was pressured to announce in September 1985 that he would resign. (He ultimately left the firm in April 1986.) Although Rae claims he had planned to take early retirement before the judge's report was made public, Hutton insiders considered him a casualty of what many call the "Great Whitewash."

When Bob Fomon saw the Bell Report days before it was released, he threatened to tear it up, to run it through the shredder. "At a special board meeting convened to discuss the Bell Report, Fomon went bananas," recalls Norm Epstein. "Shouting, slamming his fists on the table, he was incensed that they wanted Lynch and Rae's hides. 'Fuck the judge,' he said. 'Fuck the report. They're not going to do this to my people. I won't make them scapegoats. I'm not doing what the judge wants. No way.'

"But I told him, 'Bob, you have to. You ordered the goddamn report, you told the world you'd do whatever it says.' "

Fomon hardly needed Norm Epstein to tell him that. From the moment he had hired Griffin Bell he had known that he would have to carry out the judge's sentence. His credibility, what little he had left, depended on it. Then why the tirade at the board meeting? According to Tom Lynch it was all an act.

"Before Griffin Bell did an ounce of research, he decided that heads had to roll," Lynch charges. "Unless there were sacrificial lambs, the report would be labeled a whitewash. It wouldn't fly with the press. Someone had to be punished, and Tom Rae and I were singled out before Bell even met us. He told Bob Fomon that. Bob knew we were going to be scapegoats well before the report came out.

"That's not speculation. Scottie Pierce told me early on in the so-called investigation that I was on Bell's shit list. I was shocked. Shocked and angered.

"At that point I thought I could protect myself. I went straight to Bell and told him my side of the story. I told him that I didn't have responsibility for the branches, where the actual problems occurred. I didn't have responsibility for the internal-audit department or the accounting department or the cashier's department. I reminded him over and over again that none of it was mine. No way am I going to let myself be sacrificed. That's what I thought. I wasn't responsible and I wasn't going to be tied to it.

"But I was wrong. Nothing I said got through to Bell."

At this point Lynch says he cut a deal with Bell, one he claims the judge reneged on.* "The way the deal was

---

*Judge Bell denies there was ever a deal.

structured, I would surrender the title of chief financial officer, but would retain my position as vice chairman of the board, continuing to perform all the duties that went with it.

"But then the night before Bell's going to release his report to the press, I got this call from Tom Curnin. 'Bell's going to make you give up all of your titles,' he says. 'All of your management duties. It's in his report.'

" 'All of my titles! All of my duties! Damn, I never agreed to that.'

"When I hung up with Curnin, I tried calling Bell. I was dialing, dialing, dialing into the middle of the night, trying to get the judge or anyone who could get to the judge for me. But it was no use. There was a brick wall around Bell."

The following morning Thomas P. Lynch, his eyes bloodshot from lack of sleep, went before the board and the audit committee to fight for his place in the Hutton monarchy. Although there was support around the table—from Epstein, Miller, Pierce, and Fomon, who put on his loyal captain routine—Lynch couldn't get past a new force in the firm: Bob Rittereiser.

"Ritt said, 'We understand your side of the story, Tom, but we told Bell that whatever he recommended we were going to do without question. And we have to honor that—we've got to move ahead. It's a shame, but that's the way it is.' "*

It would be one of the few decisive moves Rittereiser would make. And it was a good one. In spite of Lynch's claims that he was distanced from the branch system and some of the key financial departments, he did serve as a senior financial executive, reaping the power, status, and pay that went with it. According to the Bell Report, Lynch had "failed in his responsibility to ensure that adequate

---

*Lynch was forced to relinquish his titles, but remained a member of the board and the executive committee until his retirement in 1986.

controls were established to prevent abuses in the Hutton cash-management system." If he hadn't known what was going on, he should have made it his business to know. Though the same could be said for George Ball and Bob Fomon, Ball was history, Fomon was untouchable, and Hutton was still under siege. For the siege to end, big names had to fall. If not the biggest, then second tier would have to do. Rittereiser knew that. So he insisted that Lynch be let go.

But there was more. From the beginning Rittereiser had written off Lynch as a throwback to the old partnership days when the Wall Street CFOs were little more than glorified bookkeepers. In the complex and sophisticated 1980s, when the firms traded in billions rather than millions, he saw Lynch as being in over his head. And so he wanted him replaced by a financial professional, a full-fledged CFO. Shortly thereafter he reached into the Big Eight accounting world, recruiting Deloitte Haskins & Sells partner Edward Lill.

Soon the old guard would be replaced by the new. Shocked by Hutton's sloppy structure, its lack of controls, its crazy-quilt reporting system, Rittereiser was determined to usher in a new era of sophistication. He would do it by handpicking professional managers for every one of Hutton's major functions, people with MBAs and JDs who'd worked in the right places and gone to the right schools, who'd read Peter Drucker and could recite his theories chapter and verse.

These managers would prove, virtually without exception, to be disasters.

Chapter 17

"I remember Ed Lill, Rittereiser's chief financial officer, saying that his real role in the firm was that of head referee. He said he had to bring his whistle and striped shirt to meetings of the executive committee, because all they did was fight."

—Paul Bagley

In every way 1985 was an abysmal year for E.F. Hutton & Co. The one-two punch of the guilty plea and the Bell Report transformed the firm's vaunted esprit de corps into a growing sense of anger and fear. The anger was vented at management's incompetence, and the fear stemmed from the fact that the Hutton name, once a bedrock of the sales machine, had become a liability.

If the karma was bad, so were the numbers. In the midst of a roaring stock market that saw the Big Board's average daily volume soar by 20 percent and the Dow Jones average rise to a record 1547, Hutton's bottom line was anemic. Revenues had risen past the $3 billion point, but net after-tax profits from continuing operations—the true test of the firm's performance—slid to a pathetic $11.9 million. Even these dismal numbers dressed up Hutton's financial picture. If not for a one-time $14.3-million tax benefit captured by Hutton Insurance and a $24-million gain from the sale of Hutton Credit Corp. to Chrysler Financial Corporation, consummated on August 1, 1985, for $125 million, E.F. Hutton would have reported the first loss in its history. Only four years before, the firm had earned $71 million after taxes from continuing operations on a revenue base that was one third of current levels.

Dismal, yes, but to Rittereiser it was all a matter of management, of a textbook turnaround that he would engineer once in power. With a little time and Merrill-style discipline, he was certain that he could create a new force on Wall Street. A firm in his own image.

But one of the most knowledgeable men in the securities business knew better. "By the end of 1985 I had reached the conclusion that Hutton could not survive as an independent business," says Dan Good, who was serving double duty as the head of Hutton's merger-and-acquisitions practice and as its internal investment banker. "The checking matter and aftershocks it created had done permanent damage. A merger was our only hope for survival. We needed a partner, someone with the capital and clean image to fill Hutton's most glaring voids."

With this in mind, Good identified three merger candidates—Paine Webber, Smith Barney, and Kidder Peabody. Taking his "survival plan" to Rittereiser, he urged that merger talks begin immediately.

But all he heard was a confusing bluster of Rittspeak. As had become his trademark, he appeared to endorse the plan without really doing so. From the beginning of his tenure at Hutton, senior managers had left Rittereiser's office smiling from ear to ear, convinced they had the president's stamp of approval, only to find that when it came time to collect his vote, they were left twisting in the breeze.

It worked that way for Good. Though he believed that he had Ritt's commitment to explore a merger proposal, he got nothing but foot dragging and promises.

"I brought the merger proposal to Rittereiser's attention over and over again," Good recalls. "While he seemed to endorse its merits, when it came time to act, there was always some reason to stall. He'd procrastinate. He'd postpone. Things reached his desk and just died there.

"When I heard through sources that Kidder Peabody might be up for sale, I pressed Rittereiser even harder, urging him to call Kidder Peabody president Ralph DeNunzio to set up a meeting to explore the options.

"From my vantage point, Kidder made for an ideal merger partner because its retail business didn't overlap all that much with Hutton's and because I saw opportunities for synergy in the firms' investment banking and institutional businesses. I stressed this to Rittereiser and made it clear that we had a window of opportunity. One we should seize.

"But again he failed to act until it was too late. By the time Rittereiser got around to calling, DeNunzio put him off, saying the timing wasn't right. That's an understatement. Twenty-four hours later General Electric announced that it was acquiring Kidder.

"We weren't just late, we were ancient history."

Soon after the news of the Kidder deal deflated Good's hopes for a successful merger, an unsolicited offer from Bell spinoff company U.S. West came over the transom. In a series of top secret meetings with Good, U.S. West executives proposed the purchase of a minority interest in Hutton, buying 20 percent of its stock and taking seats on the board. But the deal never qualified for serious consideration. From Good's perspective, Hutton needed a full-blown acquisition, both for the resources it would provide and for the whitewashing a prestigious acquirer could give to Hutton's tainted image.

But then two more potential suitors, Transamerica Corp. and Metropolitan Life, expressed interest in Hutton. With rumors flying that other bidders were rustling in the bushes, Good invited premier takeover attorney Joseph Flom to address the Hutton board. His message? In a corporate environment prone to hostile takeovers, Hutton must adopt defensive measures, if not to thwart an acquisition, then to give the company leverage in negotiating a favorable deal. To accomplish this, the board authorized Flom's firm, Skadden, Arps, Slate, Meagher & Flom, to amend Hutton's bylaws and structure a poison pill that would shield against a sneak attack by hostile bidders.

There is evidence Rittereiser himself hoped, from the very beginning of his tenure, for a cash-rich buyer to acquire Hutton, paying him handsomely to captain the company and supporting his efforts with financial and management resources.

"Soon after Ritt became Hutton's president," says Paul Bagley, "we were riding uptown in a limousine on our way back from a client meeting when he said quite out of the blue that I should pay particular attention to Atlantic Bell. They had a proposal out to form a partnership to buy and sell real estate properties, and he told me he wanted us to do it and that he wanted me to personally shepherd it through.

" 'Bob, I'd be happy to do it,' " I said. " 'But what's the urgency with Atlantic Bell?'

"His answer floored me. 'I hope to sell the firm to them someday and remain as chief executive officer. So I want them well taken care of.' "

Whether his ultimate intention was to sell Hutton or to manage it as an independent entity, Bob Rittereiser decided to use his position as chief operating officer to drastically alter the Hutton culture. He would transform it from a retail-driven enterprise into an investment banking house.

Like Bob Fomon before him, Rittereiser was taken by the glamour and the prestige of investment banking. If retail was basically unmanageable, why beat a dead horse? Instead he would focus on the trading and corporate financing and institutional sales where the real fortunes were made and where the great reputations were earned.

"Having joined Hutton in the mid-eighties, Rittereiser and I were the newest kids on the block," recalls Dan Good, "and we became rather close. It was a casual, open relationship. Rittereiser would wander into my office, asking for my views on retail brokerage, investment banking, merchant banking and where it was all headed.

"I suggested that he shrink the firm by closing down investment banking, that he prune away everything that didn't feed into retail. No matter how badly he wanted it, we couldn't become another Salomon Brothers or Goldman Sachs. We didn't have the talent and we couldn't get it. Not with Hutton's reputation. After the F matter I couldn't get people to come to interviews. So how were we going to build a great investment bank? Under the best conditions it would take ten years of staff building and a ton of money to hire and train the kind of talent we'd need to put an investment banking operation on the map. But by 1986 Hutton didn't have the time and it didn't have the money. Both were precious commodities slipping away.

"What we needed was a quick fix to halt the hemorrhaging and get us back on our feet while there was still time. At this point there was only one way to do that: take the strength of the firm, its retail operations, and build on them. I told that to Bob, but he ignored me. Instead he took the opposite tact, setting out to shrink retail and to build up investment banking. It was a colossal mistake, one that would prove to be Rittereiser's folly."

In 1986 Hutton underwent sweeping changes in its management structure. All at once the coterie of seasoned executives who had run the firm for twenty years were pushed aside by Rittereiser and by the lingering effects of the Bell Report.

Finding that Hutton's board was not in charge of the company and that "a great majority of the board members were simply corporate officers over whom the board should have been exercising control," Judge Bell had determined: "The board of Hutton Group should be reorganized to consist of a substantial majority of outside directors."

With Hutton publicly committed to heeding Bell's recommendations, the time had come to transform the Hutton board from a VIP lounge for top management into an independent force that would serve as a check on management.

"We had this directors' meeting after the Bell Report came out, and Fomon just told us that he was throwing everyone below the rank of president off the board," Epstein recalls. "There were about eighteen insiders on that board, and as of that moment we were ceremoniously dismissed. Deciding which of us should stay and which should go was too political, they said, so they were doing a clean sweep, leaving only Fomon, Rittereiser, and Pierce as inside directors.

"That angered us, not just because we lost our positions on the board, but because the company was now in the hands of people who didn't understand it. The men who knew Hutton best were banned from its top management body. Sure, there was a need for reform, for getting outsiders on the board, but with Fomon's action the pendulum had swung too far. I told that to Ueberroth. I said, 'If you think you're going to get an accurate representation of the company from Fomon, Rittereiser, and Pierce, you're wronger than you've ever been in your life.' "

As the old club members were shown the door, new faces were ushered into the boardroom. Joining Merrill, Edward Cazien*, Lopp, Law, and Ueberroth on a shrunken board now dominated by outsiders were:

*Fomon's friend since his days at USC Law School and a longtime attorney for Hutton.

1. William G. Milliken, former governor of Michigan, a respected member of both the political and business communities. His name, like the Good Housekeeping seal of approval, Fomon wanted to add to the board.

2. Sadao Yasuda, a senior executive with Japan's Sumitomo Life, a major financial institution whose president Bob Fomon had met on a trip to Japan.

3. J. Thomas Talbot, former chairman of Jet America Airlines and a partner in the real estate management firm of Shaw & Talbot, elected to the board, sponsored by his friend Peter Ueberroth, in 1987.

Gone were virtually all the members of the 1985 Hutton Group board, including such longtime Hutton hands as Bob Wigley, Peter Detweiler, Gordon Crary, Jr., Norm Epstein, John Latshaw, Dick Locke, Jerry Miller, Tom Lynch, Bob Witt, and Bill Clayton.

In principle, the shift to outsiders boded well for Hutton. After more than a decade of autocracy, installing a new level of authority to guide management was textbook perfect. Too perfect. In practice, textbook procedure doesn't hold weight in the rough-and-tumble of Wall Street brokerage offices. And that's where Hutton would suffer. In discharging the insiders from the board, Fomon was exiling from power and influence the men who knew the company best, replacing them in one fell swoop with a collection of impressive resumes who knew nothing of Hutton's past.

At the same time a similar shift was occurring internally. In January 1986 Rittereiser, already president of the holding company, E.F. Hutton Group, had the board name him president of the brokerage subsidiary, E.F. Hutton, Inc., relegating Scott Pierce to the corporate pastureland of a vice chairmanship.

Determined to put his own dream into place, Rittereiser went off on an extravagant shopping spree, recruiting top executives from a Who's Who of leading corporations and luring them to Hutton with whopping pay packages that dwarfed those of the senior officers who'd toiled at the firm for decades.

As an executive recruiter, Rittereiser proved to be a Santa Claus in a business suit. In the give-and-take that is traditional in high-level salary negotiations, Rittereiser's recruits found that they could take, take, take. To a man they were grossly overpaid, lavished with perks and parachutes that would make them millionaires in short order.

"To those of us who'd helped to build the firm over the years, seeing the newcomers get such incredible packages was terribly upsetting," recalls an old-time Hutton board member. "I made this point clear to Rittereiser in several meetings: 'Once word gets out about the kind of deals you've struck with your team, there's going to be a revolt here. People are going to be pissed off. They're going to want their fair share too.'

"His response was that because Hutton was a troubled firm, he had to pay top dollar to recruit qualified people. In the long run, he said, everyone would benefit because his team would make the firm more profitable. But people didn't buy that. A lot of the executives who worked for me just thought they were getting screwed."

Rittereiser's failure as a recruiter went beyond the dollar issue to the personalities and qualifications of the men he handpicked to help him manage Hutton. As events would soon prove, most were incompetent, insensitive, or ill-suited for the job. Worse yet, they would look beyond the posts they were hired to fill, fighting to leapfrog each other to emerge as Hutton's president when Rittereiser succeeded Fomon as CEO. In this wild melee of greed and ambition, they would divide the company into warring camps determined to destroy each other.

As Rittereiser's dream team took shape, the principal players included, in order of hiring:

• Chief Financial Officer Edward J. Lill, appointed March,

1986. The very image of a stuffed-shirt Big Eight auditor—
dull, straight-laced, painfully conservative—Lill had toiled
for thirty-three years as a partner with Deloitte, Haskins
& Sells. Though an acknowledged expert in securities-
industry accounting, he assumed Hutton's top financial post
with no experience on the client side. Serving as CFO
would be a new experience.

• General Counsel Stephen J. Friedman, appointed April 1,
1986. A former commissioner of the Securities and Exchange Commission and a one-time partner with the prominent law firm of Debevoise & Plimpton, Friedman was
brought on board to replace Tom Rae. But he had more on
his mind than lawyering.

"When Friedman came strolling in here, he announced in
so many words that he was leaving the practice of law and
going into business management," recalls Paul Bagley.
"From day one he's going to be deeply involved in the
operation of the firm. But hell, our legal problems were a
full-time job for a team of lawyers and he's talking about
operating businesses.

"Well, it was just talk. No matter how he may have
viewed himself, he wasn't much of a businessman. His
approach was ivory tower. The retail guys, who get on the
phone and want an answer now if not sooner, lost faith in
him very early on. He wouldn't give advice, he'd give a
treatise, and they could never figure out what the hell he
was saying.

"Look, Steve was a good enough guy, but he was a fish
out of water."

• Capital Markets chief Mark F. Kessenich, Jr., appointed
July, 1986.

Plucked from Citicorp, where he had headed their North
American investment banking operations, Kessenich had
been reasonably successful there until his department's

earnings sagged in the first half of 1986, mostly as a result of poor trading performance. It was then that he was recruited by Rittereiser to make Hutton a force in capital markets. He was paid lavishly for it. The contract Rittereiser bestowed upon him guaranteed cash compensation of $4.7 million over three years, roughly $400,000 a year more than Rittereiser himself was earning. The word around Hutton was that Kessenich couldn't have done as well if he'd negotiated with himself.

From the beginning Kessenich saw his role as the point man in Rittereiser's master plan to transform Hutton from a modern wire house into an investment bank. This was a sensitive position calling for the skills of a diplomat as well as a financial innovator. But Kessenich had no interest in diplomacy. Flaunting a cold, cocky personality that made enemies throughout the retail system, he took an adversarial approach, antagonizing the brokers at every turn.

"Traditionally, the guy in Kessenich's position serves a dual role," Bagley says. "He buys and sells securities for the firm's own trading account, and he acquires inventories of stocks and bonds for the broker to sell. For example, for the retail brokers in the Southwest to service their customers, they need issues like State of Arizona tax-exempt bond issues. So the Kessenichs of the firm buy these bonds and build an inventory for the producers.

"But Mark rejected that role. He wasn't building inventories for anyone. Instead of buying State of Arizona bonds, he'd buy World Bank issues and try to make a profit trading them. As far as he was concerned, his mandate was to trade for the firm's account.

"No way was he going to accommodate the retail system. In his book the retail system was the farm team of the Hutton organization. Why bother with them when he could make hundreds of millions of dollars trading without the brokers and branch offices and sky-high commissions he thought were bleeding the firm?"

Blessed with Rittereiser's backing, Kessenich moved quickly to build a big capital markets department, adding hundreds of traders and researchers and support staffers to his costly fiefdom. "Mark would tell anyone who crossed his path that he had carte blanche from Rittereiser to build a world-class capital markets department," Bagley says. "If that meant firing just about every executive who worked there before his arrival because they didn't meet his standards, so be it. If that meant spending millions on personnel, technology, and services, so be it. If it meant beating retail over the head, so be it.

"He'd get up at the Hutton, Inc. board meetings and announce that he wasn't going to take a single position to accommodate the retail system unless they paid him to do it. Hearing this, the retail guys would erupt. I mean, they'd go bananas. Whatever decorum there was at the meeting would give way to a free-for-all."

At one point feelings against Kessenich were running so high that Rittereiser had to restore calm by watering down Kessenich's remarks to a meeting of retail executives.

"You misunderstood Mark," Ritt chimed in. "What he said doesn't reflect our approach on this. We are a retail firm, we intend to serve the retail side, and we're going to take positions that help you do your business."

Not really. Rittereiser's comforting statement, his "clarification" of the Kessenich philosophy, was based more on his aversion to confrontation than on a genuine attempt to discipline his capital markets chief. The shrinking of the retail system, the high-handed treatment of the brokers, the adversarial attitude that poisoned the internal culture, all continued without pause. "Ritt's remarks were just a temporary palliative," Bagley says. "Kessenich continued to operate the way he said he was going to. He never changed his position to accommodate the brokers. And he irritated the entire retail system to the point that we had a war between the trading and fixed income departments run by Kessenich and the retail system run by Jerry Miller."

"It was as if Mark started his own firm within E.F. Hutton," says Norm Epstein, "a firm not aligned with or encumbered by Hutton. For the first time in the firm's history, there was a business within the business."

• Marketing Chief Jerry C. Welsh, appointed March, 1987. Plucked from American Express, where he'd earned a reputation as a marketing whiz, Welsh arrived at Hutton with a flourish of trumpets. Proclaimed a superstar by the man who hired him, Welsh was supposed to bring a new sophistication and creativity to Hutton's marketing campaigns. Singlehandedly he would cultivate new markets, enhance clients relationships, and open whole new vistas for the firm. It was on this assumption that Rittereiser vested Welsh with enormous power, anointing him senior executive vice-president for marketing and strategic development, a member of the executive committee, and a key player in the much ballyhooed turnaround that would occur once Rittereiser's team was in place.

"Welsh liked to say that brokerage is a customer-driven rather than a marketing-driven business, and that he was going to change that," recalls Jerry Miller. "He was going to 'bring marketing to Wall Street.'

"Well, Rittereiser fell in love with that idea. 'Bring marketing to Wall Street.' He couldn't hear it enough. So he gave Welsh great latitude and backed him on virtually all of his projects. The problem is that while the concept of bringing marketing to Wall Street was good in theory, Welsh never found a way to implement it in any meaningful way."

A round peg in a square hole, Welsh never fit in at Hutton, which had always focused more on salesmanship than marketing. Throughout his brief tenure at the firm, he concocted a series of campaigns that struck many as bizarre.

"I remember when he came up with this oddball program called 'The Dream Exchange,' " says a former Hutton marketing executive who reported to Welsh. "Over the years the great dilettante and self-proclaimed art connoisseur Bob Fomon acquired works of undiscovered artists and proceeded to hang them throughout the Hutton offices. Everyone was supposed to marvel at his talent for spotting the next generation of Klees and Picassos.

"Enter Mr. Welsh, who decides he doesn't like Fomon's in-house gallery and comes up with a solution for disposing of all of the paintings. They'll have a 'dream exchange.'

"It works like this: we'll auction off the art to our wealthy clients. Then we'll have the children of America put their fondest dreams into art form. Like a kid who wants a car for his unemployed father. Or another who's always dreamed of going to Disneyland but can't afford it. They'd paint pictures of their dreams and send them into Hutton, where we'd choose the winner and, using the proceeds from the auction, would make their dream come true. Something like a corporate version of *Queen for a Day*.

"Helping kids make their dreams come true. No one can find fault with that. But people around the firm had a question: 'What the fuck does this have to do with the brokerage business?'

"Then Welsh had another scheme called the '1904 Society.' The way this shaped up, our biggest clients would get a membership in a club complete with a card and a pin and a little ego massaging from management. At one point Welsh was also going to strike a deal with a French vintner, buying out its entire production and making it available to society members alone. Why any of this would turn on our major clients was never answered.

"But wait—it only gets better. The next thing you know, we're going to videotape successful people and record their little melodramas on how they'd stared down the barrel of adversity in their lives, only to fight back and overcome. The plan was to get F. Lee Bailey to do a taping. Lucille Ball was also on the list."

The end product of all this was to enlighten that ever so lucky band, the members of the 1904 Society.

"Welsh's brainstorm was to put the segments on videotape, sending them off to the society members to watch at home. Then several times a year we'd gather the membership at special events where they would press the flesh with Lucy, F. Lee, and the like.

"An interesting idea? Maybe, maybe not. These things are subjective. But no matter what you thought of Welsh or his ideas, everyone asked that same question again: 'What does this have to do with the brokerage business?' "

Naturally, from Welsh's standpoint the connection was apparent.

"When it came to marketing, Hutton was in the dark ages. The dream exchange—that was a great idea that I only wish had gotten off the ground. It would have made for great press, showing Hutton in a charitable light, and whoever thinks we didn't need our image polished must have had their head buried in the sand.

"The 1904 Society—another great idea. Segmentation is the name of the game in marketing and we needed to segment our customers, to give something special to the major investors. If we didn't our competitors would be only too happy to fill the void.

"It's easy to say we should have done nothing but that wasn't getting Hutton very far in the mid-1980s, was it?"

• Corporate Finance Chief Kendrick Wilson III, appointed April, 1987. He was recruited from Salomon Brothers, where he had served as a managing director specializing in corporate finance for the financial services industry. Having served as Hutton's outside investment banker through the first Shearson merger talks, he was a familiar face to Rittereiser, who hired him to run Hutton's corporate finance department, replacing Dick Locke, who was reassigned to public finance. Like the others in Ritt's team, his ambitions exceeded the role he was hired to fill.

"Wilson came in and announced right off that he was going to be the next president of the firm," Bagley says. "It was as if the board had held a vote, named him president elect, and never bothered to tell anyone but Wilson. He had no time for investment banking. No sir, he had to run the firm.

"The problem is, Mr. Wilson had never run a group larger than eight people. That was his training for the presidency of Hutton. Somehow he thinks with this under his belt, he can manage a firm with thousands of employees. It was a fever for power—all the guys on Rittereiser's executive committee suffered from it. They spent more time battling each other for rank and position and clout than in trying to turn the firm around."

Widely touted as an administrative miracle worker, Bob Rittereiser strode into a firm crippled by divisional feuds and personal rivalries. To get the firm moving again, he had to end this internal warfare by creating a unified organization working toward common objectives. But he failed at this. Through the people he hired and through his failure to manage them, he would exacerbate rather than diffuse the civil war that raged within the house of Hutton.

Chapter 18 ⋀⋀⋀⋀

"Because of so many years of experience, I may have more wisdom than some other people, and the fact that I may have the power to outvote others is a good feeling. Most people will not admit that there is a great satisfaction and pleasure in power."

—Bob Fomon interview
M *magazine, August 1986*

The scene was a small alcove beside the bar at New York's Le Perigord, home of the power dinner, haute cuisine style. The occasion was a private welcome party for Perry Moncreiffe, just hired by Bob Fomon to run Hutton's London office. A born patrician, Moncreiffe was just the kind of Brit who made Fomon swoon. A classy repast in one of Manhattan's premier culinary institutions would show off Fomon's good taste. Moncreiffe would know he was in the right company. Or so Fomon planned it.

With the requisite pleasantries and champagne toasts behind him, Bob Fomon turned to the serious business of drinking. Soon after he was moved to address the assembled, subjecting his guests (and others who listened in at the bar) to a tasteless monologue that savaged every minority group from Jews to blacks to hispanics. In crude, often vulgar language he espoused all the racist clichés about stupidity and laziness and sexual proclivities. Embarrassed by this verbal assault, Jerry Miller tried to nudge him back to his place, but the CEO clung to his pulpit, spitting out his cesspool of disgusting jokes and prejudiced swipes until the full impact of the alcohol overwhelmed him. He collapsed in his seat in a drunken stupor. For the men gathered around the table, the siege was over. But it was not soon forgotten. The spectacle of Hutton's chief executive behaving in public like a deranged Archie Bunker left a haunting impression.

"That night when I went to bed, I kept replaying the incident over and over again in my mind," says former general counsel, Steve Friedman. "As I was tossing and turning, one thought kept gnawing at me: 'My God, Friedman, you've associated yourself with someone really terrible.' "

Bob Fomon's years at Hutton had been littered with unsavory episodes, but to those in attendance at the Moncreiffe debacle, he'd reached a new low. This time, though, the low was caused not just by the arrogance that had marked his reign as CEO, but by a painful readjustment to his new role in the executive hierarchy. In recruiting Rittereiser to join the firm, Fomon had believed he was simply shifting the F matter storm to a harmless lightning rod. For all his talk of putting a new president in place, Fomon never expected to relinquish his hold on Hutton. Why should he? Rittereiser had come in without the title of CEO, without as much as an employment contract.

But gradually, with a subtlety that Fomon never understood, Rittereiser began to acquire power. By nagging the board to make him chief operating officer, by installing his own management team, he began to squeeze Fomon out. Where the CEO once found drinking buddies, he now saw strange faces. The power he assumed that was his for life was slipping away. And he couldn't bear it.

"Fomon was like one of those tenth-generation English dukes who still lives in the manor house, but has to run tours through it to pay the bills," says a former board member and friend. "He'd look at Rittereiser as the tour manager and say to himself, 'What is this guy doing in my house?' Even though it was Bobby who invited him there, he resented every move Ritt made. He'd been the lord and master for too long to let someone else rule the roost."

"Fomon and Ritt's offices faced each other, and were connected by a joint secretarial area," recalls Andre Backar. "Well, for years all the traffic went through the secretarial area to Fomon's office. But suddenly it was going the other way, to Rittereiser's office, and Fomon couldn't stand it.

"On more than one occasion his secretary called me and said 'Come up and have lunch with him. No one stops by anymore.' It was really quite sad.

"During the same period, Bob was getting jealous, insecure over everything. When I took a walk with him along Madison Avenue—he always loved to walk the city streets—he complained to me, 'We've been walking for half an hour and ten people have said hello to you, but no one has greeted me. Hey Christ, do you know everyone in New York?' "

The more Fomon felt Rittereiser closing in, the more he wanted to fight back. Often he resorted to cheap shots meant to belittle Rittereiser in his adopted company.

"Nothing was beyond Fomon," recalls a member of the Rittereiser team. "You'd be sitting in Ritt's office, having a private conversation with him, when Fomon would just walk in, uninvited and unannounced. Without as much as a hello or an excuse me, he'd wander around the office, chain-smoking cigarettes, eavesdropping on the conversation. Only when he'd heard all he wanted to hear would he get up and leave. Still without a word.

"After watching this bizarre routine firsthand, I thought to myself: What happens when Rittereiser's visitors don't know who Fomon is? They must sit there wondering, 'Who is that masked man?' "

Much as he had bullied George Ball during his tenure as Hutton's president, Fomon rarely missed an opportunity to put Rittereiser in his place. "Once I was in a meeting in Rittereiser's office," recalls consultant Neal Eldridge, "when Fomon barged in, screaming, 'Eldridge, get the hell out of here.' It was Ritt's office and Fomon was telling me to leave. Of course, he had no business doing that, but Ritt never answered him back. Fomon told me to leave and so I had to."

In Fomon's Machiavellian view of the world, if the CEO wanted to waltz into the president's office uninvited and unannounced, that was his prerogative. He was, after all, the chief executive. Yes, Rittereiser was wielding power, but there were limits to that. As CEO, Fomon would see to it. He would do it by serving as a thorn in Rittereiser's side, by clinging to the areas of responsibility that were still his and his alone. He countermanded Rittereiser's orders and roadblocked Ritt's executives in their efforts to upgrade the firm's systems and management capabilities.

When Steve Friedman decided Hutton needed a more experienced executive to head public relations, he commissioned a search firm to identify suitable candidates.

"I didn't need approval for this," Friedman recalls. "Under Rittereiser's organization chart, public relations was in my bailiwick. But as a courtesy I thought I'd run my plan by Bob Fomon anyway. He'd always treated PR like his private preserve, so I thought I'd get his blessing before moving ahead.

"But it wasn't that easy.

" 'How much do you intend to pay this PR person?' Fomon asked.

"I was prepared for that. A number of financial institutions had just filled similar posts for $175,000 to $200,000. So I told Bob the salary range I had in mind.

" 'That's ridiculous,' he barked. 'I can get someone for less than half that—$75,000 at the most. No way we're paying $200,000 for a PR man.' "

Reading between the lines, Fomon wasn't arguing about salaries. He was arguing about control. He was saying, "Don't step on my toes. Don't think you guys have all the power, because I'm still here and I'm still chief executive."

Whether Hutton had a burning need for an overpaid press flak at a time when it was bleeding internally is questionable. But if an executive vice-president identified a recruiting need, his proposal deserved more than a flick of the wrist. And that's precisely where Rittereiser failed his management team, the company, and himself. By refusing to stand up strongly enough to Bob Fomon, the management whiz from Merrill Lynch was creating the biggest power vacuum of all. Just who was really in charge was unclear to the employees, the senior executives, and the board.

Although Fomon was now an easy target for an aggressive contender, Rittereiser lacked the killer instinct to knock him out of the box. Yes, he did complain about him to board members. He did protest that Fomon was countermanding his orders. He did suggest that the CEO was thwarting the will of the board, acting to preserve the old crony system, the status quo, rather than positioning Hutton for a new era of growth. But fretting and whining weren't enough.

"Ritt was too weak with the directors," says a former member of Rittereiser's management committee. "He could never take aggressive action against Fomon at the board level. He always stopped short of the full-scale indictment he needed to get rid of Fomon.

"There's an old saying: 'When you strike at a king, you must kill him.' But Ritt didn't have the instinct to do it."

While Hutton was fighting for its financial survival, Bob Fomon conducted an embarrassing interview with *M* magazine, complete with glossy photos of the CEO dressing beside his teddy bear, Ralph, and playing sugar daddy to two Southampton beauties forty years his junior.

The interview offered a sordid peak at Fomon's personal life and his chauvinist values. On the topic of women, the chief executive of one of America's best-known companies established himself as a raving sexist:

> Most women of any maturity have been married and most have emotional problems. And those problems get dumped on you. I have enough emotional problems that I don't need more. I'm old enough to be grandfather to some of the girls I take out. I mean, it's just a kiss-on-the-cheek kind of date. But why not? They're decorative, nice to look at, they have keen senses of humor. I don't want every dinner conversation to be what people think about Muammar Qaddafi. . . .
>
> I'd like a girl who's not interested in my business. I'd just as soon have a wife who knew nothing about my business . . . or what's involved. Who's not demanding on my time, someone whom I don't have to explain to why I'm not going to be there. Basically, I'm very shallow when it comes to women: They have to be pretty, and that hasn't changed.

In paraphrasing another enlightened observation from chairman Bob, the magazine noted: "He's not dying to get married again, he says, but he would, grudgingly allowing that there's a certain usefulness in wives: organization, especially of the social sort."

When the story hit the newsstands, it caused a furor

inside Hutton, not only with the women but also with the men who recognized Fomon's comments for what they were: the tired prejudices of a pompous old man who'd become a major liability to the firm. By mid-1986 the glorious gunslinging days were ancient history. In many ways Bob Fomon was like the old family hound hanging around the house waiting to die.

At this point Fomon had another opportunity to step aside. He could retire to Palm Beach, where he loved to vacation. Or he could simply recede into the Hutton woodwork, taking on the role of chairman emeritus. Here he could play out his days fretting about the art collection or the number of urinals on the trading floor.

But that wasn't Fomon's style. As he stated in the *M* interview, "I love my job—I couldn't imagine doing anything else." He'd wielded power for so long that he couldn't think of surviving without it.

Without real friends or close family ties, without a wife to share his days with, Bob Fomon was as he'd always been: alone. All he had was Hutton. And he wasn't giving it up without a fight.

Internally, his position was weak. With his F matter cronies gone and Rittereiser's textbook team calling more and more of the shots, Fomon had been neutralized. But he wasn't conceding defeat. He saw one last chance to exert his power and to exact revenge on Rittereiser. He would do it by selling Hutton.

Starting in the summer of 1986, Fomon, who always fancied himself an investment banker, began to shop Hutton to a list of potential buyers. He approached Bear Stearns's CEO, Ace Greenburg. ("He kissed me off," Fomon recalls, "saying 'if it ain't broken'—"it" being Bear Stearns—'why fix it?' ") and Paine Webber's Don Marron ("He said they couldn't afford it").

Learning that Hutton was in play, Shearson Lehman

CEO Peter Cohen proposed that his client, the Chrysler Corporation, buy Hutton.

On paper the idea was sound. Like many of America's premier smokestack companies, Chrysler was seeking to diversify away from manufacturing and into financial services. The automaker had already purchased Hutton Credit Corporation and, flush as it was with cash, could afford to gobble up the big quarry, E.F. Hutton Group.

At first the deal seemed to have some promise. Responding to Chrysler's requests for background data, Ed Lill provided a packet of income statements and financial projections, which were passed along to Shearson. Soon after, a secret meeting was held in a private apartment Hutton kept at 800 Fifth Avenue. The Chrysler team—a half-dozen financial executives, including the treasurer and the CFO—appeared enthusiastic.

"They wanted to know what kind of plans we had for the firm," Lill recalls. "They also asked for our thoughts on the securities industry in general, what direction we saw it taking in the near future.

"Overall it was a pleasant meeting. You left thinking that Chrysler was genuinely interested in acquiring us."

But the air came out of the balloon when Lee Iacocca showed up at the next secret powwow, held this time at Chrysler's corporate apartment in the Waldorf Towers.

"Cohen, who set up the meeting, thought it was going to be a momentous event, but it was a dud," Fomon recalls. "No sooner do we start talking when Iacocca asks, 'Why should we want to acquire E.F. Hutton?' You knew right then that Iacocca was just going through the motions. He was there as a courtesy to Cohen and for nothing else.

"That's when I said to myself, 'Fomon, these talks are a waste of time.' And so I got out of there as fast as I could.

"We never talked price. We never got anywhere close to that. The so-called negotiations died a swift death."

About the same time Hutton was striking out with Chrysler, the investment banking firm of Morgan Stanley was also pitching Hutton to another potential suitor, San Francisco-based Transamerica Corp. Aware that Hutton was in play and that Transamerica had bought and sold big positions in Hutton's stock over the years, Morgan believed the time was right to forge a deal and to collect the investment banking fees that would rain down from it.

"Transamerica had a sort of love affair with the idea of owning Hutton," says Morgan Stanley partner Fred Whittemore. "There were real synergies there. Both were sales-oriented companies. Both had big West Coast operations. And both had major insurance operations. The latter was the real catnip for Transamerica. As the foremost retail firm in the sale of insurance products, Hutton offered a built-in distribution channel for Transamerica's products."

Hired by Transamerica to create a plan for acquiring Hutton, Morgan partners worked through the summer of 1986, meeting with client management, putting a price tag on Hutton, structuring the terms of a deal to be presented to Hutton. Though there was considerable skittishness at the prospect of getting knee-deep in the volatile securities business, Transamerica's president and CEO Frank Herringer was gung ho, convincing his senior executives and wary board members to proceed.

Testing the waters of a friendly deal, Whittemore called Bob Fomon, a longtime acquaintance. From the outset Fomon was cool to the idea, claiming that he'd explored the possibility of a Transamerica deal on his own and believed the San Francisco company lacked the financial muscle to acquire Hutton.

"But I said, 'Bob, I think you'll find Transamerica to be bigger than you think it is. Give us a chance to put a deal on the table.' "

Although Fomon remained skeptical, Rittereiser, who

saw a place for himself in a Transamerica acquisition, was receptive to the idea. Meanwhile Whittemore flew to San Francisco for a tête-à-tête with Transamerica's senior executives, Herringer and chairman James Harvey. Meeting for an hour in Transamerica's corporate apartment, the men discussed a possible acquisition of Hutton, but the talks remained exploratory. Essentially, Transamerica was sizing up the situation and setting the stage for subsequent talks in New York.

That came at a September meeting held in Manhattan's Carlyle Hotel. Cloistered in a private room, Fomon, Rittereiser, and most of the Hutton management committee sat across the table from the Transamerica team. The mood was cordial and somewhat promising, with Transamerica requesting detailed information on Hutton's finances and Hutton agreeing to cooperate fully. At a follow-up meeting a few days later, Rittereiser, accompanied by Ed Lill, presented Whittemore with Hutton's 1983–86 income statements and projections for the next three years. The documents, which were promptly dispatched to Transamerica, set the stage for still another meeting, this between Fomon, Rittereiser, Herringer, and Harvey. No lieutenants. No investment bankers. Head-to-head between the senior managers.

Responding to Hutton's concern that Transamerica lacked the resources to buy Hutton, Herringer came on strong, assuring Fomon and Rittereiser that he could put an attractive offer on the table. Though a hard price was not discussed at this point, Transamerica was hinting at a bid in the mid $40's, about a $10 premium over Hutton's current market price.

As the negotiations continued throughout the early fall, Transamerica grew increasingly comfortable with the idea of acquiring Hutton, and much of its confidence stemmed from a faith in Bob Rittereiser's management ability. Viewing Rittereiser as the management miracle worker he had been touted to be soon after leaving Merrill Lynch, Transamerica hinged its takeover plans on having Rittereiser run Hutton as a semi-autonomous division. In the process they would kick Fomon upstairs, allowing him to stay on as chairman minus the title and the power of CEO. This feat Transamerica knew would take considerable arm-twisting by the Hutton board.

But it never came to that. In meetings with Salomon Brothers managing director, Ken Wilson, then serving as Hutton's investment banker, Whittemore floated Transamerica's target price of $48 a share for Hutton's stock. Though Transamerica's board had secretly authorized a higher bid in the low $50's, Hutton never heard it. Informed by Wilson of the $48 figure, Fomon effectively cancelled the negotiations, making it clear that at that level the talks were a dead issue. Though a formal counteroffer was never made, Fomon hinted that $56 was closer to the striking point.

"There was room for continued give-and-take, but all of a sudden Hutton started nitpicking the deal, complaining that it was part stock and insisting that they wanted cash only," says a participant on the Transamerica side. "We tried to respond to this—to see what we could do in cash, how far we could stretch—but Hutton stopped returning our calls. Something was wrong, something beyond the issue of price of the payment terms. The roadblock was so bad that we thought it could only be one thing: another bidder had emerged."

The hunch was on target. Having gained an insider's view of Hutton through the abortive Chrysler talks, Shearson's Peter Cohen began to think of marrying Hutton to his own firm. An aggressive acquirer who had been trained by Shearson's former chairman, Sandy Weill, and who had already acquired the venerable investment banking house of Lehman Brothers Kuhn Loeb, Cohen set his sights on Hutton's retail network, seeing it as a synergistic fit for Shearson's brokerage business. With an 11,000-plus sales force, the combined firm would rank as a behemoth of the industry, matching leader Merrill Lynch in size and scope.

Determined to claim Hutton, Cohen met with Rittereiser to propose a merger. Rittereiser was cold to the idea, framing his objections with high-minded platitudes about the sanctity of Hutton's independence. But it's more likely that Rittereiser feared a Shearson merger because it would dash his hopes of becoming chief executive. Cohen's interest was focused on Hutton's retail force, where Rittereiser had little clout, credibility, or experience. For this reason, he would be excess baggage in a Shearson merger. Fomon, on the other hand, favored the merger, seeing it as a way to deny Rittereiser his just desserts and to earn a premium on his Hutton stock.

With both men playing it close to the vest, Ritt and Fomon attended a series of clandestine meetings held between September 26 and October 14, 1986, with Cohen and James Robinson III, chairman of Shearson's parent company, American Express. When the talks failed to proceed beyond the exploratory stages, Hutton called off the discussions. But a week later, on October 21, they were back on track again with Cohen pressing harder for a deal.

At a Hutton management meeting called to discuss the matter, Norm Epstein argued that Hutton had been independent for eighty years and that there was no reason to give that up now. The Hutton name had history and tradition, and that was something worth preserving.

The more Epstein railed against the deal, the more Fomon fumed. If Robert E.F. Hutton wanted to sell his firm, who was back-office gremlin Norm Epstein to object?

After months of watching his power slip away, Fomon reached the breaking point.

"You're a greedy bastard, a green-mailer," he screamed, halting Epstein's monologue in midstream.

"Greedy?" Epstein responded. "I'm giving up a lot to stay independent. I'd get millions for my stock. You call that greedy? More to the point, Bob, what are you giving up?"

Fomon erupted in anger: "I'll be giving up everything. I'll be giving up this firm. I'll no longer be CEO."

Turning to face Fomon, who'd been standing beside him, Epstein was shocked to see a fist come hurtling toward his face, stopping an inch short of his nose.

"Bob had lost all control of himself," Epstein recalls. "He was going to punch me out. I don't know what stopped his hand from landing a blow, but we came as close as we could get to having a fistfight."

By November 2 the second round of negotiations had reached the point that Shearson was prepared to make an offer: $50 a share, pending due diligence, providing Hutton would officially commence merger discussions.

The issue came before the board at a regularly scheduled meeting on Friday, November 7. The directors, who had learned prior to the session that a Shearson offer was in the making, expected Fomon and Rittereiser to argue in favor of the merger. After all, they had been talking with Shearson for weeks. But on the day of the meeting, the directors were shocked to find that Fomon and Rittereiser were poles apart.

"Bob didn't come out and say we have to merge with Shearson," recalls former director Warren Law. "No, he had this rather aloof attitude. But it was nevertheless clear that he was in favor of proceeding on the Shearson deal. He just sort of threw it out that we should do it."

At the same time Rittereiser lobbied against the deal.

Arguing forcefully that to sell now would be to sell from a position of weakness, he pleaded for time. Soon the roaring bull market that was enriching the brokerage business would work its wonders on Hutton. Soon his textbook management team would put their own stamp on the firm. They'd turn Hutton around. I can do it, he told the board. Hutton can remain independent.

To a man, Rittereiser's team also argued against the Shearson deal, presenting an optimistic picture of Hutton's financial outlook for 1987. In the week leading up to the board meeting, division heads had prepared cost and revenue projections. One by one they presented the numbers to the board during the Friday session. Should all the plans hold true, Ed Lill held out the prospect of a $100 million profit for the year.

"We felt that we could turn the place around," Lill says. "We'd come through the check-kiting problem, we'd put a new management team in place, and now we wanted a chance to make it work."

As the unofficial leader of the board, Peter Ueberroth listened to the confusing mix of opinions in disbelief. He had come to the board meeting expecting management to recommend the Shearson merger, but as events turned out, Bob Rittereiser and the management committee were against the deal, and Bob Fomon was in favor of it. "It was management by confusion and I can speak for the entire board when I say we were dumbfounded by it," Ueberroth recalls. "We agreed something had to be done. We couldn't leave it up to Rittereiser and Fomon.

"So we set up a meeting between the outside board members and our investment bankers from Salomon Brothers, John Guttfriend and Ken Wilson. When we asked for their advice, they said, 'Look, it's your responsibility. You represent the shareholders. You have to decide where you want to go with this.' "

At this point the board was torn between believing Rittereiser's forecast that he could turn Hutton around and their responsibility to achieve maximum value for the shareholders. Although feelings were mixed, a majority of the directors leaned in Rittereiser's favor.

"Hutton was a big company with billions of dollars in revenues," Law says. "By slashing expenses by just two percent, Rittereiser could make a major impact on the bottom line. It seemed to me that if we just stopped shooting ourselves in the foot, we could get the financial recovery we needed. The recovery Rittereiser said he could deliver. So we went with him.

"Either he did a good selling job on the board or the board was ready to be sold."

But as Guttfriend reminded the directors, they had an obligation to the shareholders. At $50 the Shearson offer was a fair one. Flatly rejecting Shearson's advances on the strength of Rittereiser's optimistic projections could be seen as a violation of the board's fiduciary responsibility. At some price, a bird in the hand would have to be taken over two in the bush.

"That price was $55," says a former Hutton executive privy to the negotiations. "At that price the directors believed the value to the shareholders was so good that it would be their duty to sell the company.

"Conversely, if Shearson didn't bite, they felt the loss would be minimal or nonexistent because Rittereiser could engineer a comeback, adding even greater value to the shares. That's why they didn't accept the $50 bid. With Rittereiser making all sorts of reassuring statements, they saw no reason to jump at Shearson's offer."

After concluding final deliberations on their own, the independent board members summoned the inside directors —Fomon, Pierce, and Rittereiser—telling them that they had decided to respond to the Shearson offer by holding out for $55 a share and by insisting that Shearson agree to execute a merger agreement by the opening of trading on Monday morning, November 10.

With the deal in Shearson's corner, the management committee, which had been informed of the board's move, gathered in a conference room to await the outcome. All, each for his own reasons, wanted the deal to self-destruct.

"Word had it that Robinson was flying by helicopter from New York to his Connecticut home and that once he arrived, we'd get Shearson's answer," recalls Norm Epstein. "Well, that was the longest wait of our lives. The clock ticked, the hours passed, the tension built, but still there was no call from Robinson.

"After what seemed like an eternity, John Guttfriend excused himself, saying he was going to another office to call Robinson. When he returned a few minutes later I asked, 'What did Robinson say?'

" 'He's out,' Guttfriend replied.

"With that one of the guys jumped up. 'That son of a bitch,' he roared. 'This is the most important thing in our lives and Robinson's not even there.'

" 'Wait a minute,' Guttfriend said. 'When I said he's out, I meant he's out of the deal.'

"That's how we learned we were staying independent."

Behind the scenes, Robinson had been elated by Hutton's response and was willing to pay the $55 to acquire Hutton. But in the eleventh hour Cohen, who had pursued the merger to this point, quashed it. Not because of the money. Although $55 was more than he wanted to spend, at roughly two times book value the deal was fairly priced. Neither was time the key factor. Hutton's bid deadline left little time for due diligence, but this wasn't as prohibitive as it appeared. Having served as Chrysler's investment bankers when the automaker sized up Hutton, Shearson had already done its homework. What really bothered

Cohen was that Ritt's entire executive committee was dead set against the deal and that the board, swayed by Rittereiser, had little enthusiasm for it.

"From Cohen's perspective, acquisitions of this size are hard enough to do when the principals want to cooperate," says Scott Pierce. "When they don't, the risks are simply too high."

In rejecting Shearson's $50 bid, counteroffering with a take-or-leave-it $55 deal, Hutton's board had bought Rittereiser's pitch that he could turn Hutton firm around. It was a heady gamble, depriving the shareholders of a substantial premium over Hutton's market price, all on the assumption that Rittereiser, who to this point had failed to manage the firm effectively, could turn Hutton around. Now it was believed he could perform miracles.

On November 8, just hours after its Friday night marathon meeting, Hutton's board convened for an unusual Saturday session, this time to discuss Shearson's rejection of the $55 counteroffer. As the directors took their seats, Ueberroth—still shell-shocked by the management melee he'd witnessed—was prepared to make a move that was long overdue. He would end the open warfare between Hutton's president and its chairman.

As the meeting opened, Fomon spoke first: "The first item on the agenda is the sale of the insurance company."*

Ueberroth pounced: "No, it's not. The first item on the agenda is who's going to run this company."

Fomon was shocked. "What do you mean, who's going to run this company?"

"Just what I said. We have to decide who's going to run E.F. Hutton. We just sat here yesterday watching you and

*The E.F. Hutton Insurance Group would ultimately be sold to First Capital Holdings for $300 million.

Rittereiser bicker and feud. You're supposed to be a management team, but you're not a team at all."

Convinced that he could bully Rittereiser into submission, Fomon looked to the president. "We get along, don't we?"

"Tell him what you think, Bob," Ueberroth urged.

Ritt scanned the room. The moment of truth had arrived. For once he couldn't hide behind a memo. He faced Fomon. "Bob, I really need to run the company. It has to be clear there's a leader here."

With that, Ueberroth instructed the two senior executives to caucus between themselves, deciding who that leader would be. At the private meeting that followed, Bob Fomon stepped down as CEO, relinquishing the top spot to the handpicked successor he'd come to despise. Immediately after, the board elected Robert P. Rittereiser as chief executive officer.

Chapter 19

"When we brought in the management committee to announce that Rittereiser had been made CEO, we said that if you guys believe so strongly in your projections, go out and achieve them. The numbers are yours. Make them happen."
—Peter Ueberroth

1986 had been another bad year for Hutton. Like the distant rumbles that announce a thunderstorm, several shocks of that year should have warned those in charge that action, drastic action, was required.

"For all intents and purposes, Hutton hadn't had a real bottom line since 1984," says former CFO Ed Lill. "While there were operating profits for 1985 and 1986, these were illusory because of bonds we issued, called upper floaters, that would ultimately have to be written down and because we had to take another write down for bad collateral in one of our biggest accounts."

The latter problem stemmed from high-flying accounts opened by forty-two-year-old trader George Aubin.

A customer of Hutton's top salesman, Don Sanders, Aubin opened numerous accounts in the Houston office in 1984 and 1985. Quickly he became one of Hutton's most substantial clients, generating commissions of more than $16 million over the period. In the Hutton sales culture Aubin and Sanders were lionized: living models of the big-buck players and brokers that had shaped Hutton's reputation since the days of "Bet a Million" Gates.

But the Houston fairy tale took a nightmarish twist when Aubin accounts racked up enormous losses in his margin accounts. When he covered $46 million in margin calls in February 1985, the problem seemed to be settled. But far from it.

Aubin's checks, which were made out to Hutton Inc. (the brokerage subsidiary), bounced. It was then that Aubin's friend, businessman J. B. Haralson, pledged his interest in the obscure Mercury Savings Association of Wichita, Texas, in exchange for a $50 million loan made by Hutton Group to another of Haralson's companies, RBI Inc. Proceeds for the loan were used by Aubin to cover his insufficient checks, and with the balance, to continue trading through Hutton.

With this, the problem seemed to be settled. Aubin's margin calls were covered, a valued customer was back in business trading and Hutton had collateral in Mercury, which was on the sales block and estimated to be worth $75–100 million.

With little or no due diligence, Hutton accepted the deal (known internally as "Transaction X").

Because Aubin's losses were ostensibly covered by the Mercury stock, Hutton considered itself safe. But it should have known better. Soon after Hutton accepted the stock as collateral, Texas banking regulators labeled Mercury a problem institution. Hutton would find out just how troubled it was. Only days after the note came due, Mercury was declared insolvent, leaving Hutton holding the bag. It was another example of the firm's lax and irresponsible management.

"Sanders was more than Hutton's biggest producer, he was a legend in the firm," says a former Hutton financial executive who came on board after the Houston problem exploded. "He'd brought a lot of money into Hutton over the years, and he served as a role model for the account executives. That's why Fomon was afraid to limit the credit the firm was extending to Sanders's client, even after that credit far exceeded the value of the underlying collateral. He was afraid that Sanders would take his accounts and his commissions and join his old friend George Ball at Prudential-Bache."*

The other write-down problem, "upper floaters," were tax-exempt bonds issued in the early 1980s. The interest rates on the bonds floated with rates of interest on short- or long-term U. S. government instruments. The floating rate was designed to allow the upper floaters to trade at or near par for the term of the notes. For this reason, investors came to believe that Hutton would maintain a market for the bonds at par. Language to that effect was included in Hutton promotional materials used to market the bonds.

But when the credit ratings of three of the bond issuers were downgraded substantially, the bonds lost value. In an uproar over this, investors cried foul, demanding that Hutton repurchase the bonds at par. This ignited an internal debate, with Pierce and others asserting that the investor had risks all along and should accept the losses, and the retail force, its phone lines burning up with hostile clients, arguing that Hutton should buy back the bonds at par and absorb the losses.

"Initially, the management committee said Hutton had no responsibility to guarantee the price of the bonds, and when we checked with our legal counsel, they confirmed this," Lill recalls. "So the management committee, myself included, said that we shouldn't take the hit. But when we

---

*In subsequent court action on the matter, a U.S. district judge found no wrongdoing and dismissed all the claims against individuals; however, RBI Inc., essentially a shell corporation with little or no assets, was ordered to pay Hutton $48 million.

heard from the salesmen, they told us that the way the bond was communicated to customers, people thought we would guarantee them at par. It was then that we reversed our position and decided to stand behind the upper floaters."

In the end, a $55 million reserve was set up to re-purchase the bonds. This was part of a 1986 write down of $132 million that included $15.7 million for pre-TEFRA zero coupon bonds that were also repurchased at a loss from investors.

On another front, the rating of Hutton's commercial paper, the firm was in far more danger than a one-time loss.

Like other brokerage firms, Hutton carried the enor-mous burden of financing its equity inventory. Assume Hutton made a market in the shares of Apple Computer. If the firm had 1,000,000 shares of Apple at $30 each, it would have to finance that $30 million inventory until the stock was sold to investors. Even after the shares were moved, investors would have seven days to settle their accounts, meaning Hutton would have to carry the stock until the settlement date. Adding up all of its short-term obligations—the cash requirements for buying, selling, and brokering securities—Hutton had to borrow a whopping $2 million a day, mostly through the sale of investment-grade commercial paper to such financial institutions as insurance companies and pension funds.

Here Hutton faced two critical problems. As the earn-ings from its core businesses deteriorated, the firm's com-mercial paper slid in July 1986 from A1 rated to A2. This meant that it had to pay more interest for its massive borrowing—this at a time when it could ill afford the added expense.

But even more troubling, rumors were flying that the debt-rating agency, Standard & Poor's, was contemplating a further reduction of Hutton's commercial paper to grade A3 or, if the firm's financial conditions continued to deteri-orate, below that to grade B.

"Standard & Poor's made it clear that they were going to monitor our performance relative to our peers in the brokerage business," says a former Hutton senior executive. "Because we were not doing very well compared to the other major brokers, the possibility of a further reduction seemed very real at the time."

This was an ominous sign. If Hutton's paper fell below A3, it would be closed out of the institutional markets (which rarely buy below investment grade) and would be forced to turn to bank borrowing to take up the slack. But with the banks already leery about Hutton's fiscal condition, the firm would be hard-pressed to come up with sufficient cash to inventory stocks and bonds, to finance brokered transactions, to conduct its business. In short, Hutton faced a liquidity crisis. But at this point, Rittereiser and his chief financial officer Ed Lill saw no reason to panic.

"We knew there was a possible liquidity problem somewhere out in the future, but in 1986 we weren't thinking of catastrophes," Lill recalls. "We thought that by taking prompt action on a number of fronts, we could neutralize our problems. We had to bolster our permanent capital, which we did by issuing $250 million in bonds, and we had to cut costs, which we were planning to do. With a little luck and some decisive action we thought we could improve our core earnings, protect our credit rating, and get the firm moving again.

"At this time, everything seemed possible. Everything seemed within range. We thought we could turn Hutton into a profitable brokerage firm."

But at E.F. Hutton & Co., things were about to go from bad to worse. Shearson's $50-a-share offer, a chance to gain fair value for the firm, would never be seen again. Hutton's stock, which had soared on the basis of merger speculation to a record high of $54.25, soon plummeted to the mid-forties. The bottom line suffered as well, showing a 1986 loss of more than $90 million.* This occurred at a time when the rest of Wall Street was earning land office profits.

At this critical crossroads in its history, Hutton needed a decisive executive who would claim power, slash the firm's runaway costs, and redirect its marketing strategies. Instead it had a man who seemed incapable of making the hard decisions he'd been hired to make.

"We had a total change in management personalities," recalls Paul Bagley. "Fomon had been autocratic, imperious, whimsical, but always decisive. No one ever accused Bob Fomon of being afraid to make a decision.

"But with Rittereiser, it was just the opposite. He simply wouldn't make a decision. After all the great expectations that greeted his arrival at the firm, nothing ever happened."

Rittereiser's approach was apparent in the way he tiptoed around the field force, a key area for meaningful cuts. From the beginning of his tenure, it had been clear that the brokers' payout, which was higher at Hutton than the industry average, was a prime target for the accountant's scalpel. After years of coddling by George Ball and a long line of retail-oriented managers, Hutton's account executives had grown accustomed to a rich share of the commission pie that could no longer be supported in an era of discounters, negotiated commissions, and cutthroat competition.

Cutting back Hutton's payout, though, was a sure-fire way to antagonize the field and provoke the very confrontation Rittereiser dreaded. From his perspective, it was a lose/lose situation. Cutting the payout meant he could no longer play the role of management's Mr. Nice Guy. Compounding the problem, he feared that trimming the brokers' take would alienate the top producers and spark their exodus.

---

*After creating a reserve for exposure on its upper floater bonds.

What action Rittereiser did take was built around a laborious cost-cutting program called NOVA (National Overhead Valuation Assessment). Similar to the zero-based budgeting process Jimmy Carter had popularized during his tenure as governor of Georgia, NOVA required that Hutton's managers review their expenses from the ground up, justifying all of them and making cutbacks where they could not be supported.

"Once the decision was made to cut costs aggressively, we had to decide just how to go about that," recalls Ed Lill, whose methodical style of financial management, the inevitable by-product of a career in the Big Eight, matched Ritt's glacial approach to corporate stewardship.

"We could just go in and say everyone cut ten percent from your budgets, but that's not an educated way to do it. You may be cutting areas like financial futures that are profitable and that you want to grow rather than shrink.

"The other alternative is the NOVA process, in which you analyze every expense and ask, 'Is this something we have to cut, and if so, by how much?' It's a thoughtful approach and one we thought was right."

As the blueprint for Rittereiser's much touted turnaround, NOVA was presented to Hutton's board in March 1987. As the plan was unveiled, fifty high-level executives would head up teams evaluating all components of overhead with an eye toward cutting expenses. According to Ritt's scenario, NOVA would begin in May and in six months of analyzing, projecting, and cutting bloated costs, NOVA would chop $100 million from Hutton's overhead.

Addressing the board on NOVA specifics, Ed Lill announced that staff reductions in public relations, product coordination, and middle-management terminations had already saved $40 million. The remaining $60 million would come from cuts in the retail payout (savings of $12 to $15 million), reductions in the retail infrastructure (savings of

$12 million), and, as Lill put it, "another $10 million here and $12 million there and it all adds up."

Perhaps NOVA was the educated way to cut Hutton's costs, but in times of crisis, education has to take a back seat to expediency. While the fifty executives were studying ways to trim the infrastructure, the picture turned ever bleaker.

"NOVA was bullshit," says a former senior member of Rittereiser's inner circle. "It dealt only with administrative and operational costs, not the costs of marketing, sales, and investment banking, where the real problems were. I remember one point they were talking about cutting back the costs of the executive dining room, which would have zero impact on the bottom line."

"The crazy thing about NOVA was that it took people from certain parts of the company and put them in charge of cutting expenses in other parts that they knew nothing about," Bagley says. "For example, a guy in mutual funds would wind up on a NOVA team looking at our trading operations, even though trading was foreign to him.

"It was like the Maoist system, where they took Chinese farm laborers and made them engineers and turned doctors into field hands. No wonder NOVA never worked.

"At the same time we were going through this nonsense, the Salomon Brothers and First Bostons and Shearson Lehmans were making big cost-cutting moves. Salomon was taking losses in municipals, so it just went out of the business. That was a major step, a decisive action. But Rittereiser's team wasn't doing any such thing. They were playing with pennies."

At this point Hutton needed a hatchet man who would take out the machete and "go in and say everyone cut ten percent." Educated? Perhaps not. But it would get results, slashing more than a quarter billion dollars from the firm's 1986 overhead, and going far toward solving its fiscal woes.

But this wasn't Rittereiser's style. His indecisiveness continued to plague Hutton.

"A big clue to Ritt's management style could be gleaned from a homily he liked to recite," recalls Scott Pierce. "If he felt an executive was ill-suited for the job he held, he'd say, 'I'll put him in a position where he can't succeed.' In other words, he'd try to embarrass the guy into leaving. Anything to avoid firing him. That took tough, sometimes painful action.

"Look, we were suffocating under our own weight. Critical moves had to be made throughout our operations, but instead of making these moves, Rittereiser commissioned studies. But studies take time and we didn't have the luxury of time."

"Whenever you asked Rittereiser to make a decision on a critical business proposal, he'd utter these platitudes about global strategy and overall direction," recalls Bagley. "You'd sit with him for an hour and he'd say these things that sounded good, but nothing would ever happen."

"At American Express, where I'd worked before going to Hutton, when they wanted to cut costs, they didn't play NOVA games," says Jerry Welsh. "They'd call the managers in and say, 'Cut $25 million from your budget and cut it now.' You did it or you were history.

"My reputation was never that of a cost cutter. Jim Robinson liked to say that I was the only guy who could outspend an unlimited budget, but at Hutton I was a fiscal conservative. I said to Lill, 'Put in a T & E policy.' I begged him to. What was his answer? That he tried and got too much flack for it. Hell, that can't stop you. We had to cut big bucks and we had to cut fast. When Jerry Welsh is the leading advocate for cost control, you know something's wrong."

Soon after the Shearson merger talks collapsed, two petty soap operas unfolded within the Hutton hierarchy. It was then that Bob Rittereiser, the newly annointed CEO, and Bob Fomon, the former CEO and current chairman, decided to make themselves takeover proof. In a series of moves that would preoccupy the board for months, the two senior officers plotted to assure themselves of millions of dollars in golden parachutes whether Hutton lived or died.* At a time when the stockholders had every right to believe the senior officers were focusing on the critical issues that threatened the firm, the fact is they were engaged in a game of supermarket sweepstakes, Hutton style.

A little background is in order. The Shearson courtship had put the fear of God in Rittereiser. With the firm nearly sold out from under him, he was left feeling vulnerable. Having come to Hutton without a contract and having failed to secure one in spite of repeated increasingly desperate pleas to Bob Fomon and the board, he knew all too well that his $1.2-million-a-year salary was as safe as a naked option. Were Hutton to be sold, odds were that a savvy acquirer à la Peter Cohen would find the Yorkville Boy Scout eminently dispensable. To hedge his bets, Rittereiser set out to protect himself. Specifically, he was looking for a three-year guarantee of his annual salary plus attractive perks and bonuses. Although the terms were within reason for a Wall Street CEO, the board, now somewhat skeptical of Rittereiser's talents, decided to hold him to his own oft-repeated theme that salaries should be based on performance rather than guarantees.

"Those of us on the compensation committee told Rittereiser to redo his proposed contract based on a sliding scale that equated compensation to the company's performance," Warren Law says. "We said, 'Do well for Hutton

---

*When it represented Chrysler in the negotiations with Hutton, Shearson Lehman agreed, as a condition for gaining access to Hutton's records, not to mount a hostile action. But other suitors would not be similarly restrained.

and you can make even more than you're asking for. We're giving you the chance to become a rich man. But it has to be based on results.' He said he'd restructure the contract that way, but he never did. He kept resubmitting variations of the guaranteed-earnings theme and we kept rejecting it."

Recognizing perhaps that he needed help with an intransigent board, Rittereiser tried to turn Fomon into an involuntary ally. "Just as I was leaving for a vacation in Europe, Rittereiser came into my office, saying, 'Bob, you should have a contract. After all the years of service you've put in, that's the least you deserve.'

"He hands me this sample contract, which I can tell at a glance is very generous. That surprised me—his being so considerate of me and all—but then he puts this other document in my hand, saying, 'While we're submitting your contract to the board, I'd like to submit this one for me.' Instantly the puzzle pieces came together. His plan was to get the board to pass my contract and, while it was in a generous mood, to have his pass through on my coattails."

Were he to have his way, Rittereiser would have been protected regardless of Hutton's fate. Were the firm to be gobbled up by an acquirer or forced into a fire sale, he would walk away a rich man. In seeking this guarantee, Rittereiser was hardly alone.

The attitude that "you work for Hutton only if you have nothing to lose" permeated the Rittereiser camp. To his menagerie of pampered executives, the notion that they should accept a measure of risk in return for the whopping salaries they collected was absurd. Though they bragged of the thrill of turning the firm around, they suited themselves in such eighteen-karat-gold parachutes that they were bound to profit regardless of Hutton's fate. In a nutshell, the men who ran the company in the Rittereiser administration had no real stake in its success. For them it was a win/win situation.

"In order for me to give up thirty years in a firm where I was one of the top ten partners, I certainly wasn't going to go without protection," says Ed Lill. "My contract guaranteed me that I would be paid $300,000 a year in salary plus an annual $300,000 bonus for three years even if I was terminated due to a change in control of the company. I wasn't going to take an economic risk to go to Hutton."

To one school of thought, Rittereiser's generosity toward his top managers was self-serving. "One of my more cynical views is that he hired all these bonus-baby contract people and paid them so lavishly—including ironclad golden parachutes—for the purpose of establishing this as a precedent," Bagley says. "These sweetheart contracts were meant to be proof that this kind of indulgence was routine and that it should be applied to him as well."

While Rittereiser was on his hands and knees begging the board for a contract, in the other ring of this two-ring circus Bob Fomon was negotiating the deal of his life. If he would be leaving Hutton—and by now the handwriting was on the wall—he would be leaving as a wealthy man.

Befitting an imperious chairman who still thought of himself as the guardian of the great name of E.F. Hutton, Fomon sought a rich package of cash and long-term compensation. For months the board labored over the issues, devoting the great bulk of its meetings to Fomon's contract. From time to time members of the management committee were called in for their opinions on various components of the package. Although there were strong pockets of resistance by Ritt's team against a rich send-off for the fallen king, in the end the board caved in, handing Fomon a settlement worth well over $10 million. According to the terms of his retirement and consulting agreement, signed in the spring of 1987, Fomon would receive

$4 million on his official retirement date (May 6), a consultant's fee of $500,000 annually for seven years, and a supplemental income lifetime pension of $465,000.

Although the board dickered over the terms of the Fomon payoff, there was never any question that the old gunslinger would depart a wealthy man. After all, he deserved it, right?

Throughout the final chapter in the Hutton odyssey, the board of directors failed over and over to honor its responsibility to the shareholders. Though the Bell Report had transformed the board from an unwieldy cabal of insiders and drinking buddies into a smaller, more independent group, for the most part they were still weak and indecisive. Disgusted with Fomon, disenchanted with Rittereiser, they were unable to make a bold move, replacing both of them with a dynamic leader capable of turning Hutton around.

"Through late 1986 to mid-1987, Rittereiser kept feeding the board a steady diet of unbridled optimism," says a former vice-president who was privy to a series of critical board meetings. "Ritt promised, 'I'll cut $20 million in X months, $40 million by Y months, $60 million by Z months,' and on and on. At the same time he predicted that the bull market would catch up to us and bail us out."

For a brief moment it seemed as if he might be on target. Swept along by a strong stock market, Hutton reported a modest profit in the first quarter of 1987. To Ritt's team this was a sign that the pendulum had swung in their favor.

"Because the results had turned positive even before our cost-cutting measures were reflected in the financials, we were quite optimistic," Lill recalls. "We felt that once the overhead was trimmed back, we could boost the profits substantially."

But the joy didn't last for long. Reflecting substantial losses in bond-trading operations, second- and third-quarter results showed a loss, and there was no reason to expect that a recovery was imminent.

"As the board meetings came and went, Rittereiser's optimism turned out to be pie in the sky," adds the former vice-president. "Through it all you could see the board losing confidence in Rittereiser. Some of the directors even talked of dumping him, but the move was never made. Maybe they never had the balls. Or maybe they just ran out of time."

Chapter 20

"We were in shock. Here you have a firm in dire financial straits, one that's losing morale and employees and profits and is desperate for solutions, and what does top management come up with? A coloring book! The stupidity of the idea was bad enough, but to see it in the Wall Street Journal *was a fiasco. You wanted to hide until it went away."*

—Rich Braugh

In the last year of its life, the brokerage firm that Edward Hutton had founded was no longer the proud financial institution its customers assumed that it was. Beneath the slick advertising (now featuring Bill Cosby) and the familiar logo was an organization divided into enemy factions that pitted the board, the management committee, and the firm's principal divisions—retail brokerage and investment banking—against each other.

Rittereiser deserves much of the blame. As usual he was wishy-washy, telling the retail camp, led by Jerry Miller, that it was the linchpin of Hutton's turnaround and then, without blinking an eye, telling the same to capital markets chief Mark Kessenich. Classic Rittereiser. Tell 'em what they want to hear.

"When Ritt first came to Hutton, he spent a couple of hours with all the senior guys one on one, trying to put together a picture of the firm, its history, its strengths and weaknesses," says Jerry Miller. "And he was good at this.

Sizing up people, seeing where they fit in, where they didn't. He had a knack for it.

"At first I thought Rittereiser was going to be good for the firm. He tried to knit us together, to put together a positive image, to give management and the employees a common purpose. Unlike Fomon, who barricaded himself in his office, Rittereiser went on the internal speaker system and gave these leadership pep talks that people in the firm needed and appreciated. Finally, it seemed, an accessible leader was in charge again.

"Rittereiser made a good impression. He was a very decent guy. Moralistic. A terrific family man—he talked about his family all the time. He had good values. When he spoke, you believed him."

In what was music to Miller's ears, Rittereiser told him to take the retail ball and run with it. For the first time in his career, it seemed, he could build a brokerage business in his own image: sans George Ball, sans Bob Fomon.

"Ritt says to me, 'I've got tremendous problems all over the firm, particularly in the capital markets side, so I can't spend time on retail. I need someone who can hold that together. I want you to rebuild the whole retail system.' "

With this mandate from the president, Miller began to breathe new life into retail's sagging morale. The account executives were delighted to have an ally back in charge again. They knew that to Jerry Miller, "E.F. Hutton" was just another way to spell "stockbroker." If Rittereiser and his textbook team were going to rush off half-cocked trying to turn the old wire house into a Salomon Brothers, at least there was a broker's broker there to keep the scales balanced. Or so it seemed.

"With Jerry Miller back in charge of retail, we felt that there was someone there who knew how to do the job," recalls Tony Malatino, "someone who was competent and who understood how the company worked. And that was a good feeling.

"Whether there was still time for Jerry to do something, to make a difference, that we didn't know. It was like being behind 14 to 0 in the bottom of the ninth and suddenly Sparky Anderson is called in to be your manager. You know you have the right guy in the dugout; the only question is, are you too far behind to catch up?"

But there was another problem. Yes, Miller was in the dugout, but his power to manage the club was limited. The first hint that things were not the way Rittereiser had said they would be, or the way Miller and the brokers had interpreted what he said, came with the hiring of Jerry Welsh. Suddenly Miller's carte blanche had limitations.

"Ritt calls me up one morning and says, I've hired this guy, Jerry Welsh. He's coming from American Express and he's in charge of marketing. When I asked, 'What marketing, retail or corporate?' Ritt said, 'Well, you know, retail marketing . . . I think.'

"He thinks! I said, 'That's a pretty important issue to me, Bob. Do I still have retail marketing or don't I? If I don't have it, I should know it because I have to coordinate marketing with my product guys.' Ritt's answer: 'I'm not sure.' Can you imagine that? He's the CEO, he's hired a senior executive, and he's not sure what he's hired him to do—or not to do.

"I pressed on. 'What did you tell this new guy? How did you describe his responsibilities? Did you tell him he's in charge of retail marketing or not?'

"Well, Ritt danced around that one, too. Instead of answering the question, he sent me a goddamn press release. From the release I could see that Welsh's duties are extensive. He has responsibility for marketing of retail products, which I assumed was in my bailiwick as head of retail. When I asked Rittereiser face-to-face how he could do this, he didn't answer, and I gleaned from the silence, this ominous silence, that I wasn't going to get the autonomy I had been promised. I could sense that retail was going to be the whipping boy. Sooner or later the other shoe was going to drop."

The "other shoe" would be the carefully calculated plan to extract the bulk of NOVA savings from the retail organization. As Rittereiser's cabinet deliberated on the fate of the firm, they saw a drastic reduction of the retail arm as the best hope for salvation. Because they were outsiders with little or no retail experience, they had no loyalty to the component of the Hutton machine that had been the firm's great strength since 1904 and that, rampant inefficiency notwithstanding, was the only thing it did well.

As Rittereiser's team set out to shrink the retail division, an "us versus them" attitude poisoned the relationship between management and the brokerage ranks. The rift was split along emotional and philosophical lines. On an emotional level, the account executives felt neglected, shortchanged, and mistreated by a management that used them as scapegoats for the corporation's woes. To their way of thinking, they would make the money only to have headquarters blow it on ostentatious office buildings and enormous bond-trading losses.

"We saw that no matter how much money we were making in retail, the guys in New York were finding ways to blow it," says Hutton's one-time star producer Tony Malatino. "When you saw the kind of losses Kessenich's department would sustain, your morale would hit bottom. At one meeting when we were told of the most recent bond losses, I turned to my colleague Bruce Tuthill and said, 'We're not going to make it.'

"Rittereiser and his people thought they were above the brokerage business. They wanted to mingle in the glamour world of investment banking. And so they moved the firm from what was basically a risk-free business, brokerage, into the high risk business of trading. And those risks came to haunt us."

On philosophical grounds, retail split with Rittereiser on

his plans to pare back the number of account executives in the branch offices. To Jerry Miller, who was as bullheaded about limiting retail reductions as his adversaries were in achieving them, the idea that you could save money by slashing the head count in a given office was preposterous—the sign of a naive management that knew little about the finances of stock brokerage.

The clash came to a head in the summer of 1987. With Rittereiser under intense pressure from the directors to deliver anything near the projections he'd made, the CEO began to meddle in Miller's domain.

"He said that when he ran a region at Merrill, he fired about a third of the sales force—the low-end producers—and this left him with the best of all worlds: lower costs and higher productivity per account executive," recalls a former retail vice-president. "I knew what was coming next. He said, 'Why don't we do the same at Hutton? If we can wipe away the bottom third of each branch, we'll be left with the most profitable and productive producers.'

"Sure, sure, and the moon is made of cream cheese. This kind of simplistic thinking showed me how little Rittereiser really knew about retail. There were two major flaws in his strategy. First, say a branch office has fixed costs of $1 million and revenues of $4 million. If you fire the bottom third of the office's account executives, shrinking revenues by $500,000 in the process, you've just lost a half million dollars in very profitable, incremental dollars. Because it's hard to bring down fixed costs in a branch office, you'll have given up income without achieving a corresponding decline in expenses.

"Second, Rittereiser believed that in cutting away a third of the account executives, he could slash the headquarters costs needed to support them. While there would be some savings there, what he didn't realize is that by closing offices and firing brokers en masse, we'd be cutting away revenues before we could net enough savings to make up for that lost income. In the condition we were in, that would be perilous."

Miller's approach was to reduce retail operations by selectively closing down the dog branches and gradually peeling away those brokers at the low end of the production curve. It was a streamlining rather than a radical surgery. And it was too small and too slow for Ritt.

"The way I saw it, he wanted to sacrifice retail for the sake of trading and corporate finance," Miller says. "And I told him I thought that was the biggest mistake he could make. He was cutting away the only proven part of the firm."

To the Rittereiser camp, this was the born salesman talking, one who thinks he can always sell his way out of financial crises. And there is some truth to this. As the commanding officer of the retail forces, Miller had an obligation to support his troops. But as an executive vice-president of the firm, as a member of the management committee, and as a future presidential contender, Miller should have looked beyond the impact of his troops to the welfare of the firm.

"Jerry Miller had a myopic view of the firm—all he saw was retail's point of view," says Ed Lill, who clashed openly with Miller. "Contrary to what Jerry believed, you don't necessarily make a retail office profitable by filling empty desks. If an account executive isn't generating a minimum level of commissions in three years, he should go, whether his seat is left vacant or not. Keeping a poor producer in place adds to the variable costs: wire costs, telephone costs, support staff costs."

Essentially the rift between Miller and the Rittereiser camp boiled down to the last broker in a branch office. Whereas Miller saw him as a source of incremental profits (all the expenses were already covered, the last man could only contribute to the bottom line), the Ritt team saw him as a poor performer whose presence and the costs to support him drained the bottom line. The accountant saw it as half-empty, the salesmen as half-full.

"With all respect to Jerry Miller, he is a productive guy," Lill says. "Truly a salesman. I say whenever you let a salesman manage, you're in trouble.

"For years the retail people assumed they were making money, but they weren't. Before I came on board, only part of the operating costs generated by the retail division were allocated to it. They had this simplistic approach that would take fifteen percent of each branch's revenues and say that was retail's share of the operating costs. But that failed to reflect how much money the retail network was costing the firm. Some of their expenses were never subtracted from their revenues. So what looked like profits was just a mirage. Beginning in the early eighties, retail was only marginally profitable, if at all.

"But a system that had been spoiled for years didn't want to hear about it. So when we asked for more substantial cost cutting from retail, Miller objected. From his perspective the picture looked much brighter than it really was."

By July 1987 the management and brokerage camps were barely talking to each other. A fuse that had been lit at the now infamous DAC meeting in the summer of 1985 was now ready to explode.

"Everyone was screaming at everyone else," Miller recalls. "Rittereiser's people were telling me to cut retail drastically. But I said, 'Not when capital markets is hiring truckloads of MBAs. You want my guys to make all the sacrifices while the head office wastes all the money we make.' "

But the worst was yet to come. In mid-July, an outrageous incident would leave the firm humiliated. In the process it would reveal a Rittereiser more naive and out of touch with the Hutton culture than his worst critics had believed him to be.

It was going to be the corporate gala to end all corporate galas. More than that, it would be Bob Rittereiser's moment in the spotlight. He would knit together the factions dividing Hutton, rallying them around the management flag. Rittereiser would do the impossible. He would make Hutton great again.

With this grand ambition Ritt brought together Hutton executives from across the country for a two-day revival meeting in Washington, D.C. He would officially introduce his star-studded management team (rounded out only months before with the addition of senior executive vice-president Ken Wilson) to the boys in the field. He would explain the greater glories of NOVA to an awestruck congregation of employees. He would celebrate the turning point in the history of the modern Hutton. It would be the official coronation denied him in Hutton's sullen boardroom.

"Jerry Welsh had put together this incredible multimedia presentation complete with a film on Hutton's history going back to 1904," recalls Jerry Miller. "He'd done a first-rate job. The event promised to be a real success."

But as the curtain was about to go up, a misguided Santa spread presents through the hotel suites where the Hutton executives were staying. "I went to sleep the night before the meeting thinking that the get-together was a good idea—just what we needed to gain momentum again," says Rich Braugh. "But when I awoke the following morning, I found that something was askew. Hanging from my door was a package containing a copy of the *Wall Street Journal,* and, of all things, a coloring book. Thinking that the coloring book was some kind of hotel flyer, I tossed it on a table, tucked the *Journal* under my arm, and went down to breakfast.

"But when I opened the *Journal,* there it was again, a story about the coloring book. The guy I'm eating with says, 'Have you seen this?' It turned out we were giving out these things called *The Hutton Neighborhood Coloring Book,* as some sort of gimmick. Jerry Welsh, who'd dreamed up the idea, thought it would make a good publicity stunt and would help to highlight Hutton's problems for those employees who, by some freak of nature, weren't already painfully aware of them."

The approach was more suitable for Mr. Rogers's audience of preschoolers than for a gathering of war-scarred brokerage executives. With an accompanying box of crayons, Hutton executives were actually supposed to color in little pictures that illustrated in an allegedly humorous way some of the difficulties Hutton was facing.

Learning of the coloring book only hours before its release, Jerry Miller tried desperately to halt it, but ran into a brick wall with Rittereiser. "When we got to Washington, Ritt held a management meeting to go over the agenda for the event," Miller recalls. "It was then that he first mentioned, 'We have this coloring book.' When I said, 'What?' he repeated, 'We have this coloring book.'

"Well, I demanded to see it before it went out, so he let me have a sneak preview. Two pages were all I had to see. One shows a little girl at a lemonade stand with the sign E.F. Hutton at the top. The caption says, 'Last year we did a lot of business, but we lost a bundle of our lemonade.' Another shows our offices being dismantled under the caption, 'If we don't fix our problems soon, someone could even take our home away.' At the top, in parenthesis, it says, 'Color this gloomy.'

"I threw the book on a table. 'This is a disaster,' I screamed. 'How can you put this out? Every paper in the country and every one of our competitors is going to pick up on this. If we admit we're in trouble, that we're not the best on the Street, we're going to have everyone in the business prospecting for our AE's. What am I going to tell my people? That we're second-class and that we've decided to announce it to the world? This is a major problem, Bob. A major problem.'

"But Ritt wouldn't hear of it. He was going ahead with the thing no matter what I said.

"The next day the story came out in the *Wall Street Journal.* My managers went crazy. They jumped all over me, demanding to know how I could let this happen. But I said I didn't let it happen. It was out of my control.

"That same day Rittereiser passed me in the hotel and asked me how things were going. I said, 'Worse than you think.' He said, 'You're overreacting.' But I wasn't. It was absolutely the dumbest thing I'd ever seen anybody do."

Here again, Welsh saw himself as the savvy marketing guy forced to operate in an environment that knew nothing of marketing.

"The coloring book was doing something no one else at Hutton was doing," Welsh says. "It was addressing the fact that we had serious problems. The company was going bankrupt. The company was hemorrhaging. The coloring book was a whimsical way to say things that couldn't be said otherwise. It was unpopular because it tried to make the company deal with the serious problems it faced. And so no one wanted to do that."

At the time of the meeting, Welsh took most of the heat for the coloring book, but as the shock wore off it was Rittereiser who suffered the greatest damage.

"When we learned that Ritt knew about the coloring book before it came out and that he didn't act to stop it, we lost all faith in him," says a branch manager who attended the Washington meeting. "We came to the realization that he didn't have what it would take to run E.F. Hutton. We believed that he was in over his head."

Rittereiser was under siege from his board as well. As the months rolled by, and as his Pollyanna projections fell consistently short of the mark, the board grew disenchanted with their messiah.

"In principle, Rittereiser's plans weren't bad, his budgets weren't bad, NOVA wasn't bad," says Warren Law. "But it became increasingly apparent that the man couldn't act.

"Although the board never discussed Rittereiser, not formally at least, we were giving him all kinds of signals that our faith in him was waning. One of the reasons we failed to approve his employment contract was because we figured: why get tied up for three years with a guy we may have to get rid of?"

If a candidate had emerged as a likely savior, it was Peter Ueberroth.

From the beginning, joining the Hutton board had turned out to be more, and less, than Ueberroth had suspected. Recruited in 1984 by Bob Fomon, who suspected that the simmering F matter scandal would blow up in Hutton's face, Fomon saw in Ueberroth a white knight whose *Time* magazine Man of the Year of 1984 credentials would help to deflect negative publicity. Acting through his buddy Dick Jones, Fomon arranged a meeting with Ueberroth and pitched the board seat to him. Thinking the Hutton name a prestigious one to add to his resume, Ueberroth accepted.

Soon after, the lid blew off the F matter, leaving Ueberroth, a man deeply concerned with his public image, seething. He'd been left in the dark about the checking investigation, and hadn't realized how poorly Hutton was managed. As conditions at the firm continued to deteriorate over the years, as Fomon was exiled and as Rittereiser failed to take command, Ueberroth began to play an even larger role as the leader of the board. Insiders, from Warren Law to Jerry Welsh, pressed him to play an even bigger role.

"Peter was ambivalent about running Hutton, either as chairman or as CEO," says a former board member. "On one hand, I think he relished the opportunity. He was a competent, aggressive man who was confident that he could do a better job than Rittereiser. But on the other, he feared rolling around in the mud of Hutton's politics. Plus he worried that if he couldn't structure a turnaround, his image would be permanently damaged."

By the time Ueberroth had the reins of power in his grasp, the firm was rushing headlong to ruin. Filling the power vacuum that left Hutton virtually leaderless would entangle him in a corporate Vietnam from which he could not emerge with his image intact. And so he would resist the temptation to step in as chairman.

The issue came to a head when Bob Fomon stormed from his last board meeting in May 1987, stripped of his power and determined to wreak revenge on Bob Rittereiser. Thus he challenged the only man who could usurp Rittereiser's power to put his money where his mouth was, to take the kind of decisive action he had castigated the others for failing to take. He nominated Peter Ueberroth to be chairman.

The challenge Ueberroth declined. It was then that Fomon, shades of the old gunslinger, responded in his own inimitable style. Staring eyeball to eyeball with Ueberroth, he had a parting message:

"You're a wimp."

"It's not that Peter didn't want to be chairman, he did," says Scott Pierce. "But Bob Rittereiser killed the idea. Learning of the threat to his power, he asked Ueberroth not to accept the chairmanship, holding that would send the wrong signal to the new management team.

"Perhaps the most significant thing isn't Peter's failure to become chairman but the board's refusal to bestow that title on Rittereiser. He asked for it at that very meeting, but was denied. Clearly, that was the board's way of indicating that they lacked faith in Rittereiser."

By the early fall of 1987, control of the firm had subtly shifted from Bob Rittereiser to Peter Ueberroth. As the de facto chairman of the board, and as an action-oriented man impatient with delays and excuses and the endless stream of false hopes that came out of Rittereiser's office, his natural instinct to take control led him to fill the vacuum left by the man who called himself CEO.

"Peter would hold private meetings in Rittereiser's office, where he would get real tough with him, demanding to know: 'What are we going to do about this and this and this?' " says consultant Neal Eldridge. "After a few of these sessions Ritt began to see Peter closing in on him. Once he screamed at Ueberroth, 'You're not going to use this company as a platform to the Senate.' "

Had Ueberroth wanted the role of Hutton's chairman, by now there was no doubt that the job would have been his hands down. As a businessman, as a leader, and as the one director forceful enough to take control of a drifting company, he was the best person on board to fill the post.

But he was more convinced than ever that Hutton was too far gone to save. Even his own considerable talents would fall short of the task at hand. Instead he began to favor a sale of the firm as the best way to salvage its assets.

Soon there would be no other choice.

Chapter 21

"Rittereiser and his managers were running around like Chicken Little, saying, 'The sky is falling, the sky is falling.' That's how they dealt with the crisis. Rather than making decisions on how to weather the storm, they ran through the halls creating a climate of panic that would make it impossible to salvage the firm."

—Paul Bagley

On October 19, 1987, the impossible happened. Nearly sixty years after the stock market crash of 1929 stunned the nation, the market crashed again, plummeting 508 points in a single day.

History had repeated itself. The worst nightmare of the financial community had turned to reality. In spite of the checks and balances built into the system to prevent a devastating decline, the market collapsed under the weight of its speculative fever.

In the course of a dark and dismal afternoon, the Dow Jones averages leveled the coup de grace to Rittereiser and his management team. Their NOVA-based plan to turn Hutton around had run out of time.

Until the wee hours of Black Monday, Rittereiser's tenure had been a management by faith in the market's ability to sustain superheated prices and to generate record volumes and burgeoning commissions. Faith that all of this would give the CEO time.

265

"Back in the late summer of '87 Ritt and I had formulated a plan to reorganize top management, making Ken Wilson the number two man and giving him control over capital markets as well as corporate finance," recalls Neal Eldridge. "The idea was to get someone in there who could bring some control to the organization.

"Well, Ritt went to Bermuda, promising to act on the plan when he returned. But he never did. Like so many other moves he said he would take, this one never left the drawing board."

Whether he ever really planned to act on Eldridge's plan is immaterial. The day the market crashed, he ran out of time.

"We knew a bear market was coming, but we thought it was six to nine months off when it struck," recalled Ed Lill, who seemed perplexed that the stock market would veer from Hutton's projections, spoiling what was a neatly drawn scenario that called for gradually cutting expenses and improving the company's core earnings by year end 1987. "Abruptly the crash threw our plans out of whack."

The worst fallout from the crash was the fear it unleashed. Haunted by visions of their life savings being smothered in an avalanche of sell orders, small investors panicked. They were not alone. Financial professionals suffered severe bouts of anxiety and disillusionment. In the space of an afternoon the ticker tape in the sky had wiped away generations of wealth. Suddenly blond-haired patricians with tiny replicas of the Federal Reserve Board building embossed on their ties thought of stuffing their money in a mattress. Fear, as Franklin Roosevelt had warned, was the real enemy.

It proved that way for E.F. Hutton & Co. An incident that began a few days after the crash—and that seemed, in the scope of things, like a minor event—would unleash a reign of fear that would lead to the end of the beleaguered firm.

In the tense days following the crash, the world crossed its fingers and waited for the dreaded repercussions. Could the giant brokerage houses, whose expenses had mushroomed along with the meteoric rise in the Dow, absorb the impact of Black Monday and continue as going ventures? Were the rumors of impending doom at some of the most venerable houses just that? Or were they harbingers of even greater disasters?

With speculation running at a fever pitch, Cable News Network (CNN) decided to explore how investors would fare if their accounts were trapped in an insolvent brokerage house. In preparation for the broadcast, a CNN producer called Standard & Poor's brokerage analyst Clifford Griep to ask how the crash had affected the brokers' credit ratings.

In response Griep read a press release issued by S&P days after the crash. The tone was reassuring. "The financial strength of the brokerage firms S&P rates hasn't been materially affected by recent stock market events," and as such S&P is "taking no rating action at this time." But Griep added that the agency was watching the industry closely, especially those firms with the lowest credit ratings: Paine Webber, Oppenheimer & Co., Bear Stearns, and E.F. Hutton.

To a world ready to take bad news and blow it out of proportion, this was the worst thing that could have happened to Hutton. Just when it needed to instill investor confidence, it was described as a weak link in the financial chain: the last place a prudent investor would want to keep his money. In a climate of wholesale panic the message got around fast.

"Right after the CNN broadcast, our phones rang off the hook," says Standard & Poor's vice-president Byron Klapper. "It turned out that the network aired a chart highlighting the four lowest-rated firms, indicating that they had 'weak balance sheets.' We never said anything about the firms' balance sheets, but in an environment of fear, people believed what they wanted to believe."

To many the CNN report was a red flag that Hutton's commercial paper rating, already at A2, would be further reduced to A3, the lowest investment grade.

"CNN's report triggered a deadly crisis for us," recalls director Warren Law. "To understand how that could happen, you have to put things in context.

"After October 19 rumors were swirling about every kind of bank and brokerage house being in big trouble. Certainly Hutton wasn't spared. Our stock had plummeted to $11 and many feared it would sink lower. The rumors didn't help. There were rumors that Hutton was closing its doors. Rumors that the firm was going into Chapter XI. At a board meeting at another company where I was also a director, I heard a rumor that Bob Fomon had committed suicide. The rumors were awful.

"Then to top it off, the CNN program leads people to believe that Hutton will be downgraded by Standard & Poor's. The impact was devastating."

Nowhere more so than in the retail trenches, where customers, alarmed by the CNN report, began to pull their accounts from Hutton. "We had a mini run on the bank," recalls Jerry Miller. "Fearful that we were going under, investors started withdrawing their money, switching their accounts to other brokerage firms. It was a tense situation that could easily turn into a catastrophe.

"Understand, fear was spreading through the ranks. It gripped the account executives as well, causing a sharp rise in defections and prompting a lot of others to think about leaving, too. At this point we were vulnerable to systemic losses."

The picture also looked troubling to the money markets where institutional investors bought and sold Hutton's commercial paper and where bank lines kept Hutton alive. "In the weeks after the crash I spent at least half of my time on the phone with the banks," recalls Ed Lill. "Every time a rumor spread about Hutton going into bankruptcy or becoming illiquid, I'd have to reassure the bankers that none of this was true. I'd do it by going through all the financial data with them, showing that we could still meet our obligations and that we were worthy of additional funding."

For the most part the hand-holding worked. Except for Bankers Trust and a small number of banks in Europe and Japan, Hutton's lead lenders stayed with the firm. Most active were Morgan Guaranty, Citibank, First Chicago, Bank of America, and Security Pacific.

But then, like a self-fulfilling prophecy, rumors of the S&P downgrading appeared to be coming true. Alarmed by Hutton's deteriorating financial condition, S&P informed Rittereiser (who, in turn, informed the board) that Hutton's credit rating was coming under close scrutiny. News that S&P might act on Hutton shocked the board, coming as it did only weeks after Ritt had posted another in his string of optimistic reports.

"In a post-crash briefing session Rittereiser's team told the board that Hutton had come through the debacle in relatively good shape," says Jim Freund. "In spite of the rumors about a lot of firms being hit hard by Black Monday, they indicated that Hutton had been spared the worst. So the directors felt they had reason to breathe easy."

"In the weeks following October 19, the directors had held a series of telephonic board meetings," recalls Peter Ueberroth. "For a company as big as Hutton, a company that was not meeting its projections, it was important for us to talk often and keep up to date on what was going on.

"And what was going on, we were told, was okay. Hutton's market losses, management assured us, were minimal. There was no crisis at hand."

It was in this mood of remarkable optimism that the board met for a regularly scheduled meeting on November

10. Although Law and Ueberroth had immersed themselves in the numbers and asked tough questions about Hutton's financial condition, the answers they got made it seem as if the crash had been little more than a tempest in a teapot.

"According to Rittereiser and Ed Lill, who made presentations to us, the company was in the best capital position and the most liquid position it had been in in two years," Ueberroth recalls. "They said, 'We've weathered October 19. In spite of the rumors, we're not being downgraded by the credit agencies—we've confirmed this with Standard & Poor's—and everything is really good.'

"So we told Rittereiser and his team to go after those NOVA projections and make them work. And with that we concluded the meeting, thinking everything was okay.

"But two days later I got a call from Rittereiser. 'You have to come over here,' he says. 'I need to see you. Now!'

"Well, I rarely went to Hutton save for board meetings, but judging by the urgency I detected in Rittereiser's voice, I went to see him.

"Incredibly, I found the picture that had been drawn for us 48 hours before was now dramatically different. We had some real setbacks. The credit agencies had reversed their position and Hutton's commercial paper wasn't turning over. We had a crisis here, a crisis there. Faced with these pending disasters, Ritt says, 'We'll have to organize a meeting somewhere down the line.'

"I said, 'No, we're going to organize it right now because you just told me things I don't want to know alone.' So we set up a telephone conference informing the board of current conditions and how perilous they were. I told the directors, 'You have to hear what I've just heard. It's night and day from what we were told on November 10.' And with that I put Rittereiser and Ed Lill on the line to run down the problems they'd run down for me."

For the first time Rittereiser's team recognized that they were facing a crisis.

"On the Tuesday after the stock market crashed, Rittereiser got on the firm-wide communication line to tell us all that rumors and press reports of Hutton's financial difficulties were absolutely untrue," says a former broker in Hutton's Brighton, Michigan, office. "He said just go out and conduct your business as usual.

"But only a few days later, there was a complete about-face. The office, they said, was being closed. We had ten days to sew up our affairs and clean out our personal belongings. But then a day after that they said, no ten days—you'll have to be out of here in two days. In less than 48 hours, the office that had been told that everything was hunky-dory was shut tight."

"Suddenly we found ourselves in a hole that promised to get deeper and deeper," Lill recalls. "With the small investor spooked out of the market, our retail revenues were down 30 percent. For a firm that relied on retail commissions for 85 percent of our income, that was devastating. Worst of all, we knew that this precipitous decline in commission revenues was not going to be a short-term blip. It would be a fact of life for at least a year. Although we'd been cutting costs, with revenues down by a third there was no way we could cut enough to make up for that loss of income.

"In my presentation to the board I made it clear that we didn't have the resources to sustain the firm through this kind of long-term siege. The way I figured it, by early 1988 our capital would be depleted to the point that we would be in very serious straits.

"To complicate matters, the credit rating agencies called to say that a downgrading of our commercial paper to A3 was imminent. With this in mind, they wanted to meet with me to see our plans and projections. But when I assembled the data they wanted, I came to a terrible conclusion. When they saw the numbers, they would downgrade. There'd be no changing their minds."

Faced with this prospect, Lill informed the board that Hutton would have difficulty turning over $500 million of its commercial paper. Some of this could be made up with bank loans, but in any case Hutton would be pressured to cut back on its operations, mostly reducing inventories of securities available to the brokers. This would slash expenses, yes, but it would also cut revenues at a time when Hutton could ill afford it.

One reason for the coming crunch was that Hutton had already spent its employees' own money, and would have to replace that capital.

"Part of the firm's capital base was in the form of employees' deferred compensation—money employees kept with the firm to defer taxes on it," Lill says. "While this was an attractive strategy when personal tax rates were in the 40 to 50 percent range, it became much less attractive when individual tax rates dropped to 28 percent. So a good many employees made the determination to withdraw their deferred compensation, about $280 million, which after the required one year's notice would be coming out in February 1988. We'd made provisions to replace some of that money in 1987, but with 1987 losses coming as they were, we had eaten into that replacement capital. So we knew that in February, we faced a very big hit."

The picture was turning ugly. The threat of S&P action was looming over the firm, threatening to interrupt its commercial-paper financing. Hutton's most valuable asset, its top brokers, were jumping ship, taking their clients and their commissions with them. That's when everyone recognized that a merger was inevitable.

"As soon as word of our S&P problem leaked out to the Street, competitors started chanting, 'Hutton is going under, Hutton is going under,' " recalls Warren Law. "They were vicious about it, chasing after our brokers, warning them that 'Hutton's going belly-up, and when it does, your clients will have their accounts frozen. That means they can't trade. That means you can't make money.'

"If you don't think that has an impact, you've never worked in this business. Rumors about a financial institution going under have the same effect as yelling fire in a theater: everyone heads for the exits. All of a sudden we were losing brokers. Lots of brokers. Top brokers. Some left because they feared for themselves, others because they were forced into it by frightened clients. Swept up in the wave of rumors, clients would get hysterical. 'Look, I don't want to get caught in a mess,' they'd say, 'If you don't leave, I'll find another broker.' So the brokers left. We lost sixty in one week."

Just as things seemed to be as bad as they could get, they got worse. Another devastating rumor spread: the SEC was going to freeze employment, prohibiting brokers from switching employers for six months. For account executives sitting on the fence, this was a catalyst for action. They wanted to get out before the freeze took effect.

"Putting the pieces together, we knew that if the current trends continued, the firm would be decimated in a matter of weeks," Law recalls. "There'd be nothing left to sell. Our competitors had deep pockets to bail them out. They had Sears and American Express and Prudential Insurance behind them. But we had no one. We couldn't survive as an independent any longer, not in the shape we were in. Not in the shape Wall Street was in. It was sell now or lose it all. If Hutton was to be sold for any semblance of value, a deal would have to be closed quickly."

Throughout the late summer and early fall of 1987, Bob Fomon—now exiled from the company he considered an extension of himself—had searched for a buyer who would snatch Hutton away from Rittereiser. As always with Fomon, money was a motive, but not the only one. Equally important to a proud man who'd been evicted from his castle, selling Hutton would give him the last word. Even from retirement he would strike out, proving that Robert Fomon still called the shots.

Acting as his own investment banker, Fomon made the rounds with two former Hutton executives, Pru-Bache's chairman, George Ball, and Drexel Burnham's chief, Fred Josephs. His pitch, one he would also make to Bear Stearn's Hank Greenberg, Paine Webber's Donald Marron, and American Express's Jim Robinson, was that Hutton's retail business was still strong and profitable. Adding this force to their own brokerage network would create a formidable power on Wall Street.

Ball, who had his hands full trying to ignite a still sluggish Pru-Bache, brushed off the idea, and Joseph, who was dealing with an insider trading scandal at Drexel, recognized that the last thing he needed was to join forces with another tainted firm.

"Fred said he'd like to do it, but the problems were too great to surmount," Fomon recalls. "He worried about all the negative publicity such a deal would unleash. It would be like the pimp marrying the whore."

Fomon's sales pitch struck the most promising chord outside of the brokerage industry, piquing the interest of Sanford Weill, chairman of Commercial Credit Corp. A Wall Street legend who'd built Shearson into a brokerage giant and then sold it to American Express (only to be forced out in a power struggle with Jim Robinson), Weill dreamed of a triumphant return to the business he loved best. Purchasing Hutton would provide the ideal vehicle.

The more Fomon talked, the more Weill liked what he heard. With Hutton's very survival on the line, it was in desperate need of a strong and imaginative leader. Of a Sandy Weill. He could see the headlines: "WEILL REVITALIZES A SAGGING HUTTON. THUMBS HIS NOSE AT SHEARSON LEHMAN."

Fomon, who relished the idea of selling Hutton out from under Rittereiser—and the prospect of earning a $3 million investment banking fee—convened a secret powwow in the first week of November at his New York co-op. Seated in his handsomely appointed den overlooking Central Park, amid English equestrian paintings, antique andirons, and hand-painted porcelain bowls, Fomon introduced Warren Law, Dina Merrill, and at least one other director to the man who would buy the company. Shortly after, he flew his white knight out to Los Angeles to introduce him to Ueberroth and director Tom Talbot.

"Ueberroth had agreed to attend the meeting," Fomon says. "But at the last minute he backed out.

"He said he was going to be out of town but I heard he was close by at the Century Plaza Hotel. So I called him there repeatedly, but he refused to answer my calls. I even had some materials sent over to the hotel, but he failed to acknowledge this too. It was amazing to me because he'd always told me he thought Sandy would be a good choice to acquire the firm. But when the time came to act on that, he backed off. Why? Because he didn't want to ruffle Rittereiser. So we held the meeting without Ueberroth."

At these sessions, kept secret from Rittereiser, Weill outlined his interest in Hutton and how he proposed to acquire the company.

"At this point Fomon thought he'd found his buyer," recalls Paul Bagley. "I happened to speak with him after the New York meeting and he told me he thought the deal was a shoo-in. He was really excited about it."

But the deal Weill proposed, a cautious one that reflected Hutton's sorry state, would be hard to sell to the board. In essence, he offered to swap Commercial Credit stock for Hutton stock, merging Hutton into Commercial Credit, where he would preside over the combined entity as CEO.

"But he would only pay market value for Hutton's shares, and that was the stumbling block," says James Freund. "Because there was little or no premium for the shareholders, there was no incentive for the board to accept the deal."

When word of the Weill talks reached Rittereiser, he was furious over Fomon's continued meddling.

"The night before its November 10 meeting, the board had a dinner at a Manhattan restaurant," Ken Wilson says. "Ritt went in expecting to talk about the need to search for capital—which was a euphemism for finding a buyer—and about some management restructuring he wanted to do. But before he could get a word out, some of the directors told him they'd met with Sandy Weill and that they thought there might be an opportunity to sell the company to Commercial Credit.

"Well, Ritt was dumbfounded by this. Though he'd heard some rumors about Weill's interest, he had no inkling that directors had met with Sandy. He was blindsided by it, and it shook him to the core.

"The next morning he came into my office with this horrible look on his face like he was going to die. The thing upset him so badly because I think it was then that he realized how low his stock had sunk with the board."

Instructed by the board to further explore the Weill offer, Rittereiser met with Commercial Credit's CEO twice that week, once in New York and then over the weekend at Weill's home in Greenwich, Connecticut. Although Weill, who can be as charming as he is shrewd, implied that there would be a place for Rittereiser should Commercial Credit acquire Hutton, it was clear to most that an acquisition by a brokerage titan of Sandy Weill's stature would knock Ritt out of the CEO's box.

Writing a new rule that forbade corporate officers past or present from trying to sell the firm or its assets, Rittereiser had the rule printed out and sent to Fomon.

Rittereiser's communiqué by photocopy amounted to a not-so-veiled threat: keep up the sales pitch and your retirement income (which requires that you abide by corporate rules) will be cut off.

Rittereiser also hired his own investment banker, commissioning Pete Peterson, former chairman of Shearson, now head of the boutique M&A firm the Blackstone Group, to represent him.

"Ritt had been talking with Peterson and his partner at Blackstone, Steve Schwarzman, about arranging for a capital infusion at Hutton, when Schwarzman suggested that because Hutton was in play, it would be a good idea for Ritt to hire Blackstone in an advisory capacity," recalls an investment banker who was privy to the discussions. "And Ritt agreed to this, not only to have Blackstone search for a buyer, but even more important to gain Peterson's help in dealing with the board.

"The way Ritt saw it, he could borrow from Peterson's prestige to regain the credibility he'd lost with the directors. He thought that if he could say, 'I want to take this particular action, or talk to this particular buyer, and Pete Peterson thinks it's a good idea too,' he could get the board to side with him. In effect, he was hiring Peterson as a corporate ally."

At the same time, Ritt (urged by Ken Wilson) directed Hutton's long-time investment bankers Salomon Brothers to join Blackstone in the search for a suitable buyer. If Hutton was to be sold, he would arrange the deal.

"For a while Rittereiser saw salvation in U.S. West, a Denver-based company that was one of the seven Bell Telephone spin-offs," recalls Paul Bagley. "Because U.S. West was known to be interested in acquiring financial service businesses, Rittereiser dispatched Ken Wilson to meet with West's president, Jack MacAllister.

"Rittereiser and Wilson were practically on their knees to U.S. West. But the deal fell apart. There just wasn't enough interest at West to make the acquisition."

*   *   *

In the week November 16–23, the investment bankers offered Hutton to a hot list of prospective buyers, all united by a common thread: they were known to be interested in buying or expanding into the financial services sector and they had the resources to gobble up a company the size of Hutton. In hastily arranged meetings, the bankers called on U.S. West, Equitable Life, Bell Atlantic, General Electric, Xerox, and leading European and Japanese securities firms.

At this point negotiations with Transamerica resumed again, bringing some promise, but that faded quickly. Transamerica was interested, but their interest never developed into an attractive bid. Essentially, they were offering to make a modest cash infusion that would have to be repaid in part with Hutton's earnings, which would be an additional drag on the bottom line.

Going from bad to worse, one of the Salomon Brothers partners sneak-previewed the deal to Standard & Poor's, hoping that the proposed arrangement with Transamerica would forestall a downgrading of Hutton's credit rating. But when he raised the $64,000 question, 'Will this transaction bolster Hutton's credit standing?' S&P had only bad news. From their standpoint the deal would do nothing to help Hutton.

At the outset Salomon and Blackstone hoped to keep the Hutton deal away from competitors in the brokerage community. With the sharks already circling the waters, smelling blood in Hutton's wounded credit rating, announcing that the company was up for sale would only play into the hands of George Ball or Merrill Lynch, helping them to pick off more and more of Hutton's biggest producers. Blackstone also believed it could fetch a higher price for Hutton away from the securities industry.

But corporate America wasn't buying a brokerage firm in the post-crash environment of November 1987.

"This was the worst time to be selling a brokerage company," Freund recalls. "Everyone was still in a state of shock. The last thing these companies wanted to do was buy into the securities business. They said, 'In effect, we don't know where the market's going and we're not about to gamble on it.' "

At this point Sandy Weill made an appearance at Hutton's offices.

"With the directors, the management committee, the lawyers and investment bankers all gathered on the twenty-ninth floor, Sandy put his offer for Hutton on the table once again," recalls Ed Lill, who met with two of Weill's lieutenants. "He offered to do a deal mostly with Commercial Credit stock. But because that stock wasn't very strong, and because the sum he was willing to pay for Hutton wasn't attractive, the board formally rejected his offer. There were a lot of uncertainties during this period, but one thing we knew: we wouldn't be selling the firm to Commercial Credit."

Clearly, the best chance for a sale rested in the very arena Hutton had been avoiding: in the snake pit of the securities business. These firms were in the best position to assess the risks and rewards of a Hutton acquisition. These companies had long coveted Hutton's retail system. In short, other brokerage firms were the most logical buyers. With Hutton's financial condition deteriorating day by day, it was a card that had to be played.

By now all the critical decisions were being made by Ueberroth. Stepping in to fill the management vacuum, he had decided (1) the firm had to be sold and (2) he would direct the sale. As Blackstone and Salomon and Skadden Arps put the machinery of a deal in motion, what many had suspected for some time was now confirmed: Ueberroth was the boss.

Unofficially, the changing of the guard had taken place after the board meeting of November 12. It was then that a group of directors asked Ueberroth to assume the chairmanship. When he declined, Jim Freund came up with the novel idea that Ueberroth serve instead as a committee of one, representing the board in the sale of the company. Though his decisions would be subject to board approval, Ueberroth would have wide latitude in structuring a deal. On this basis he accepted the offer. He would sell E.F. Hutton and, because he believed he had precious little time to act, he would sell it quickly.

And so on the morning of November 23, a reluctant Bob Rittereiser got on the telephone to his Wall Street competitors. His message was straight as an arrow: Hutton is up for sale. I'm giving you a chance to bid. If you're interested, you'll have to act fast. We'll need your best offer by December 1. That's the deadline, period.

Chapter 22

"When the company was sold, it was three or four weeks away from insolvency. I was surprised at how the balance sheet could deteriorate so rapidly.

"It struck me what effect this collapse, were that to happen, would have on Wall Street. To the public there was no difference between an E.F. Hutton and a Shearson Lehman or a Paine Webber. They were all major firms and if any failed, it would have caused a run on all of them. That's the story that's never been told."

—Peter Ueberroth

It was enough to make Ed Hutton turn over in his grave. Eighty-three years after its founding, the company he'd launched with a Western Union wire across the Rockies, that had survived the great depression, backed J. Paul Getty, and served as trusted brokers to the nation's elite from Palm Beach to Palm Springs, was being picked over like a used Chevy on the dealer's back lot.

For all intents and purposes, E. F. Hutton & Co. was no longer a private company. From the moment three potential acquirers—Merrill Lynch, Dean Witter, and Shearson Lehman Brothers—responded positively to Rittereiser's phone call, Hutton was an open book on the auction block.

"On November 25, we sent a letter to the prospective bidders, inviting them to submit a written offer for the acquisition of the firm," recalls Jim Freund. "The letter was very specific. It said that we preferred a cash deal, that we wanted to consummate a transaction quickly, and that offers had to be submitted by the strike of noon on December 1. With that, we opened our doors to them, saying we would cooperate fully in their due diligence."

Within hours, intelligence units from Merrill, Witter, and Shearson descended on Hutton demanding financial statements, operating reports, customer lists.

"The guys who came up were all in the brokerage business, so they knew the questions to ask, the red flags to look for," Lill recalls. "The teams I met with wanted detailed information on our capital position and on our costs and revenues by product line, by division, and by branch. The meetings were intense. We were working eighteen- to twenty-hour days just to give the prospective bidders the hard information they needed to arrive at a decision."

Divided into three separate teams, the prospective buyers were sequestered in offices and conference rooms, each serviced by squads of Hutton financial executives, lawyers, and investment bankers.

"We were operating in perilous waters," Warren Law recalls. "By announcing that a sale was in progress, we ignited a chain of events that could reduce Hutton's value as a corporate entity. With each passing day, as the bloodletting of clients and brokers continued, our value could plummet to the point where we would have very little to sell. So we had to move with great dispatch, demanding that all parties observe the December 1 deadline."

It was this point that Law, playing out the prospect of a worst-case scenario, asked Ueberroth if he would take over the company as CEO should the auction fail to produce a satisfactory bidder.

"He indicated to me that he would," Law recalls. "He said that though he wasn't seeking the job, he'd take it if that's what he had to do to keep Hutton from going under."

But soon after this a surprise development emerged from the negotiations to sell Hutton. In a telephone call to Jim Freund, Shearson attorney Jack Nussbaum, a partner with the New York firm of Willkie, Farr & Gallagher, intimated in the course of a wide-ranging conversation that Shearson might be able to sweeten its offer for Hutton were it given the opportunity to make a preemptive bid before the auction deadline.*

"I reported this to management and some of the board members and we had a meeting to discuss it," Freund recalls. "The consensus was that we should explore this further, seeing just how much higher Shearson would go. Ueberroth wasn't at the meeting but when we called him at home and briefed him on our thinking, he agreed that we should see what Shearson had in mind."

Hutton then presented Peter Cohen with a challenge. Make a strong preemptive offer for the firm and the quarry is yours. We'll shut down the auction before the others have a chance to bid.

This was just what Cohen had in mind. As an astute negotiator who'd already engineered a string of savvy mergers in his young but brilliant career, Shearson's chairman relished the idea of snatching up Hutton before Merrill or Witter placed their bids, sewing up a deal without the give and take of an auction.

It was in the mood of cautious optimism that high-level negotiating teams from both sides converged at Willkie, Farr's offices just days before the auction deadline. In attendance were Ueberroth, Rittereiser, Wilson, Freund, Peterson, Salomon Brothers managing director Lee Kimmell, and from the Shearson side, Cohen, president Jeffrey Lane, and Nussbaum.

Both teams were there ostensibly to make a deal, but

*Similar reports from other sources had reached Hutton's investment bankers.

they were also there to snooker each other, to rob each other blind. For its part, Hutton hoped to scare Shearson into a deal. "Act now," the line went, "and the company is yours. But wait until the auction and you run a risk that there'll be a higher bid.

Shearson's gambit was to come to the negotiations smiling away, only to bare its teeth once the bargaining started. It would do so by shocking Hutton with a bargain-basement bid, a strategy Cohen believed would throw fear into the Hutton camp, forcing Ueberroth et al. to lower their expectations and, with a bit of negotiating, to accept a lowball offer.

"The Shearson guys proceeded to dump all over Hutton's balance sheet," Freund says. "They said some of the assets were overvalued on the books and some of the liabilities weren't fully reflected."

Cohen did most of the talking and his presentation was designed to take the wind out of Hutton's sails, setting up Ueberroth for a low bid. When the offer came, it was to pay in the low twenties for each share of Hutton stock. But that wasn't even close. Not for a preemptive bid.

At this point Ueberroth told the Shearson team that for a deal to be consummated, "the successful bid will have to have a number three in front of it." Ueberroth was clearly thinking in terms of $30, a number Shearson still believed was too high.

Price was not the only issue dividing the parties. As a condition of sale, Hutton required that offers to buy Hutton be ironclad. Once a bidder committed to purchase the firm, that commitment had to be firm. Except for the most extraordinary circumstances, there could be no turning back.

"In a deal like this, there's usually a merger agreement that provides for a tender offer," Freund explains. "The tender offer is used because it speeds the process. But in its standard form, the tender offer carries certain conditions that must be met for the guy making the tender offer to be bound by it. If these conditions are not met, he can walk away from the deal.

"A typical clause gives the purchaser leeway to get out of the deal if there's a material adverse change in the target company's business during the twenty business days the tender offer is in effect.

"Well, there was no way we could let Shearson get off the hook on that condition. We were bleeding. And as soon as we announced a deal, we'd be bleeding even more. Competition would step up their raids. More brokers would leave. Conditions were bound to get worse before they got better. We were going to bleed throughout the tender period. There was no question about it. No way we could allow this to be a reason for calling off the tender offer.

"From our perspective, once the deal was set in motion, it had to be done. It was as if we were jumping out of a plane with a parachute. It has to be done right the first time, because if it isn't, there is no second time.

"So once we made a deal with someone, that deal had to fly because if we lost a month fiddling around with a prospective buyer, only to have that guy back out, we could lose our only chance to sell for a decent price."

But as much as Hutton demanded an airtight contract, Shearson held out for a series of "what ifs" built into the language, giving them a chance to renege should the risks suddenly mount.

"As the talks were unfolding, a bill drafted by Ways and Means Chairman Dan Rostenkowski threatened the economics of corporate acquisitions by denying some of the tax deductions that usually go with them," Freund recalls. "Worried about this, Shearson proposed that the usual clause be included in the conditions to the tender offer, providing that any negative legislation such as if the Rostenkowski bill was passed, or was likely to pass, they could cancel the tender offer."

It was just the kind of escape hatch that Ueberroth would not accept. His position was firm: once Shearson signed a deal, it would have to be a marriage that could be reversed only if the parties were enjoined by the courts (a contingency Freund knew was remote). From Ueberroth's perspective, the deal would have to be signed in blood or not at all.

Aware by now that they were facing a formidable opponent in Peter Ueberroth, Cohen held out an olive branch. In the interest of making a deal, Shearson would agree to a more or less airtight contract without escape clauses, and would raise its bid to acquire Hutton to $25 a share.

But Hutton wasn't biting.

"We said, 'Thanks, but no thanks,' " recalls a member of the Hutton negotiating team. "At $25 the offer's still not preemptive. If that's the best you can do, make a bid at auction and we'll consider it."

While poker-faced Ueberroth was toughing it out with Shearson, the outlook for a successful auction was growing dimmer. Most worrisome, news leaking out of the Merrill Lynch camp was disheartening. Until that point Rittereiser's alma mater had been considered an ace in the hole.

On paper, Merrill had every reason to make a strong bid for Hutton. From a strategic standpoint the two retail systems would fit together like synchromesh gears. And from a competitive tack, taking Hutton out of play would deprive Shearson, Merrill's main competitor, of the opportunity to narrow the lead Merrill still retained. But as the bidding deadline approached, word had it that the giant of the brokerage industry was too much of a bureaucratic behemoth to make a quick decision. Lawyers inside Merrill were concerned about the contingent liability of lawsuits pending against Hutton (one by shareholders angry over the failure to accept the Shearson offer of a year before). Given the short time frame Hutton was demanding, a Merrill bid was unlikely. As Rittereiser had proved since he'd come to Hutton, quick action wasn't part of the Merrill culture.

"The Witter and the Shearson guys were all over Hutton, meeting with the department heads, checking the books and the records, really getting into the guts of our business," recalls a former member of the management committee. "But the Merrill guys had this laid-back attitude. They weren't nearly as aggressive or as thorough in their due diligence.

"I saw the difference firsthand. In the meetings I had with the Shearson guys, I sat across the table from their senior executives. They wanted their top brokerage executives to get a fix on Hutton. But when it was Merrill Lynch's turn to meet with me, they sent some functionary in the planning department. Instinct told me they wouldn't be bidding."

Word from the Witter camp was equally gloomy.

"During the due diligence period, I came into my office one morning expecting to meet with a team from Dean Witter," recalls Ken Wilson. "I waited and waited and waited until it was apparent they weren't showing up. When I called over there to find out what was up, the Witter guys were surprised to learn that I thought the meeting was still on.

" 'Haven't you talked to Ueberroth?' they asked.

"It turned out that Witter's CEO Philip Purcell had called Peter the night before, telling him they were backing out of the auction process. They didn't like the whole bidding mechanism Jim Freund had set up and they weren't going to participate.

"That moment was the most desperate of my Hutton career. There we were auctioning a crippled firm and it looked as if we'd have only one bidder—or none if Shearson found out what was going on. I don't remember being as frightened of anything since my Vietnam days.

"Determined to get Witter back into the auction, I grabbed

Ueberroth and we went to see Purcell, trying to convince him to stay in the hunt. We were desperate, but we couldn't let on to that. Instead, we said we were interested in working with them and that if they didn't like the auction process not to worry about it, we'd work around it with them. They listened, but I wasn't optimistic."

Wilson's instinct was on target. As the directors assembled on the morning of December 1, there was more of a negotiation than an auction. On the table was a bid from Shearson and a complicated "expression of interest" from Dean Witter.

This time Shearson offered to pay at least $25 a share and offered to up the ante if Hutton would sign a definitive agreement to sell the company the following day, on December 2. The deal would be all cash (as the board preferred) and would be free of contractual escape clauses (as the board demanded). Given Shearson's apparent flexibility on the purchase price and its willingness to make an airtight commitment, all of the elements for a deal were on the table. But the Witter proposal thickened the plot.

In a meeting with Ueberroth, Purcell came up with a jerry-built package that offered cash plus stock in its parent company, Sears Roebuck, for each share of Hutton's stock.

Just how much money the shareholders would actually wind up with depended on further negotiations aimed at valuing key assets and liabilities on the Hutton balance sheet. And therein lay the rub. Depending on the outcome of these valuations, Witter's offer could be higher or lower than Shearson's $25-plus bid.

As the board mulled over the offers, Ueberroth—who was clearly in command of the auction—leaned toward the Shearson package. From the outset he'd wanted a solid deal, one that would bind the acquirer to specified terms and to a set price.

That's why the Witter proposal fell short. In spite of its

upside potential (given the highest valuations, the final price could climb to $30 or more), the deal was too murky, too open to surprises and disappointments at a time when Hutton could ill afford the suspense. With the company continuing to deteriorate, the deal would have to wade through intensive negotiations on asset values, would have to survive deliberations by the Witter board, and, because it was a stock offer, would have to endure a ninety-day registration process.

Adding it up, the unknowns, the uncertainties, the unpredictables were greater than the Hutton board was willing to risk. But the Witter proposal proved invaluable nevertheless. It gave Ueberroth what he needed most: a bargaining chip, a bid to play against Shearson's offer.

"For a while, it looked like the auction wasn't going to produce any bidders besides Shearson," says a Hutton adviser. "It was like we were having a party and no one was coming. That was disappointing because we knew that without other bidders we'd be hard-pressed to get Shearson to boost its offer.

"But when Ueberroth came out of his meeting and told us what Witter had offered, we were pleased even though the offer itself wasn't as good as we would have liked it to be. At least we had something to negotiate with."

Although Hutton's board greatly preferred the Shearson bid, Cohen didn't have to know that. As long as there was another player at the table, he could be moved to raise the ante. With this in mind, Ueberroth invited the Shearson team to return to Hutton on December 1 for further negotiations. If Hutton was willing to sign a deal the following day, by how much would Shearson raise its $25 bid? By $1? By $2? Secretly, Ueberroth was still clinging to his target price of $30 a share. Could he move Cohen that high?

"We told Cohen that we had a proposal from another solid and respectable bidder that probably would exceed the offer he'd made to us," Freund recalls. " 'Unless you come up in your price,' we said, 'we will feel obligated to pursue that other offer. But if you do substantially better, then the board will have a basis for doing a deal with you without further pursuing the other offer.' "

Shearson lawyer Jack Nussbaum recalls the thinking in his client's highest councils.

"If anything worried us, it was that we might be bidding against ourselves. While Ueberroth, like any good auctioneer, made it seem that there was plenty of interest in Hutton, we had our doubts. We knew there was another offer but we had no way of judging how high that offer was or how serious they were about going through with the process.

"All we could do was set a ceiling on a price we would be willing to pay and go, if need be, to that limit. If it would turn out that we overpaid, that would be a fact of business life we would have to live with. You have to understand that Hutton was an asset Shearson wanted very much— had wanted for more than a year. The objective at this time wasn't to pay the lowest price. No. The main thing was that when the day was over, we wanted to own Hutton."

In an intense bargaining session—with the parties coming and going, caucusing, huddling in the hallways—Ueberroth and Lee Kimmell pressed Shearson's chairman to increase his offer dollar by dollar, climbing steadily to the $30 figure before Cohen stopped short at $29.25, 85 percent to be paid in cash, 15 percent in notes.* Here Cohen froze the negotiations, making it clear that Shearson had gone the limit. The deal would be inked the following day at $29.25 or not at all.

---

*The debt portion was 10-year senior subordinated debentures. A shareholder with 100 shares of Hutton stock would get $85 in cash and $15 in debt.

Faced with Shearson's final offer, Ueberroth polled the Hutton board. The vote was unanimous. The firm that Edward F. Hutton had founded eighty-three years before would be sold for $960 million.

"Voting in favor of the merger was an emotional thing for me," Warren Law recalls. "I'd been a Hutton director for about sixteen years and through all that time we'd always prided ourselves on having the same name since the firm was founded. Almost all the other brokers had merged and lost their original identity, but not Hutton. Not until that single vote wiped away all those years of independence. That got you in the pit of your stomach."

Epilogue

"Rittereiser remained upbeat throughout the auction process, up to and including the sale day. I think that's because he knew he couldn't stay at Hutton anyway, and that it would look better on his resume if he left because of a change of control rather than because he was fired."

—*Warren Law*

Overnight a proud name slipped into the oblivion of a glued-together corporate patchwork: Shearson/Lehman/Hutton–American Express. It was a sign of the times. Where once there had existed business builders, now there were asset shifters.

With the ink still wet, Shearson's big broom swept through 31 West 52nd Street, dismissing 1,450 employees in a blitz of pink slips that left secretaries weeping and lifelong employees mourning for the fate of their families. As armed security guards roamed the halls (including a pair of bodyguards assigned to Rittereiser), staffers who had devoted all of their working lives to Hutton were searched as they left the premises. In a month 4,800 employees were lopped from the payroll.

But from the financial carnage a handful of millionaires emerged. Ironically, the great beneficiaries of the Hutton collapse were those who had served for the briefest period and who by their arrogance, pettiness, and blatant failure to take affirmative action, had taken Hutton to its grave.

Blessed with golden parachutes that insulated them from the firm's woes, the bickering, back-stabbing group that had served as Rittereiser's cabinet emerged from the rubble with aggregate payments of $13.5 million. (Rittereiser, still stranded without a contract, had to rely on Shearson's mercy for his payoff. When it came, he would be $1.2 million richer.)

"It's tragic, but the guys whose plan provided a short path to the oblivion of E.F. Hutton were generously rewarded for it," says Norm Epstein.

Even Jerry Welsh admits that the management committee was overpaid. "We all cashed our checks," he says, "but we didn't do the job. We were incompetent."

If the specter of an incompetent management walking away rich from the Hutton fiasco wasn't bad enough, the directors decided to celebrate their Pyrrhic victory by bestowing on Ueberroth a $500,000 gesture of appreciation.

"Given the adverse circumstances, the directors were very happy with the transaction," Freund says, "and they felt that Peter deserved much of the credit for accomplishing it. Operating in a crisis atmosphere, he had remained cool and effective and obtained a good price for the company. For that they believed he deserved special consideration."

Because the terms of the merger agreement precluded the board from increasing a director's fee without Shearson's approval, a director was dispatched by the board to get Cohen's blessing. Days later, Shearson authorized the payment.

The gift was uncalled for. In negotiating the Shearson deal, Ueberroth acted in the capacity of a director, not an investment banker. Had he wanted to run the company as its chairman, and be paid accordingly, the job could have been his. But he rejected it. Getting the most for Hutton was hardly an act of charity. As a director, it was his fiduciary responsibility to the shareholders.

With so much money floating around—millions to the Rittereiser team, millions to Salomon Brothers and the Blackstone Group and Skadden, Arps and Willkie, Farr— Rittereiser was willing to take his share too. This he defends by touting his role as a negotiator.

"It's no fun having the weak hand in a tough, tough poker game. Hutton was going to negative net worth so fast it made your head spin. The firm could easily have been sold for $10 a share, or zero dollars, rather than the nearly $30 we got. In my negotiating the deal vis-à-vis someone else doing it, I think the shareholders got nine figures more for the company."

Though all hands agree that Ueberroth performed effectively in Hutton's closing weeks by extracting the best possible deal from Shearson, the argument that he saved the shareholders "nine figures" is questionable. From the shareholders' perspective, they collected $600 million less than they would have collected had the board seen through Rittereiser's optimism and sold Hutton in the fall of 1986.

What's more, there is question whether the auction approach, favored by Ueberroth and the Blackstone group, against the advice of Salomon, worked for or against Hutton's shareholders.

"With the auction, we came within a hair of winding up without a single bid for the company," says an investment banker active in the sale. "Had Cohen found out that he was going to be the only hard bidder, he might well have backed out, let Hutton's stock nosedive to $18 and then make a bid soon after for $21.

"The fact is, the auction was a dumb and dangerous idea and though Salomon pointed that out, Freund and Ueberroth were determined to go that route. And I think Hutton went for less money because of it. If they'd gone to Cohen first and said, 'Look Peter, we'll give you the chance to make a preemptive bid before anyone else has a chance to look us over,' I think they could have gotten more than $29.25—maybe $31 a share."

"Should I have been paid?" Ueberroth muses. "You can make an argument that I shouldn't have. But it was offered by both parties to the transaction after the transaction was consummated and after I was off the board.

"I don't know how many points you get for turning down a half million dollars."

Before the directors boarded up Hutton's windows, closing the books on a once glorious institution, they capitalized on an obscure clause granting them a lump-sum payment equaling ten times their annual fees for serving as board members; in effect, a golden parachute for directors. As a final act they wrote themselves checks totaling $2,192,500: Dina Merrill $307,500; Ed Cazier $420,000; William Milliken $295,000; Sadao Yasuda $245,000; Warren Law $370,000; Peter Ueberroth $420,000.*

This was the same board that had slammed the door on longtime officers whose fates were in their hands. Under the terms of the executive officers' plan in effect at the time of the Shearson acquisition, officers' interests would vest gradually over a period of five years. In the event of a change of corporate control, however, the board was empowered, at its discretion, to authorize immediate vesting.

As Shearson prepared to take over Hutton, this "change of control" seemed to be sufficient grounds to kick off the accelerated vesting. But because this would add $45 million to its acquisition cost, Shearson made its $29.25 bid contingent on the board's agreement not to vest the plan. This request the board honored, feeling no shame that it did so while lining its own pockets with lump-sum payoffs.

The day the *Wall Street Journal* carried the headline: "SHEARSON SIGNS DEFINITIVE PACT TO BUY HUTTON," those

*In addition to his $500,000 bonus.

who had worked for Hutton throughout its modern history, those who had helped build the firm and then watched it collapse, felt an extraordinary loss.

"For over a quarter of a century the company had been more than an employer," recalls Norm Epstein. "It had been Mother Hutton. For a whole group of us who had started together and built our careers together, seeing that Hutton existed no longer was like a sudden death in the family."

Where They Are Today

Paul Bagley—Chairman, Silver Screen Management

George Ball—CEO of Prudential-Bache Securities

Andre Backar—Senior Director, International Business & Investments, Bear Stearns

Clarence Catallo—Director of Paine Webber's North Central division

Ed Cazier—Partner with Morgan, Lewis & Bockius

Gordon Crary, Jr.—Financial Consultant, Shearson/Lehman/Hutton (L.A.)

Neal Eldridge—President, Eldridge Associates Inc.

Norman Epstein—Chairman of ILX Corp.

Bob Fomon—President of Robert M. Fomon & Co., investment banking

Steven Friedman—General counsel for The Equitable

Arthur Goldberg—Partner with Neuberger & Berman brokerage firm

Fred Josephs—CEO of Drexel Burnham Lambert

Ed Lill—Partner with Deloitte, Haskins & Sells

Dick Locke—Executive Vice President, Capital Guaranty Insurance Co.

Jim Lopp—Chief Executive of Financial Security Assurance

Tom Lynch—Retired

Tony Malatino—Senior Vice President, Account Executive, Dean Witter

Jerry Miller—Vice Chairman of Shearson/Lehman/Hutton

Scott Pierce—Chairman of Asset Management at Prudential Insurance

Humbert Powell—Senior Managing Director of Corporate Finance, Bear Stearns

Tom Rae—Counsel with a Wall Street law firm

Bob Rittereiser—Self-employed

Don Sanders—Chairman of Sanders, Morris, Mundy, Inc.

Loren Schechter—Executive Vice President, General Counsel, Prudential-Bache Securities

Al Sched—President, Monterey Farming Corp.

John Shad—Former chairman of the SEC; Ambassador to the Netherlands

Bruce Tuthill—Senior Vice President, Prudential-Bache Securities

Peter Ueberroth—Former commissioner of major league baseball

Jerry Welsh—President of Welsh Marketing Associates, Inc.

Ken Wilson—President, Ranieri Wilson & Co., a New York investment firm

℗ Plume

By the year 2000, 2 out of 3 Americans could be illiterate.

It's true.

Today, 75 million adults...about one American in three, can't read adequately. And by the year 2000, U.S. News & World Report envisions an America with a literacy rate of only 30%.

Before that America comes to be, you can stop it...by joining the fight against illiteracy today.

Call the Coalition for Literacy at toll-free **1-800-228-8813** and volunteer.

Volunteer Against Illiteracy. The only degree you need is a degree of caring.